COINS

COINS

Ancient, Mediaeval and Modern

VOLUME THREE

Coins of America, Africa, Australasia and Asia

R. A. G. CARSON

Deputy Keeper in the Department of
Coins and Medals at the British Museum

Radius Book/Hutchinson

HUTCHINSON & CO (*Publishers*) LTD
178–202 Great Portland Street, London W1

London Melbourne Sydney
Auckland Johannesburg Cape Town
and agencies throughout the world

First published August 1962
Second impression November 1963
Third impression November 1966
Second (revised) edition November 1970
Radius edition in three volumes February 1971

© R. A. G. Carson 1962
© Additional material R. A. G. Carson 1970

This book has been set in Bembo type, printed in Great Britain
on smooth wove paper by Anchor Press, and
bound by Wm. Brendon, both of Tiptree, Essex
The illustrations have been printed by The Cotswold Collotype Co. Ltd.

ISBN 0 09 104830 3 (cased)
0 09 104831 1 (paper)

CONTENTS OF VOLUME THREE

Introduction
vii

THE NEW WORLD
415

AUSTRALASIA
457

AFRICA
461

THE NEAR EAST
471

THE INDIAN SUB-CONTINENT
499

THE FAR EAST
537

Select Bibliography

List of Coins Illustrated

Index
Following page 559

Introduction

This third section is concerned with coinage outside Europe. The coins of the New World, of Australasia, of most of Africa, and even parts of Asia have their antecedents in the coinage of Europe, for it was the colonizing activities of the great mercantile nations of western Europe from the sixteenth century onwards which introduced coinage to these areas.

Asia itself was not unfamiliar with coinage. The Near East had known the coinage of Greece and Rome and from the seventh century onwards had used the successive forms of Muhammadan coinage. In the sub-continent of India, in addition to the coins of the Greek kingdom of Bactria and the later Scythic and Kushan kings in the north-west, native coinages had proliferated elsewhere and been influenced by the innumerable invasions, such as those of the Moguls in the sixteenth century.

As in so many fields, China is credited with the invention and earliest use of coinage; for the earliest Chinese coins, tradition says, date from the second millenium B.C. Early types of coinage were simply small-scale reproductions in bronze of everyday objects such as knives and spades, previously exchanged in barter. These pieces began to be inscribed from about the middle of the first millenium B.C., and, though this form of coinage probably lasted down towards the beginning of the Christian era, coins of conventional round shape, with a square hole in the centre, and inscribed with characters, began to come into circulation some centuries before that date. These bronze cash continued, with modifications, to furnish the staple coinage of China down to the nineteenth century, and to influence the form of coinage in Annam, Korea and Japan.

THE NEW WORLD

★

North America	416
Canada	416
Newfoundland	419
The United States	419
Central America	428
Mexico	428
Guatemala	432
British Honduras	433
Honduras	433
Nicaragua	434
Salvador	434
Costa Rica	435
Panama	435
South America	437
Colombia	437
Venezuela	439
Ecuador	439
Peru	440
Bolivia	441
Chile	441
Argentina	442
Uraguay	443
Paraguay	444
Brasil	444
The Guianas	446

The Caribbean   448
Haiti   448
Dominican Republic   449
Cuba   450
Danish West Indies   450
Dutch West Indies   451
French West Indies   452
British West Indies   452

The New World

THE first discovery of the New World was made by the Northmen who, in their Iceland voyages in the eleventh century, made land-fall on the coast of North America; but their knowledge received no general publication and quickly passed into oblivion. In 1492, however, Christopher Columbus, with his three ships, accomplished his great expedition and reached the Bahamas and West Indies in his endeavour to sail across the Atlantic and reach India and China. By an award of Pope Alexander VI in 1492, further formulated the following year by the Treaty of Tordesillas, a north to south boundary in America was agreed between Spain and Portugal. The outcome, briefly, was the establishment of Portuguese authority in the area represented approximately by modern Brasil and the extension of the Spanish empire in the course of the sixteenth century over the remainder of South America, Central America, the Caribbean and a considerable area of North America. It was in the north that other European powers, principally Britain and France, were quick to follow the example of Spain and Portugal and establish New World colonies.

As a result of the great colonial wars of the eighteenth century France was compelled to relinquish her American possessions to Britain, although in Canada, above all, the influence of French civilization has persisted till the present day. Later, in the eighteenth century, the disastrous colonial policy of Britain led to the revolt of her American colonists and the creation of the independent United States of America in 1776. A century of steady expansion west and south enlarged the new republic more or less to its present-day boundaries. In Central and South America the percolation of the ideas of the French Revolution and the severance of communications during the Napoleonic wars loosened the ties between Spain and Portugal and their colonies and began the movement which culminated in the establishment in the nineteenth century of the independent republics of today.

The pattern of coinage in the New World mirrors the historical development of the continent which has just been sketched in its barest outline. The great Spanish empire from the sixteenth century was served by a more or less uniform coinage modelled on that of the home-land but struck by a chain of mints, spread throughout the territory, until the creation of the new republics gave rise to a whole series of independent coinages. In the Caribbean, possession of the several islands changed hands on more than one occasion until today's position has been reached of a number of independent states with their individual coinages, while other areas, still administered as colonial possessions, are provided with a colonial coinage. In the north the individual coinages of the several colonies were super-seded by a single national coinage on the creation of the United States in 1776 and in Canada the earlier provincial coinages were eventually replaced by a new coinage for the whole country. These coinages will now be examined in some greater detail in geographical succession from north to south.

NORTH AMERICA

CANADA

It is not certain whether the voyages of the Norseman Lief Ericson in the eleventh century brought him to Canada but in 1497, only five years after Columbus dis-covered the New World, John Cabot made land-fall in Canada. It was left to the French under such adventurers as Cartier and de Champlain to begin the settle-ment of the Canadian mainland along the St. Lawrence. In 1670 the Hudson's Bay Company was formed and English settlements were made in Hudson Bay, Nova Scotia and Newfoundland. Rivalry between France and England culminated during the Seven Years' war in the capture of Quebec and the French surrender at Montreal in 1760. In 1791 the settled portion of Canada in the east was divided into Lower Canada, predominantly French, and Upper Canada, mainly British, but the two were united in 1840. Expansion westwards in the nineteenth century, accelerated by the great railroad constructions, led to the formation of the other provinces and to the eventual formation of the Dominion of Canada in 1867.

The majority of these happenings find their expression in the coinages current in Canada. The more active French policy of exploration and settlement at the outset of Canada's development is reflected in the provision of a coinage for colonial use, particularly in the Americas. In 1670 in the reign of Louis XIV a series of such coins was struck at Paris in denominations of 15 and 5 sols in silver with types of royal portrait and French arms, similar to those of the ordinary French issues but with a reverse inscription *Gloriam regni tui dicent*. In 1717 copper coins of Louis XV were struck at Perpignan in denominations of 12 and 6 deniers for the American colonies. The obverse carried the usual royal portrait and the reverse a four-line inscription *XII/deniers/Colonies/1717*. Later, in 1721, copper pieces of 9 deniers had as obverse two L's in saltire, crowned, and *Colonies françoises* and the date on reverse (Pl. 772).

For the remainder of the eighteenth century after the submission of the French no specific, official coinage was issued in or for Canada and even the trade-token coinage, of which there is a great variety, where it is dated is, at the earliest, of the first part of the nineteenth century. A series of token coins of a somewhat more official character also made their appearance in the early decades of the nineteenth century, the types varying for each of the several provinces.

In Lower Canada a bilingual series of bank tokens began issue in 1837. The obverse figure in winter clothing has given rise to the name Papineau for this series, after the Papineau who led an uprising in that year and was said to affect this style of dress. The obverse is inscribed in French, *Province du Bas Canada*, with the value (one or two sous), while the reverse is inscribed in English, *Bank Token*, with the value one penny or a halfpenny around arms of St. Andrew's cross with thistle, shamrock, rose and beaver in the angles and the name of the particular issuing bank below (Pl. 773). Another series with a similar reverse but with an obverse giving a view of the bank and inscribed *Bank of Montreal* was issued in 1837-9 and 1842. Quebec Bank tokens of a penny and a halfpenny value in 1852 used the obverse of the first series described but had, on the other side, a personification of Quebec seated below the Heights of Abraham by the edge of the St. Lawrence. The 'bouquet' series of halfpenny or sous tokens takes its name from the bunch of flowers on the obverse which has a variety of inscriptions such as *Trade and Agriculture* or *Agriculture and Commerce*, together with the name of the province of Lower Canada—sometimes in French. The reverse gives the value in either English or French in a wreath. The union of the two portions into the province of Canada in 1840 was followed by an issue of silver cents in 1858 of value 5, 10 and 20 with head of Victoria and value crowned within a wreath (Pl. 774).

In Ontario or Upper Canada a series of halfpenny tokens in copper in 1823 carried the name of the province around the head of George IV, while the seated figure of Britannia on the reverse was accompanied by the value. Between 1850 and 1857 penny and halfpenny tokens of the Bank of Upper Canada had as types St. George and the Dragon and a complex of anchor and sword in saltire above two cornuacopiae, all crowned and with part of the Union flag to the right (Pl. 775). The penny and halfpenny tokens of Nova Scotia bear the name of the province and the portrait of George IV or Victoria and appropriate to the name of the colony, a Scottish thistle as the reverse type (Pl. 776). Later coinage of the cent and its half in 1861 has the portrait and title of Victoria on obverse and crown with date surrounded by wreath border, value and province. The New Brunswick tokens resemble those of Nova Scotia but for the name and the substitution of a sailing ship for the thistle on the reverse, while copper cents in 1861 are identical but for the name. The issues of Newfoundland, which until 1949 remained outside the Dominion, are dealt with below. In British Columbia extremely rare gold pieces of 20 and 10 dollars were struck in 1862 with a crown and the name of the province on obverse and the value in wreath on reverse.

The union of the provinces in 1867 to form the Dominion of Canada brought to an end the series of provincial coinages and the issue of a single coinage for the whole of Canada. Coinage in silver of denominations of 5, 10, 25 and 50 cents was of simple design in the reign of Victoria. Her portrait head in diadem was accompanied by her name and title and the word Canada on obverse, while the reverse carried the value and date within a wreath of maple-leaves, closed by a small crown (Pl. 777). The bronze cent had a similar obverse but with the inscription enclosed within two circles of dots and similar circles on the reverse enclosed a circlet of maple-leaves. The issues of Edward VII were identical except that the obverse bore his portrait bust in imperial robes and crown and the word Canada was transferred to the reverse. The coinage of George V introduced new designs, denominations and metals. Between 1911 and 1919 gold sovereigns struck in Canada with the conventional types were distinguished by a small letter C on the reverse and gold was also coined between 1912 and 1914 in denominations of 5 and 10 dollars with imperial obverse and the arms of Canada flanked by branches of maple on the reverse. The 10, 25 and 50 cent values followed the traditional designs as did the bronze cent initially. The 5 cent, in silver till 1921 and thereafter in nickel, and the bronze cent from 1920 replaced the reverse wreath by two maple-leaves. A silver dollar with reverse showing two voyageurs in canoe in front of a small island with the Northern Lights in the background was first struck for the king's Silver Jubilee in 1935 (Pl. 778).

In common with the coinages of other British dominions and colonies in the reign of George VI the Canadian issues develop a series of reverse types of greater variety and picturesqueness. The dollar retained its type of the voyageurs and on the 50 cents or half-dollar appeared the arms of Canada with lion and unicorn supporters holding, respectively, the Union flag and the fleur-de-lis banner of France. The 25 cents showed a caribou head, the 10 cents a fishing schooner, the 5 cents a beaver and the cent piece maple-leaves. On all these issues the obverse carried a bare-headed portrait of the king. On special silver dollars in 1939 the Parliament buildings commemorated the royal visit and in 1949 the ship of John Cabot marked the entry of Newfoundland into the Dominion. The first coinage of Elizabeth II retained the existing types, but a special silver dollar with Indian totem pole reverse celebrated the centenary of British Columbia in 1958. In 1967 the new royal portrait was paired with a complete set of new reverses of fish, animals, and birds on the coinage issued to commemorate the confederation centennial. In 1968 the denominations from 10 cents upwards were issued in nickel, and the 50 cent and dollar coins were reduced in size.

NEWFOUNDLAND

The coinage of Newfoundland was first struck in the reign of Victoria in 1865 and the denominational system consisted ultimately of values of 50, 20, 10 and 5 cents in silver and a cent piece in bronze. The silver pieces carried the royal portrait and title and *Newfoundland* on the obverse and the value within a circlet of leaves on reverse. The cent had as reverse a crown with the value and colony name in a circular inscription. Gold coins of the value of 2 dollars had an obverse similar to the silver coins but on the reverse, carrying the value as a type, had a circular inscription *Two hundred cents—one hundred pence*. The coins of Edward VII and George VI showed the imperial bust common to all commonwealth and colonial issues of their reigns and while retaining the established design of the cent piece had simplified reverses for the other values, the circlet of leaves being replaced by the inscription *Newfoundland*. Only the 5 and 10 cent pieces in silver were struck for George VI, continuing the conventional types but with crowned head and not bust on the obverse. The reverse of the bronze cent was altered to a flower design. The decision of Newfoundland, taken by referendum in 1949, to join the Dominion of Canada was commemorated by the issue of the special silver dollar already described in the Canadian coinage (Pl. 779).

THE UNITED STATES

The story of the settlement of that part of the North American continent which is now represented by the United States of America is one of considerable complexity. England laid claim to North America by virtue of the discovery by John Cabot in 1497 but no extensive settlement took place from England until the early seventeenth century, and that limited to the eastern seaboard. In the meantime other European nations had not been slow to embark on colonization: the Spaniards had pushed north into California and New Mexico, the French had established themselves on the Gulf of Mexico in Louisiana and laid claim to the great hinterland stretching north to the Great Lakes and the Dutch had erected a settlement at New Amsterdam, now New York. Some mention has been made in the Canadian section of the coinages issued by France for her American colonies and those of the Spanish colonial empire are dealt with below (see p. 428). Attention must now be directed to the British settlements in the east and the local coinages which served them.

The first serious attempt at English settlement in America was that of the colonists sent out by Raleigh late in the reign of Elizabeth I but the venture failed, though it still has its memorial in the name of Virginia which was given to the settlement in honour of the virgin queen. A second venture in the reign of James I resulted, eventually, in more permanent settlement, followed by the planting of colonies by the Pilgrim Fathers and others in New England, Massachusetts and Connecticut. The territory granted to Lord Baltimore by Charles I was named Maryland after Charles' queen, Henrietta Maria, while, after the Restoration of 1660, lands to the south of Virginia granted by Charles II were named Carolina in his honour and the Quaker William Penn in 1682 obtained land on the west of the Delaware to which he gave the name Pennsylvania. In 1732, in the reign of George II, a final colony of Georgia was founded in the south. At the end of the great colonial wars France in 1763 gave up her claims to the territory west of the Mississippi.

Unlike France, Britain undertook no coinage for the use of her American colonies and, indeed, in the early stages the primitive circumstances rendered a monetary medium of exchange unnecessary. When the growth of settlement and trade created the need for coinage, these requirements were met here, just as later in the settlements of Australasia and Africa, by the great international trade coinages, particularly the Spanish dollar or piece of eight and its subdivisions which continued to play a part in American coinage till as late as 1857. Although such coinages facilitated exchange where comparatively large sums were involved, there was a growing need for small change for everyday transactions and in default of official provision of such a coinage the defect was remedied by a number of locally produced coins in the various colonies or states as they came to be termed.

Of these one of the earliest, the series known as Hog money after the obverse type, was struck in 1616 not specifically for the continental settlements but for the Sommer Islands in the Bahamas. The coinage in brass was in four denominations, shilling, sixpence, threepence and twopence, and had on the obverse a pig and the value in Roman numerals and a fully-rigged sailing ship on the reverse (Pl. 780). Probably the earliest coinage to be issued in the North American settlements was ordered to be struck near Boston in 1652 for New England. These coins were rough silver disks with nothing but a rectangular stamp with the letters NE on obverse and the value in Roman numerals on the reverse. The denominations were the shilling, sixpence and threepence. Since such a coinage lent itself to forgery and clipping it was replaced in Massachusetts in the same year by a series of the same three denominations but using complete types on either side. There were three varieties of tree which formed the obverse types, namely the willow, the oak and pine. The tree on obverse was accompanied by the inscription *Masathusets in* continued on the reverse *New England An Dom* with the date and value in Roman figures in the centre (Pl. 781). Although only the date 1652 appears on this coinage, it continued to be issued for some thirty years, the three varieties most probably being struck in the order in which they have been named. An extremely rare shilling of the same fabric as the tree coinage used the same types also, except on the obverse which illustrates the story of the Good Samaritan. For Maryland Lord Baltimore produced a coinage of shilling, sixpence and four-pence in silver. The obverse carried his portrait and title *Caecilius Dns Terrae Mariae & ct* and the reverse his arms separating the value in Roman figures with inscription *Crescite et multiplicamini* (Pl. 782). A copper penny, designed but apparently never issued, had a coronet with two pennants on its reverse. Token halfpennies struck in 1694 for Carolina have an elephant on obverse and a five-line inscription *God/preserve/Carolina and/the Lords/Proprietors/* on the reverse.

In addition to these coins and tokens issued for specific states or colonies other series were produced by private enterprise to meet the demand for small change. A series which gained official sanction and wide currency in New Jersey was that of the St. Patrick halfpence and farthings said to have been originally struck in Dublin in 1678. On one side of the halfpenny a kneeling king plays a harp with crown above and is inscribed *Floreat rex;* on the other, St. Patrick inscribed *Ecce grex,* with crozier preaches to a crowd. On the reverse of the farthing inscribed *Quiescat grex* St. Patrick with cross stands before a church. Two other series, in a base alloy principally of brass, were produced by William Wood for more general circulation in America. The obverse of the specifically American series had the bust and titles of George I and a rather attractive reverse design of a full-blown rose inscribed *Rosa americana-utile dulce* (Pl. 783). Denominations of two-pence, penny and halfpenny carried no indication of value but, as in the case of British coppers, were distinguished only by their module. Issues were made in 1722–4. A very similar coinage but with a seated figure with harp, inscribed *Hibernia,* was produced by Wood in the same years. This coinage was originally intended for circulation in Ireland but, proving unpopular there, was shipped to America.

The revolt of Britain's American colonies and the Declaration of Independence in 1776 was followed two years later by the Articles of Confederation which, amongst other measures, left to each state the right to strike coin under the general authority of Congress. In the ten years which elapsed until the legislation of 1792 which provided for a uniform coinage a number of states did, in fact, issue their own coinage in a variety of forms. New Hampshire in fact anticipated events by authorizing in 1776 a coinage of copper cents equivalent to the English halfpence. This coinage with types of a pine-tree and a harp apparently never reached more than pattern stage. The next state to produce coinage was Vermont in 1785 and 1786. Its copper cents had as obverse a plough with mountains and a rising sun in the background with inscription *Vermont respublica* or *Respublica Vermontensium*. The reverse has rays and stars from a central eye while the inscription *Stella quarta decima*—the fourteenth star—alludes to the fact that Vermont was not one of the original thirteen states of the confederation. A new issue begun in 1786 had as types a laureate bust reminiscent of that on British coppers but inscribed *Vermon auctori* and a Britannia-like figure on the reverse with inscription *Inde et Lib.*

Copper cents current in New York were produced, not officially but by private enterprise, in 1786 and 1787. One series copying the laureate bust and Britannia figure of British copper coins was inscribed on obverse *Nova Eboraca* and on reverse *Virt et Lib.* On another an Indian warrior with tomahawk and bow stands on the obverse and an eagle with spread wings on the reverse. In Connecticut copper cents produced between 1785 and 1788 by a private firm under official contract were also based on the types of Georgian copper coins with inscriptions *Auctori Connec* and *Inde et Lib.* Massachusetts, on the other hand, set up its own mint to strike cents in 1787 and 1788 with types of Indian and eagle as at New York but inscribed *Common Wealth* and *Massachusetts.* New Jersey's copper cents struck in 1786–8 by contrast had on obverse a horse's head above a plough with the state name Latinized into *Nova Caesarea* and a shield with inscription *E pluribus unum* on the reverse. In addition to these coinages, which were to a greater or lesser degree official issues, the requirements of small change were met by an extensive series of token pieces of considerable variety. One of the more prolific was the series with a portrait of George Washington coupled with reverses bearing a seated figure, an eagle or a sailing ship. The first coinage of the United States issued by Federal authority was struck in 1787 and is commonly known as the Franklin cent, as it is believed that Benjamin Franklin provided the designs and inscriptions. On one side thirteen linked circles, representing the component states, surround an inner circle inscribed *United States* and containing the words *We are one*; on the other is a sun-dial with sun above, with inscription *Fugio* and the date with, in the exergue, *Mind your business.*

In the discussions which preceded the issue of the first regular coinage for the whole of the United States it was decided that the unit should be the dollar which, in the form of the Spanish dollar or piece of eight, was the most familiar piece of currency in circulation. It was further decided that a decimal system of coinage should be adopted, as advocated by Thomas Jefferson and approved by Washington. In 1792 legislation was passed specifying a coinage system which was to comprise a dollar, its half, quarter, disme or tenth—later popularized into dime—and a half-disme, all in silver. The denominations in gold were the eagle of ten dollars with its half and quarter and token pieces in copper of a cent, the hundreth part of a dollar, as well as a half-cent. A mint for the production of this coinage was established at Philadelphia. Several rare patterns were produced in 1792 but the regular issues date from the following year, though a few years passed before the whole denomination system was produced.

The first gold eagles struck in 1795 carried on the obverse the bust of Liberty wearing her distinctive cap, within a circle of stars representing the states, together with the inscription *Liberty* and the date. The reverse which gave its name to the piece showed an eagle with spread wings on a branch and holding a wreath in its beak with inscription *United States of America*. This reverse was changed in 1797 to a heraldic eagle grasping arrows and an olive-branch in its talons and with shield on breast; above it were the state stars and small clouds as well as the motto *E pluribus unum*. Since this gold coinage was undervalued in relation to prevalent world values, it tended to disappear from circulation and its issue was suspended in 1804. The half-eagle duplicated the types of the eagle itself until 1807 when a left-facing bust of Liberty with round cap inscribed *Liberty* on the cap-band was introduced. At the same time the reverse design was altered: the heraldic eagle was shown three-quarter facing, the motto was raised to a position under the inscription and the value 5 D. was added at the bottom. These types continued substantially unchanged until 1838. On the quarter-eagle the types and their pattern of change were exactly those of the half-piece. Following a reduction of the weight of standard gold in 1834 new mints, established at Dahlonega in Georgia and Charlotte in North Carolina near the sources of gold, joined Philadelphia in the striking of half- and quarter-eagles, their products being marked with their initial letter on the reverse.

The silver dollar was first struck in 1794 with designs similar to those described for the gold coins but with a head of Liberty with long hair on the obverse and an eagle within a wreath on the reverse. A bust of Liberty was introduced in 1795 and in 1798 the heraldic eagle type described on the gold pieces was adopted on the dollar (Pl. 784). Striking of this denomination was suspended in 1803. The half- and quarter-dollar, the dime and its half followed the types of the major piece but, just as in the case of the subdivisions of the gold, continued to be struck after the suspension of the major piece. Issues after about 1807 changed their types to those introduced at that time on the lower gold denominations, including the addition of the value at the bottom of the reverse. The activity of the Philadelphia mint was supplemented from 1838 by the mint at New Orleans which marked its products with O on the reverse. These designs were maintained till the late 1830's.

The copper denominations were the earliest pieces to be struck, both the half-cent and cent being issued in 1793. On the obverse of the half-cent was a long-haired head of Liberty with the Cap of Liberty on a pole behind her head with inscription *United States of America*; the value in words at centre was enclosed in a wreath, while the value, expressed as a fraction $\frac{1}{200}$ (of the dollar), appeared below. The 1793 cent had originally only a head of Liberty on obverse and on reverse a circular chain design enclosing the value in words and as a fraction. Later in the year types identical with those described for the half-cent were substituted. After 1797 the Cap of Liberty disappeared from the obverse and in 1808 a new bust of Liberty with a head-band inscribed with her name was introduced. A circle of stars was also added on the obverse and on the reverse the fractional mark of value was removed. These types remained substantially unchanged till 1857 (Pl. 785).

A new coinage act in 1837 prescribed, amongst other regulations, changes in the precious-metal coin types and was followed shortly afterwards by resumed striking of the gold eagle and the silver dollar. Issues of the eagle began again in 1838 with a coin of reduced weight and module and with modified designs. The obverse in fact carried a type similar to that on contemporary coppers, a head of Liberty with her name inscribed on a head-band instead of round the circumference of the coin which now consisted of a circle of stars. On the reverse was the heraldic eagle with the value, *Ten D*, below. The half- and quarter-eagles had received these modified designs in 1834 but acquired a smaller obverse head on issues in 1839 and 1840 respectively. The quarter retained these types till 1907, the half and the eagle itself until 1866. Additional mints at New Orleans and San Francisco marked their coinage with initials O and S. More obvious changes of type were effected on the silver coins on which the obverse from 1837 onwards showed a seated figure of Liberty holding cap on pole and resting her hand on a shield inscribed with her name. The reverse, as on the gold, was the eagle with value below on the dollar, its half and quarter. The dime and its half had a simple reverse, the value within a wreath. These issues continued until 1866, some issues being marked with the initials of New Orleans or San Francisco.

The coinage of the copper half-cent and large cent was discontinued in 1857, the former for good. The latter was replaced in 1859 by a coin of smaller module in cupro-nickel with an Indian-head obverse and value within wreath on the reverse. A small shield was added at the top of the wreath in 1860 and from 1864 the metal used was bronze. Right up to 1909 these popular types kept the field with only minor variations on lettering (Pl. 786). A new denomination, the 2 cents in copper introduced in 1864, was discontinued in 1872. The obverse with shield type is of interest as being the first instance of the use on coinage of the motto *In God we trust*, on a ribbon above the shield.

Other new smaller-value coins were the 3 cent pieces issued in silver between 1851 and 1873 with types, a shield within a six-pointed star and a roman III within the initial C. The necessity for this unusual denomination appears to have been the fixing of the postal rate at three cents. The denomination was also struck in nickel (1865–95) with Liberty head obverse and III within a wreath on the reverse. Of more moment, however, was the authorization in 1849 of a gold dollar following the great discoveries of gold in California in 1848. The types initially were a Liberty head with riband and value in wreath, changed in 1854 to a head with feathered head-dress (Pl. 787). A multiple piece of 3 dollars with identical types was struck from 1854 to 1889. The gold dollar was also issued until 1889 but the double eagle in gold also introduced in 1849 had a much longer life. The reverse of this piece until 1866 was an ornate heraldic eagle with stars and rays above and value below.

In the Civil War (1860–4) lack of supplies of bullion held up the coinage which was planned by the Confederate States. A small issue of silver half-dollars was in fact prepared in 1861 but never released. This was very much an issue of expediency, consisting of the removal of the reverse type from the national coinage of half-dollars of 1861 and restriking the reverse with a new type. The obverse, therefore, still showed the usual seated figure of Liberty but on the reverse, inscribed *Confederate States of America*, was placed a shield of seven stars and stripes with Cap of Liberty above between two branches. An issue of cents was also planned with value in wreath on reverse and a Liberty head with Confederate inscription on obverse. The cents likewise were never put into circulation and Confederate currency consisted of paper money only.

In 1866 a minor modification was effected in the reverse design of the gold eagle, its double and half as well as the silver dollar with its half and quarter, namely the addition of the motto *In God we trust* first used on the 2 cent piece in 1864. No other change of note was made on the gold pieces till 1907 or on the silver dollar till 1904. An additional mint was opened at Carson City in Nevada in 1870. The half- and quarter-dollar acquired in 1892 a new head of Liberty, treated in more modern style on the obverse and a more frontally presented eagle with stars above on the reverse, types which persisted till 1916. The same obverse head was also used on the dime from 1892 but the half-dime ceased to be struck in 1873, its place having been effectively taken by a new 5 cent piece introduced in 1866 and struck in nickel, the familiar name by which the denomination has come to be known. The types, at first a shield and value in a surround of stars and rays, were changed in 1883 to a Liberty head and a roman V in wreath. Two denominations issued in the later nineteenth century remain to be noted. A 20 cent piece with types of seated Liberty and eagle, struck briefly between 1875 and 1878, was withdrawn because of its similarity to the quarter-dollar. A special series of silver dollars was struck from 1873 for trade in the east. Liberty seated to the left holds a branch on the obverse; on the reverse, with usual eagle type, is inscribed the weight and fineness (480 grains, 900 fine) and the words *Trade Dollar*. Issues ceased in practice in 1878.

The coinage of the United States for something over a century had been extremely conservative and its international impact was due in part to the important part which American commerce had increasingly played throughout the world, and in part to romantic fiction which had rendered the names of its coins familiar to all. The twentieth century, however, brought a striking break in the hitherto conventional and conservative coin designs. Some were extremely successful, others not so inspired but all were at least attempts to break away from the heraldic conventions which still shackle much of modern coinage. Perhaps the most outstanding of these new designs was that for the double gold eagle introduced in 1907. A facing figure of Liberty with torch and branch stands on the obverse while on the reverse is an extremely effective eagle in flight, a design which clearly owes its inspiration to similar types on Ancient Greek coins. Less happy is the standing eagle on the reverse of the half- and quarter-eagle, a reminiscence, surely, of the eagles on Ptolemaic and Seleucid coinage, coupled with an obverse head of Liberty in Indian war-bonnet. Another standing eagle in defiant but clumsy pose was adopted for the half-dollar in 1916 with standing Liberty with flowing drapery on obverse, but the eagle, again in flight, on the quarter is more graceful. Ancient coin types also inspired the designs of the 1916 dime on which the Liberty head wears the winged hat of Mercury and the fasces of the Roman consul occupies the reverse. The nickel of 1913 draws on American types, an Indian head and a buffalo (Pl. 788). The portrait of Lincoln adopted for the obverse of the cent has maintained its popularity until the present day (Pl. 789). The silver dollar, coined again between 1921 and 1935 and presenting a modern rendering of the head of Liberty in radiate crown and a perching eagle, was first issued in 1921 to mark the return of peace.

The economic crisis of the 1930's brought to an end the issue of gold coinage and also of the silver dollar, leaving in circulation the half- and quarter-dollar, the dime, nickel and cent. As legislation of 1890 decreed that changes in coin design should not be made more often than once every twenty-five years the types on some of these remaining denominations, changed after the last war, are likely to go unaltered for a considerable period. The trend in modern times is towards honouring America's famous sons on the various denominations. Lincoln, on the cent, was joined on the quarter-dollar by Washington in 1932, while portraits of Thomas Jefferson appeared on the nickel in 1938, Franklin Roosevelt on the dime in 1946 and Benjamin Franklin on the half-dollar in 1948.

The normal coinage series which has been described has been enlivened from the late nineteenth century by the issue of commemorative pieces, usually of half-dollar value, for such occasions as the tercentenary in 1920 of the landing of the Pilgrim Fathers. These, however, have normally been struck in restricted numbers, presumably for the delectation of coin-collectors. Another and more substantial subsidiary is formed by the gold issues by some of the states and even private companies during the great gold era of the late mid nineteenth century. In 1965 the metal of the 10 and 25 cent coins was changed from silver to cupro-nickel. On the new silver half-dollar introduced in 1964 the obverse carried the portrait of the late President Kennedy and the reverse the American eagle arms. In 1965 this was issued as a 'clad' coin with only 40% silver.

CENTRAL AMERICA

It is perhaps not geographically accurate to include Mexico in Central America but since political and numismatic history has separated it firmly from the North American states and linked it equally firmly with Central America and the Spanish New World it has been thought permissible, and certainly desirable, to treat it in this latter context. In addition, since the first mint in the New World for the coinage of the Spanish empire was established at Mexico City and since the issues of that mint were amongst the most prolific and continuous, it will be convenient to give a fairly detailed account of its coinage which will be of general application in the other regions of the Spanish empire in Central and South America.

MEXICO

Shortly after the penetration of Mexico by the Spaniards under Cortès in 1519 the Aztec city of Mexico was captured and destroyed but was soon rebuilt to form, eventually, the capital of the Spanish vice-royalty of New Spain. In 1536 a mint for the Spanish coinage was opened in Mexico City which continued to strike up to and during the war of independence (1810–21). Other provincial mints were established during this unsettled period but Mexico City continued to be the mint for the first Mexican empire of Iturbide (1822–3) and for the republic from 1823 till the present day, as well as for the interlude of the second Mexican empire under Maximilian (1864–7).

The first coinage of the Mexico City mint was in the names of Charles I (the emperor Charles V) and his mother Johanna (1521–56) and consisted of silver coins of 4, 2, 1 and a half-real values. The obverse type, inscribed *Carolus et Iohana Reges*, bore the royal arms of Spain, quartered with the lion of Leon and the castle of Castille, with the small pomegranate of Granada at the point of the shield; to the right appeared the initial M of the mint, surmounted by a small O and to the left the initial of the mint assayer. The reverse, continuing the royal titles *Hispaniarum et Indiarum*, had as type the Pillars of Hercules (representing the Straits of Gibraltar) crowned and standing in the sea, with the motto *Plus Ultra* across the field, and the value, e.g. 4, between the pillars (Pl. 790). Copper coins of 4 and 2 maravedis with the initial K on obverse and I on reverse, each flanked by lion and castle and with the value under the I, were struck but proved

428

so unpopular that they were withdrawn and extremely few examples have survived. Copper was not coined again until the nineteenth century.

The coinage of Philip II (1556–98), in silver only, was furnished with new types. The obverse was still the royal arms crowned but these now bore the quarterings of the many additional states of which Philip was the ruler; beside the shield of arms the value in Roman or Arabic numerals was placed in addition to the initials of the mint and the assayer. The reverse carried a cross with the lion-and-castle device in alternate angles. The half-real, instead of the crowned arms, has a monogram of Philippus. The five values enumerated above continued to be struck, though some pieces of 8 reales have been attributed to this reign. Most of the coinage was of the 'cob' type, that is, not quite circular in shape but somewhat angular, since the flans were produced by slicing from a bar of silver. Under Philip III (1598–1621) and Philip IV (1621–65) the same range of coinage was struck with the same types and since many of the surviving examples of coins of these three Philips are struck on such irregular flans that much of the obverse inscription is often missing, particularly the ordinal number of the king, the exact attribution of these coins is often extremely difficult. An additional difficulty is that the practice of placing the date on the reverse inscription which had begun under Philip II was not always observed.

The first gold coins of the Mexican mint were struck for Charles II (1665–1700) in 1679. The types were almost the same as those of the silver coins except that the lion-and-castle devices in the angles of the reverse cross were replaced by fleur-de-lis and the cross is in the form of a Jerusalem cross. The denominations were the 8 and 4 escudo pieces with a rare 2 escudos also reported. Silver of the established types continued to be struck. For Philip V, the first of the Spanish Bourbons, in his first reign (1700–24) both gold and silver coinage was produced as before, the gold now in four denominations of 8, 4, 2 and 1 escudo pieces (Pl. 792), but not all these denominations have been confirmed for Louis I who succeeded on his father's abdication in 1724. On Louis' death after a reign of only a few months, Philip V resumed the crown and reigned till 1746. New types were introduced on both gold and silver in this second reign and the majority of the coinage was now of circular shape and not of the angular 'cob' variety. The coinage of gold escudos now carried the royal bust and titles on the obverse, while the crowned shield of arms was transferred to the reverse, where the 8 escudo piece had, as an addition, the chain of the Order of the Golden Fleece. The mint mark was also moved from the field to a position in the circular inscription. The silver reales still retained the crowned shield on the obverse but the reverse showed two globes crowned between the Pillars of Hercules on each of which a riband bears a portion of the motto *Plus Ultra* (Pl. 791). On the silver also, the mint initial was incorporated in the inscription. On the silver of Charles III (1760–88) new types appeared in 1773: the obverse had the royal portrait, the reverse crowned arms between pillars with the mark of value now also placed in the inscription. The silver quarter-real or cuartilla was first issued by Charles IV in 1796 with lion on obverse and castle flanked by the mint initial and value on the reverse.

During the revolution which broke out against the Spanish authorities in 1810 royalist provisional mints were established in other cities. Of these only Guadalajara in Nueva Galicia struck gold 8 escudo pieces with mint-mark, initial G accompanied by a small A. Silver was also issued by this mint as well as by mints at Chihuahua, Durango, Guanajunto, Sombrerete and Zacatecas, each of which marked its products with its initial letter. At Chihuahua some of the earliest issues were produced by casting copies from coins of the Mexico City mint. At other cities, such as Nueva Vicaya and Oaxaca, emergency issues with individual types were struck.

The coins issued by the Mexican insurgents include a series in all three metals struck by Morelos, the leader in the south. The types, which have a great number of variations of detail, represent, basically, on the obverse a roughly drawn bow and arrow and the word *Sud* (South) and the value and date on the reverse, accompanied sometimes by the initial M of Morelos. Other coinage was produced by the Supreme National Junta in the years from 1811 to 1814. The first issue of silver 8 real pieces, produced in 1811 by casting, had on obverse an eagle on a bridge of three arches, and was still inscribed with the name of Ferdinand VII; the reverse, a hand holding a bow and arrow with sword and quiver in saltire, was inscribed *Provicional por la suprema junta de America*. On die-struck pieces in 1812 the obverse inscription reads *Vice Ferd VII*, etc. Pieces of 1 real were also produced, as well as some 8 real pieces in copper. Both royalist and insurgent commanders on occasions found it necessary to countermark coinage already in circulation.

When the insurgent forces captured Mexico City in 1821 the Spanish vice-royalty of New Spain ceased to exist and the country assumed the name of Mexico. Augustin Iturbide became head of state, first as a regent and then, in 1822, as emperor of Mexico. On gold coinage of 8 and 4 escudos pieces the new emperor's head was accompanied on the obverse by the inscription *Augustinus Dei Providentia*, while the reverse, showing an eagle perched on a cactus, surrounded by arms or in an oval frame, was inscribed *Mex I Imperator Constitut*. Silver from 8 reales down to a half-real had similar types, the reverse not so elaborate. When Iturbide was compelled to abdicate and flee the country in 1823 Mexico was declared a republic, the form of government which it has maintained with the exception of the years 1864–7 and despite repeated civil wars.

A coinage was struck for the republic of Mexico in gold, silver and copper in the years 1823–64 both at the mint of Mexico and at some eight or nine provincial mints such as Chihuahua and Durango. Gold denominations which included pieces of 8, 4, 2, 1 and ½ escudo had as types a hook-necked eagle with outstretched wings, holding a snake in its beak and standing on a cactus, all between branches of oak and laurel and inscribed on the obverse *Republica Mexicana*. The reverse inscribed *Libertad en la ley,* together with the denomination and the mint initial, showed a hand holding a book surmounted by the Cap of Liberty. In silver the major piece was the 8 reales or peso with smaller values of 4 reales, 2 reales or peseta, 1 real and a half-piece. These had a similar obverse to that of the gold coins but the reverse type was a Cap of Liberty with a background of rays (Pl. 793). The copper cuartino or quarter of a real and the eighth, still with eagle obverse, had value in wreath on reverse. The provincial mints struck these copper denominations in a range of more individual types.

Mexico which had been the scene of one of the earliest European conquests in the New World also witnessed the last European adventure into New World affairs. In the civil dissensions of 1861 Miramon, overthrown by Juarez, appealed to the Catholic powers of Europe and in response Napoleon III of France despatched an expedition which set up a new Mexican empire with the Archduke Maximilian, brother of the Emperor Francis Joseph of Austria, as its emperor. The imperial coinage was based on the decimal system which had already been proposed in 1861. The unit was the peso, divided into 100 centavos. The coinage issued for Maximilian consisted of the peso and pieces of 50, 10 and 5 centavos in silver and a centavo piece in copper. On the peso and its half the portrait head of Maximilian on obverse was inscribed *Maximiliano Emperador*, while the reverse with legend *Imperio Mexicano* and value carried the imperial arms crowned (Pl. 794). The United States, emerging from its own civil war in 1865, refused to recognize Maximilian and ordered Napoleon to evacuate Mexico. The imposed régime, unpopular and deprived of outside support, ended with the execution of Maximilian in 1867 and the restoration of the republic.

The coinage of the restored republic included a range of gold coins of 1, 2½, 5, 10 and 20 peso values with the conventional eagle type on obverse but with the scales of Justice and Cap of Liberty on the reverse. The silver peso and its portions used similar types, though the lower centavo values in silver and the 1 and 2 centavo pieces in copper had simply the value in wreath on the reverse. Nickel coins of 1, 2 and 5 centavo values with bow and quiver obverse were struck only in the years 1882–3. The old piece of 8 reales with eagle and Cap of Liberty type also continued to be struck up to 1897. The official designation of the country, *Estados Unidos Mexicanos*, was placed on the coinage from 1905 but the types suffered little change. The Mexican Civil War of 1913 to 1917 gave rise to a whole range of coinage struck at the mints of the several provinces by the various parties and states which continued to make use of the traditional eagle and Liberty types. The official issues included gold pesos with eagle type and a head of Hidalgo, the leader of the original revolt against Spain. The silver coinage up to 1917 had on the reverse a mounted female figure with wreath and torch and, from 1918 till 1945, the inevitable Cap of Liberty with rays. A special 2 peso piece in silver was first struck in 1921 with a standing figure of Victory on the reverse to com-memorate the centenary of independence. A new coinage in 1947 honoured some of Mexico's heroes; the 5 peso bears the head of the Aztec king Cuauhtec and the 1 peso the portrait of Morelos, the revolutionary leader in 1821. Of the very recent Mexican issues silver pieces of 5 and 10 pesos carry the head of Hildago on the reverse, while Cuauhtec in his elaborate head-dress appears on the 50 centavo piece. A special issue of the silver 25 peso coin in 1968 commemorated the Olympic Games held in Mexico City.

GUATEMALA

The captain-generalcy of Guatemala in the Spanish empire comprised the modern states of Guatemala, Costa Rica, Nicaragua, San Salvador and Honduras. A mint was opened at Guatemala in 1733, signing its products with the letter G, and, when a new city of Guatemala was built, the mint, transferred there in 1777, signed NG (Nueva Guatemala). The silver coinage from the reign of Philip V (1700–46) onwards is, apart from the mint-mark, identical with that described under Mexico, much of it until about 1753 being of the rough 'cob' variety. Gold was coined from 1751 onwards, its variations of type being parallel to those of the Mexican issues. The Mexican war for independence was not without its influence in Central America, and Guatemala declared itself independent of Spain in 1821 and became the Confederation of Central America which endured until it splintered in 1832 into the present Central American states. The confederation struck a coinage of pieces of 8 reales and lower values down to the quarter-real in silver. A range of mountain peaks and a rising sun on the obverse is accompanied by the inscription *Republica del Centro de America*, while the reverse with motto *Libre cresca fecundo* has a single tree parting the indication of value (Pl. 795). Nueva Guatemala in Guatemala signed its coins with NG, Tegucigalpa in Hon-duras with T, Leon in Nicaragua with NR, and San José in Costa Rica with CR.

After the dissolution of the Union in 1832 Guatemala did not issue its own coinage till 1859. The series of peso or 8 reales and divisionary pieces in silver bore the portrait, name and title of its president Rafael Carrera on the obverse and the state arms and value on the reverse. These types were preserved after the death of Carrera in 1865 but his portrait now had the title of *Fundador de la republica de Guatemala*. Later nineteenth-century coinage had as the most persistent types either a head or a seated figure of Liberty and a scroll on crossed arms. The coinage reform of 1924 created a new unit the quetzal in silver with subdivisions and with multiples in gold. The types were on obverse the quetzal, a Central American bird of the parrot family with long tail and resplendent plumage, on a pillar with the value and the same bird perched on a scroll on crossed arms (Pl. 796). Later reverses on the 5, 10 and 25 centavo coins are respectively a tree, a monolith, and portrait bust in local dress. From 1965 these denominations have been issued in nickel-brass.

BRITISH HONDURAS

This British enclave in Spanish Central America grew from original buccaneer settlement, and was finally recognized by Spain in 1798. It acquired colonial status in 1862 but the first coinage was not struck until 1885. This first issue consisted only of copper cents with the head of Victoria and on the reverse the figure 1 with an inscription *British Honduras One Cent* and the date. Higher values of 10, 25 and 50 cents in silver were added in 1894 with equally simple types. Apart from the portraits of the successive monarchs the coinage has remained unchanged till the present day but several metals have been used, including the cupronickel of the current coins (Pl. 797).

HONDURAS

Rare silver 2 real pieces were struck at the mint of Tegucigalpa in 1823 with the Spanish arms between two pillars accompanied by the mint name, value and date on obverse, while the reverse carried a cross with lion and castle in the angles. The same mint issued various real values of the republic of Central America in 1830 and 1831 (see p. 432) and the types of mountain peaks and trees were retained on the provisional coinage of Honduras after 1832. Coins of denominations from 8 reales downwards were struck in base metal and inscribed on obverse *Provisional del Est. de Honduras*. In 1869–70 the real and its portions in cupronickel carried a harbour scene between two flags on obverse and the value in wreath on reverse (Pl. 798). On the gold peso, with occasional multiples up to 20, issued from 1888 to 1922, there was a Liberty head on obverse and on the reverse arms consisting of a triangle within a circlet inscribed *Republica de Honduras*. The silver peso and lower centavo values from 1882 repeated the arms type on the reverse but showed on obverse a seated figure of Liberty holding flag and scroll. Lower centavo values in bronze with arms-type obverse had a simple value reverse. The coinage decree of 1926 instituted a new unit—the lempira—which, together with the 50 and 20 centavo values, was struck in silver. The types were an Indian head and the Honduras arms, while on the lower centavo pieces in bronze or cupro-nickel the types were the arms and value.

NICARAGUA

Under Spanish dominion the mint of Leon in Nicaragua struck a coinage of silver reales in several values from the later seventeenth century and very rare gold in the later eighteenth century. The types were the standard Spanish colonial designs (see pp. 428–9) and the coins were marked by the signature of the mint NR, usually ligatured. While Nicaragua formed part of the republic of Central America the mint at Leon issued silver 2 real pieces with mountain peaks and tree types (see p. 432) in 1825. In the later nineteenth century the monetary unit was the peso of 100 centavos and silver coinage of 50, 25 and 10 centavos and lower values in cupro-nickel or bronze had as types a triangular frame enclosing mountain peaks, surmounted by a Cap of Liberty on obverse and value in wreath on reverse. In the present century a new unit the cordoba of 100 centavos was created. The new unit took its name from the obverse type the portrait of Cordoba, used on all denominations—the cordoba in silver and centavo values in cupro-nickel or brass. The reverse continued to show the range of mountain peaks with a sun rising behind them (Pl. 799).

SALVADOR

After the break-up of the Republic of Central America a rare provisional coinage was issued for Salvador in 1833–5 of silver 2, 1 and ½ real pieces with volcano on obverse inscribed *Moneda Provisional* and a crowned column on the reverse with inscription *Por la libertad Salv.* Later nineteenth-century coinage was issued with the silver peso of 100 centavos as the unit. Coins of 1 and 3 centavos in copper in 1889 carried the head of President Morazan on the obverse and the value on reverse. The issue begun in 1892 comprised a silver peso and a 50 centavos piece with head of Christopher Columbus on obverse and the arms of Salvador on the reverse and lower centavo values with arms-and-value types. From 1913 the low-value coins revived the obverse portrait of Morazan. The new unit, the colon, taking its name from Colon the Spanish form of Columbus, was instituted in 1925. The colon in silver and the special gold 20 colones piece issued in 1925 celebrate the fourth centenary of Salvador with jugate busts of the early Spanish commander Alvarado and of President Quinonez on the obverse and arms type on the reverse (Pl. 800).

COSTA RICA

As one of the component states in the republic of Central America formed in 1821 Costa Rica participated in the coinage described above under Guatemala (see p. 432). The Costa Rican mint was San José which signed its products with the letters CR. Even after the Central American Federation dissolved, Costa Rica continued to use this same coinage of 2, 1 and ½ real pieces with its types of mountain peaks and tree (Pl. 801) as well as a coinage in gold of 8, 4, 2, 1 and ½ escudo pieces with similar types to those on the silver. In 1849–50 a silver real coinage appeared with new types and inscriptions. The obverse with a facing female bust was inscribed *America Central*, while the reverse, still with the single tree-type, carried the state name *Republica de Costa Rica*. The peso of 100 centavos was adopted as the monetary unit in 1850. The gold escudo, struck also in several multiples as well as in the half-piece or gold peso, now bore the state arms on obverse and an Indian leaning against an inscribed column on the reverse. Silver in the form of the half-peso and similar fractions also had the arms-type obverse but retained the traditional tree-type on the reverse. From 1864 gold coins had the value expressed in pesos as the reverse type though silver coins, expressed in centavo values, continued the arms-and-tree types, changing in 1885 to arms-and-value types.

A new unit, the colon, introduced in 1897 took its name from Cristobal Colon whose portrait appeared on the obverse, accompanied by arms on the reverse on gold pieces of 2, 5, 10 and 20 colones. The divisionary coinage in silver was now expressed in centimos. More modern issues from 1937 onwards with arms-and-value types have been struck in cupro-nickel in denominations of 1 and 2 colones and 50 and 25 centimos. The most recent colones coins are issued in steel.

PANAMA

The isthmus of Panama broke away from Costa Rica in 1903 to conclude with the United States the treaty which enabled the Panama Canal to be constructed. The unit is the balboa, named after the Spanish conquistador whose portrait occupies the obverse of many coin issues. The first coinage in 1904 was of silver centesimos of various values from 50 to 2½ with portrait of Balboa and the arms of Panama on the reverse (Pl. 802). Later minor coins had arms-and-value types but a new coinage in 1930 consisted of a silver balboa and fractions with helmeted bust of the conquistador and standing figure of the republic or arms. Minor values were in base metal with bust of Balboa and value. The fiftieth anniversary of Panama was celebrated in 1953 by a coinage with similar types with an additional inscription *Cincuentenaria* under the bust of Balboa.

SOUTH AMERICA

The early part of the sixteenth century witnessed the gradual conquest of South America by the Spaniards, until by 1541 the whole territory belonged to the Spanish crown, with the exception of Brasil which Portugal had occupied. When, in 1542, Central America was formed into a vice-royalty, a second vice-royalty was set up in South America with its capital at Lima. In 1718 the vice-royalty of New Granada, comprising the northern part of the sub-continent, was created and in 1776 a fourth vice-royalty was established in the south with its capital at Buenos Aires. Coinage for the Spanish empire was struck at a number of South American mints of which the more important were Lima and Potosi. The products of these mints will be described in the separate geographic sections below. During the Napoleonic wars when the Spanish control of the South American colonies was less effective, independence movements began from about 1810 but the establishment of the modern independent states of South America came only a decade or more later.

COLOMBIA

In the Spanish empire Colombia formed part, first of the vice-royalty of Peru and from 1718 of the new vice-royalty of New Granada (Nuevo Reino de Granada). The Spanish mints in this territory were at Popayan and Santa Fé de Bogota. The latter mint began operations in 1622, marking its products with the letters NR, the initials of the province of Nueva Reina. For the first century silver only was coined in real pieces of various values with types, the shield of Castille and Leon on one side and the Pillars of Hercules on the other. The first gold coins were struck in 1756 in the reign of Ferdinand VI with types, portrait bust and arms.

The coinage was, in effect, closely parallel to that described in detail under Mexico (pp. 428–30) and shows the same changes in types. An oddity of the mint was that the coinage for Ferdinand VII up to 1820, though bearing his name and title, continued to have the portrait of his predecessor, Charles IV. The mint at Popayan began coining in 1758, its products being marked with P or PN and, apart from a brief cessation between 1763 and 1767, was active until the end of Spanish dominion under Ferdinand VII. At Popayan as at Bogota coinage was mainly of gold escudos of various values, though silver in the form usually of reales and cuartillos was also issued. The types and their changes followed the pattern of the issues of the Mexico City mint.

The vice-royalty of New Granada made itself independent of Spain in 1811 and struck a coinage of silver pieces of 8 reales and subdivisions. The Indian head on obverse is inscribed *Libertad Americana* and on the reverse the name *Nueva Granada* accompanies a pomegranate, the traditional badge of Granada in Spain (Pl. 803). The Republic of Colombia, formed in 1819 and consisting of Venezuela and Ecuador as well as the modern Colombia, had a coinage of silver reales similar to those just described but with *Republica de Colombia* on obverse. An issue of copper cuartillos with the portrait of Bolivar and the word *Colombia* on the obverse and either a seated or standing figure of Justice with sword and scales carries no date but was produced in 1831 in Birmingham for Colombia (Pl. 804). Gold escudo pieces with multiples up to 8 were also struck with a Liberty head on obverse and the fasces between two cornuacopiae on the reverse, a type which from 1834 supplied the obverse of the silver series which now had a value reverse. The union, however, did not long survive the death of the liberator, Bolivar, in 1830, and split again into its component states in 1836, Colombia adopting now the title of Republica de la Nueva Granada. The Liberty head remained on the obverse of the gold, accompanied by the new state title, while the reverse was formed by the state arms and an inscription giving the value in pesos, together with the mint name of Bogota or Popayan. Silver real denominations showed a condor in flight above a cornucopiae on obverse and value on the reverse. In 1847 as a step towards a decimal coinage the peso was divided into 10 reales of 10 centavos. On the gold denominations a Liberty head and condor above arms supplied the types, the latter type appearing also on the major silver pieces with a value reverse. The republic of New Granada was replaced by the Confederacion Granadina in 1858 but apart from the inscription no change was made in the coin types.

Yet another change, made in 1861 when the title Estados Unidos de Colombia was adopted, brought little alteration to the coins which were struck by a new mint at Medellin, as well as the former mints at Bogota and Popayan. Nickel coins of $2\frac{1}{2}$ and $1\frac{1}{4}$ centavos in 1874 and 1881 had as types a Cap of Liberty and value. In the early twentieth century the title reverted to Republica de Colombia. From 1919 gold pesos and silver centavo pieces bore the portrait of Bolivar and the arms of Colombia (Pl. 806). The uniformed bust of Bolivar forms the obverse of post-war 50 and 20 centavos coins, and an Indian head that of the 10 centavos. A similar series but inscribed 1810–1960 commemorated the rising against Spain. A special 5 peso coinage was issued in honour of the Eucharist congress in Bogota in 1968.

VENEZUELA

The last Spanish captain-general was deposed in 1810 but only some rare emergency coins were issued at that time and, though Venezuela joined in the formation of the republic of New Granada in 1819 (see p. 437), Caracas, held by the Spanish till 1821, struck a few silver reales with lion and castle arms and Pillars of Hercules types. Venezuela became an independent state in 1836 but only in 1843 and again in 1852 did coinage in the name of Venezuela appear in the form of copper centavo and half-centavo pieces with Liberty head and value types. A new currency system, instituted in 1857, was based on the gold venezolano, equivalent to the French 5 franc piece with a silver peso or 10 reales, divided into 100 centavos. Silver only was struck at this time with the head of Liberty and the arms of Venezuela, while the previous copper centavo issue was continued but in reduced module. With the adoption in 1871 of the new title Estados Unidos de Venezuela came also a new coinage. The new monetary unit was the bolivar, taking its name from the liberator, Simon Bolivar, whose portrait appeared on the obverse of gold pieces in multiples from 5 to 100 and in silver from 5 down to ½ bolivar (Pl. 806). The reverse was the state arms which also provided the obverse for cupro-nickel coins in lower centavo values which formed the reverse type. This system lasted until 1947, and the new coinage of 1954 also retained the Bolivar arms types on the bolivar and 50 and 25 centimos in silver. In 1965 the metal was changed to nickel for these coins and to cupro-nickel for the lower centimo values.

ECUADOR

For Ecuador as part of the republic of Colombia a coinage of gold escudos and of silver 2, 1 and ½ real pieces was struck at the mint of Quito in 1833 and 1835 with types, fasces between two cornuacopiae inscribed *El Ecuador en Colombia* and the mint name on obverse and a sun above two mountain peaks on the reverse. A similar coinage from 4 to ½ real was struck after the establishment of Ecuador as a separate republic in 1836 with only the necessary alteration of the obverse inscription to *Republica de Ecuador*. A bust of Bolivar and the arms of Ecuador appeared on 4 real pieces in 1844, while a Liberty head obverse was adopted for the range of real pieces from 8 downwards from 1846 onwards. Gold escudos between 1838 and 1843 had Liberty head and mountain-peak types and Bolivar head and arms types from 1845. A new coinage, introduced in 1884, was based on the silver sucre which took its name from the portrait of Sucre, one of Bolivar's lieutenants, which formed its obverse (Pl. 807). The unit was divided into 10 decimos or 100 centavos. The reverse on the silver coins was the state arms as also on 10 sucre pieces in gold struck in 1899 and 1900. On lower value centavo coins the types were arms and value. These have continued to be the types of Ecuador's coins in the twentieth century, though, following the trend in world coinage, the metals used have become baser, the sucre and its divisionary centavo pieces being from 1946 in cupro-nickel, and from 1963 in nickel-clad steel.

PERU

The original vice-royalty of Peru comprised the whole of Spanish South America until the creation, in the eighteenth century, of the vice-royalties of New Granada in the north and that of the south with its capital at Buenos Aires. The two great Spanish mints were at Lima and Potosi, the latter now in the territory of Bolivia. The latter mint was set up in 1575 for the striking of silver signed with the letter P (Pl. 808). The types on the various real denominations are similar to those struck at Mexico City (p. 428). Gold coinage was first struck in 1779 and continued until 1808 with brief recurrences in the last years before the end of Spanish dominion in 1824. The Lima mint began striking silver at an earlier date, in 1568, with types in general similar to the usual Spanish-American types. The mint was burnt down in 1620 but reopened briefly in 1659 and then from 1684 struck continuously until 1820. Gold coinage began in 1697. With some slight variations the types are as those on the Mexican issues.

Peru declared its independence in 1821 and a coinage of 8 and 4 real pieces was struck at Lima with Virtue and Justice on the obverse and the new state arms consisting of a llama, a tree and a cornucopiae on the reverse. It was not, however, until 1824 that, with the assistance of San Martin, the liberator of Chile, and Bolivar, the liberator of Colombia, that Spanish rule was finally ended. The subsequent coinage of the Republic of Peru included some half-escudo pieces in gold with the state arms on obverse and the value and mint name on reverse and a standing figure of Liberty and the state arms on the escudo and its multiples. These same types were used on the silver real, its multiples and divisionary pieces. The ¼ and ⅛ peso in copper in 1823 had on obverse a llama with mountains and sun in the background and the value on the reverse (Pl. 809). These issues were normally struck by the mint at Lima. Other mints at Arequipa, Cuzco and Pasco issued some silver with these types but also struck silver with a sun as obverse and value on reverse.

In 1857 a new decimal coinage was instituted with the silver sol as the monetary unit. The types now were a seated Liberty and arms on the sol and its portions, including the small dinero and its half. A sun and the value provided the types on the nickel or bronze centavo pieces. These types continued with little change through the nineteenth century and into the twentieth. The gold libra, equivalent to 10 soles, issued from 1898, showed the head of an Inca chief on obverse but still maintained the arms on the reverse, and on coins of 5, 10 and 20 centavos in nickel or brass a head of Liberty or the republic, wearing corn-wreath, appeared on the obverse with a branch and value on the reverse. A special gold 50 sol coin in 1930–1 had as obverse the head of the Inca, Manco Capac. The special multiple gold soles, from 1950 on, with Liberty and Arms types represent bullion not currency. On the new coinage of 1966 the state arms obverse has as reverse on the centavo coins a flower and value, and on the sol and its half a llama.

BOLIVIA

General Sucre, one of Bolivar's lieutenants, detached Upper Peru in 1825 and created a new republic with the name of Bolivia. Potosi, one of the great mints in Peru in the Spanish period, was situated in this territory and was used to strike the new Bolivian coinage, supplemented later in 1853 by another mint at La Paz. Gold escudos and multiples honoured Bolivar by placing his bust in uniform on the obverse, clearly labelled with his name below and with an inscription *Libre por la Constitucion*. The reverse showed a mountain with rising sun and a llama in the foreground. The silver sueldo with multiples up to 8 and divisionary pieces also bore the portrait of Bolivar but had a different reverse, two llamas recumbent at the foot of a tree (Pl. 810). A decimal coinage, introduced in 1863, had as its unit the peso or boliviano in silver, divided into 100 centavos with types, an oval shield, flanked by flags and surmounted by a condor on obverse and the value on reverse. Copper centavo values in 1878 had the condor only on the obverse. In 1893 the 5 and 10 centavo pieces in nickel began to be issued with the arms, which are formed from the reverse type of the original Bolivian coins, as obverse and a staff of Aesculapius and value on reverse. The 1951 coinage of 1, 5 and 10 bolivianos had a value reverse and arms or Bolivar obverse. The currency reform of 1962 equated 1,000 bolivianos to the new peso of 100 centavos. The 1966 coinage revived the mountain, sun and llama obverse of earlier issues.

CHILE

Chile was not settled by the Spanish with such expedition as the more northern parts of South America and, though the city of Santiago de Chile was founded in 1541, a mint was not established there till about 1750. The earliest issues, bearing the signature S accompanied by small O, were gold 8 escudo pieces of Ferdinand V and gold of various escudo values continued to be struck with some regularity down to 1817, the types and their changes following fairly closely those described in detail for the Mexican mint. Coinage of the several real values in silver began in 1754.

The struggle for Chilean independence began in 1810 and Spanish control, reimposed in 1814, was finally broken in 1817. The obverse on the coinage of gold escudos, begun in 1824, was a variation of the popular South American type of a mountain range, but here it includes two active volcanoes. On the reverse was a column with two flags in saltire. The silver-real series showed a single volcano on obverse and the column without flags on the reverse (Pl. 811). New types were introduced in 1835 for the gold escudos, a hand resting on the book of the Constitution on obverse and the star shield of Chile with llama and condor supporters. In 1839 the obverse was altered to a figure of Liberty standing by the altar of the Constitution. Silver also received new types in 1838, arms on the obverse and a condor on the reverse. The types of the decimal coinage based on the peso of 10 decimos or 100 centavos were, on silver, arms and a flying condor with a broken chain in its beak, but the gold types remained unchanged. In 1867 the silver peso and its parts took as its obverse a condor beside an oval shield and, as reverse, value in wreath, while low-centavo values with value reverse had a republic head in corn-wreath on obverse. In 1896 a Liberty head and arms were introduced as the types of the gold peso multiples and on silver the obverse was changed to a defiant condor on a mountain peak, a type which persisted till the 1930's. Gold coins were struck in 1926 in denominations of the condor, equivalent to 10 pesos. From 1942 coinage of the peso and centavo values in copper had the portrait bust in uniform of the liberator, Bernardo O'Higgins, on obverse and value reverse. From 1954 the peso and multiples in aluminium have been issued with the same types. The 10 peso coins of 1956 in aluminium have a condor on the obverse and, in a wreath on the reverse, the value 10 *pesos* = 1 *condor*.

ARGENTINA

The movement for independence from Spain began in 1810 and in 1813 a coinage in gold and silver was struck for the Provincias del Rio de la Plata at the mint at Potosi. The Spanish monetary system of gold escudos and silver reales was continued but new types were adopted. The obverse showed a beaming sun and the title *Provincias del Rio de la Plata*, the reverse the new arms, two hands holding a staff surmounted by the Cap of Liberty, accompanied by the inscription *Union y Libertad* (Pl. 812). When Upper Peru was retaken by the Spaniards in 1815 and the mint at Potosi could no longer be used, other mints in the provinces, particularly Rioja, which signed its coins RA, were set up. When de Rosas became dictator in 1836 the name of the state was changed to Republica Argentina Confederada and the types on both gold and silver were altered to the mountain Famatina above crossed flags on obverse and the arms on reverse, flanked, in the case of gold coins, by flags. A brief issue at the outset of the coinage had carried the portrait of de Rosas on the obverse.

The striking of coinage languished from the 1850's and was replaced almost entirely by paper money until a new decimal coinage was decreed in 1881 to be struck by the mint at Buenos Aires. The unit, as elsewhere in South America, was the silver peso of 100 centavos. On gold coins of 5 and $2\frac{1}{2}$ pesos, known as the argentino and its half, as well as on the silver and the low centavo pieces in copper the types were a Liberty head and state arms. In 1896 the 5, 10 and 20 centavo pieces struck in nickel carried the Liberty head and value. These continued to be the principal coins struck up to 1950, though the types were modernized in 1942 and a 50 centavo piece added in 1941. In 1950 the obverse type was changed to a portrait of the liberator San Martin whose centenary, then being celebrated, was mentioned on the reverse also. In recent years higher value 5, 10 and 25 peso coins have been added to the series.

URUGUAY

in the course of the independence movements in South America Brasil occupied the left bank of the Rio de la Plata which, after recapture by the new independent state, later Argentina, fell again to Brasil which set up a Cisplatine republic in 1821. In 1828 the independent Republica Oriental del Uruguay was created. Coinage was not issued until 1840 and for long consisted only of 5, 20 and 40 centesimo pieces in copper with a sun obverse and value reverse. In 1869, 1, 2 and 4 centesimos in copper were struck with these same types and in 1877 the silver peso with divisionary pieces in centesimos was added with arms and value types. The gold peso and multiples with identical types was issued in 1870. In 1916 the bust of Artigas, the hero of the liberation, was placed on the obverse of the silver coins and the arms were transferred to the reverse (Pl. 813). The small centavo coins remained unchanged until 1938 but on the 1930 10 centavo piece a Liberty head marked the centenary of liberation. The silver peso, re-issued in 1942, still had the Artigas reverse but now with a jaguar on reverse. The new coinage of centesimos from 10 downwards, begun in 1953, has the same obverse but a simple value reverse. The 25 and 50 centesimos and the peso, added in 1960, and the 5 and 10 pesos in 1965, had the state arms as reverse.

PARAGUAY

The earliest coinage of Paraguay, the only completely inland state of South America, consisted of an issue of the copper $\frac{1}{12}$ real with types, a lion standing in front of a staff surmounted by the Cap of Liberty on obverse and the value on reverse. Other copper pieces of 1, 2 and 4 centesimos struck in 1870 had a star between two branches on obverse and value reverse, but in 1889 came the first coinage of silver pesos combining the lion and Cap of Liberty and the star types. All the silver issues of the twentieth century till the last war reverted to star-and-value types. On the new coinage in aluminium-bronze, begun in 1944, the various centimo values have had each a different obverse such as the lion and Cap of Liberty on the 50 centimos (Pl.814) or an orchid on the 10 centimos piece The most recent issues begun in 1953 have a scalloped edge and all use the lion type on obverse.

BRASIL

By an award of Pope Alexander and the Treaty of Tordesillas in 1493 the New World was divided by a north to south line, all territory to the east of this line being allocated to Portugal. In exploiting this award the Portuguese discovered Brasil in 1500 and had taken possession of it by 1503. Apart from the seizure of the north of the country by the Dutch between 1624 and 1654 the whole of Brasil remained firmly in Portuguese hands. In the early stages of the development of Brasil such currency requirements as arose were met by the use of coinage from the home country and, towards the end of the seventeenth century, by counter-marking Spanish colonial issues. Eventually in 1694 a coinage for circulation in Brasil was decreed by Peter II. This new coinage, comprising both gold and silver, was modelled in the Portuguese coinage system. The basic denomination in gold was the milreis or piece of 1000 reis with multiples of 2000 and 4000. The pataca of 320 reis was struck in silver, together with its double and half as well as the subsidiary coins known as vintem (20 reis) of which larger 2 and 4 vintem denominations were also issued. The types, also, were analogous to those of the Portuguese coinage. The gold denominations carried on obverse the Portuguese arms crowned, and the reverse, a cross within a quadrilobe. The royal title *Petrus II Dei gratia Portugaliae rex/et Brasiliae dominus* formed a continuous inscription of both obverse and reverse. Silver coins had a similar obverse together with the royal titles in more abbreviated form but the reverse was formed by a globe superimposed on the cross with broad ends, characteristic of Portuguese coinage, and had as inscription an abbreviated form of *Subque signo nata stabit* (Pl. 815). The mint for this first coinage was at Bahia but was transferred in 1699 to Rio de Janeiro.

In 1703 the types of the Portuguese gold coinage were adopted for the Brasilian issues also, differentiated by placing the initial of the mint, R, in the angles of the reverse cross. The initial of Bahia was similarly employed when the mint there was reopened in 1714, while the letter M marked the product of a new mint set up at Villa Rica, the capital of the province of Minas Geraes, in 1724. A specific copper coinage for Brasil was struck from 1715 in Lisbon and from 1729 in Bahia. The obverse bore the royal title and had as type a large crowned X indicating the value. The reverse repeated the globe-on-cross type of the silver but had its individual inscription *Pecunia totum circumit orbem* (Pl. 816). Following the lead of the home coinage Brasilian gold issues changed their types from 1727 to show the royal portrait on obverse and a shield of arms, ornamented and crowned, on the reverse. The Brasilian issues were differentiated by the addition of the mint letters of Rio, Bahia or Minas under the bust.

No essential change of types took place throughout the remainder of the eighteenth century or in the first two decades of the nineteenth, though small modifications were introduced, following the pattern of the home coinage. When John VI, who had been exiled from Portugal by the Napoleonic wars and had remained in Brasil after Napoleon's defeat and his country's liberation, finally returned to Portugal in 1821 he left the government of Brasil to his son, Peter, who was proclaimed emperor of Brasil in the following year. Gold coinage bore his portrait and title as emperor of Brasil on the obverse, while the reverse carried as the arms of Brasil a shield with the globe-on-cross device with the value in reis below. On silver and copper the types consisted of the arms of Brasil and the value in a wreath. Peter I abdicated in favour of his son, Peter II, who reigned from 1831 to 1889, issuing a coinage substantially the same as that of his father (Pl. 817).

In 1889 Brasil was declared a republic with the official title Estados Unidos de Brasil. The types on gold coins issued between 1889 and 1922 were, on the 20 milreis pieces, the head of Liberty in her Phrygian cap on obverse and the five stars of the Southern Cross within a circle of stars on the reverse, and on the 10 milreis piece a similar obverse but with the Southern Cross design of the reverse superimposed on a large five-pointed star. Silver coins of values 500, 1000 and 2000 reis repeated the types of the larger gold denomination and lower values of reis in nickel or bronze took the Southern Cross type as obverse and had simply the value in figures on the reverse. A special issue of the silver denominations in 1900 honoured the fourth centenary of the discovery of Brasil with an obverse showing a galleon of 1500 and round the value on the reverse an inscription 4° *Centenario do descobramento do Brasil*. Another special issue in 1922 commemorated the centenary of Brasil's independence from Portugal with an obverse showing the jugate busts of Peter I, the first emperor of Brasil, and of President Pessoa. The reverse of the silver 2 milreis piece carried the arms of the empire of Brasil and the republic side by side. Yet another commemorative issue was struck in 1932 on the occasion of the fourth centenary of the colonization of Brasil with types showing John III and other personalities connected with the event, a map of South America, marked with the dividing line of Pope Alexander's award in 1493, and a sixteenth-century galleon. Many of the issues of the 1930's carry the portraits of famous Brasilians but the nickel coinage of the new government of President Vargas, set up in 1938, has only his portrait on the obverse and value in a wreath on the reverse. Famous Brasilians were honoured on issues of the 1930's but the coins of the Vargas regime from 1938 on carry only his portrait and a value reverse. On the new coinage of a cruzeiro of 100 centavos in 1942 the cruzeiro values have a map of Brazil as obverse. On all values between 1956 and 1962 the country's symbol, the Southern Cross forms the obverse. The coins of the revalued system of 1,000 old cruzeiros equal to 1 new cruzeiro in 1967 have a head of Brasilia as obverse.

THE GUIANAS

The area on the north-east coast of South America known as Guiana was discovered about 1500 and this was the one area in South America where European nations other than Spain and Portugal succeeded in establishing colonies in the course of the seventeenth century. The Dutch secured a foothold in 1613, the English in 1650 and the French in 1656.

GUYANA (BRITISH GUIANA)

The early currency needs of Guiana were met by the use of the ubiquitous Spanish colonial issues and other major international commercial coinages. Towards the end of the eighteenth century the British settlements at Essequibo and Demerara countermarked Spanish pieces of eight with the letters E & D and the value, expressed in terms of Dutch currency, as 3 guilders. A central piece was punched from these Spanish dollars and itself stamped with the value '3 bits'.

The supremacy of Dutch coinage in the area is reflected in the issue in 1809 of a coinage for Essequibo and Demerara consisting of pieces in silver of 3, 2, 1, $\frac{1}{2}$ and $\frac{1}{4}$ guilder and in copper in 1813 a stiver and half-stiver piece. The types were the bust and titles of George III on obverse with on the reverse the value crowned and the names of Essequibo and Demerara (Pl. 818). A second issue of the silver with slightly modified types was made in 1816 and a similar coinage was struck for William IV. On the issue of 1836 the description on the reverse was changed to British Guiana and the 3 and 2 guilder denominations were abandoned. In the reign of Victoria the only coinage issued specifically for British Guiana was the silver fourpence with types, the royal bust and value in wreath. This denomination has continued to be issued in succeeding reigns up to the present. The first coinage of independent Guyana in 1967 has a value reverse and on the 50, 25 and 10 cents the state arms as obverse; on the 5 and 1 cent coins the obverse is three circles of decoration.

FRENCH GUIANA

Uniface billon coins of value 1 sou with a crowned C as type, struck for French Guiana, known as the colony of Cayenne, are undated but were struck in the reign of Louis XV (1715–74). Under Louis XVI billon double sous were issued for Cayenne with his name and title on obverse and, as type, a crown above three lis The reverse, inscribed *Colonie de Cayenne*, bore the value and date (Pl. 819). Copper 10 centimes were issued by Louis XVIII and Louis Philippe with a crowned monogram on obverse and the value on reverse, inscribed *Cayenne française*.

SURINAM (DUTCH GUIANA)

This territory, recognized as a Dutch colony by the Peace of Breda in 1667, normally used either Spanish colonial coinage or that of the home country. In 1679, however, a series of copper doits was issued by the governor Johannes Heinsius. These were in denominations of 4, 2 and 1 stuiver and had on the obverse a small parrot on a branch with the date below (Pl. 820). The reverse was normally smooth but the major piece sometimes was ornamented with a tree design on the reverse. Between 1941 and 1943 coinage of 25, 10, 5 and 1 cent pieces with the types used on the coinage of Holland were struck for use in Surinam and Curaçao by the mint at Philadelphia in the United States which marked its products with a small letter P. Surinam, granted equal status with the Netherlands in 1954, issued a coinage of 25, 10, 5 and 1 cent pieces in 1962 with arms and value types.

THE CARIBBEAN

The coinages of the islands scattered throughout the Caribbean have usually been issued by the European colonial powers who have at various times possessed them. A number of the larger islands have, however, achieved independence at various times from the nineteenth century onwards and have issued their own individual coinage series.

HAITI

The island of Haiti originally comprised a French colony of St. Domingo in the north-west and a Spanish colony of the same name in the south-east. The whole island was ceded to France in 1795 and until 1804 a colonial coinage in billon was struck for the island. It consisted of billon pieces of 2 escalins or gourdin, an escalin and its half, all with standing figure of Liberty and inscription *République française* on obverse and the value in words on the reverse, inscribed *Colonies de Sainte Domingue*. The north-western portion declared itself an independent empire of Haiti in 1804 under a negro emperor, Jacques Dessalines. He was succeeded in 1806 by a president, Henri Christophe, who issued a base-metal coinage of 15 sols (2 escalins) and 7½ sols (escalin) with types a shield with the monogram of the president and inscription *Libertas Religio Mores* on obverse and standing Liberty, inscribed *Monnoie d'Hayti*, on reverse. The copper cents struck in 1807 show a facing bust of Henri Christophe in uniform and cocked hat on obverse and are inscribed on the reverse, with the value in the field, *Le Gouvernement de Hayti* (Pl. 821). Henri took the title of king in 1812 and ruled as such until 1820, issuing a coinage of silver pieces, mainly the gourde with an occasional double gourde piece. The obverse shows Henri's portrait, the reverse a shield, crowned within a collar, while the inscription *Henri I par la grace de Dieu/Roi d'Hayti* is continued from obverse to reverse and completed by the date, both in its normal form and as an era date from the achievement of independence in 1804.

The south-west portion of the island became a separate republic in 1807 under Alexandre Pétion. The initial coinage of 6, 12 and 25 centimes in silver had as types a palm-tree and trophy of arms and flags, while the reverse, inscribed *République d'Hayti*, had the value enclosed within a ring in the form of a snake. In 1817, or year 14 of independence, Pétion's portrait and name appeared on the obverse, the type with palm-tree and arms being transferred to the reverse, accompanied by the state name and value. Pétion was succeeded as president in 1818 by J. P. Boyer who was recognized in 1820 by the north-western portion, previously ruled by Henri Christophe, and by the eastern portion, which declared itself independent of Spain in 1822. Boyer ruled until 1843 and issued a coinage similar to that of Pétion but with additional denominations of 50 and 100 centimes. Copper coins of 1 and 2 centimes value had as types a fasces dividing the value on obverse and the value within a wreath on reverse.

On the death of Boyer in 1843 the eastern portion broke away and established itself as the Dominican Republic (see below). The north-west portion preserved the name, Republic of Haiti, and its coinage under successive presidents was mainly of copper centime pieces with the fasces type until Faustin, who had been president since 1847, proclaimed himself emperor in 1849. Copper coins of the unusual denomination of $6\frac{1}{2}$ centimes have the crowned bust of Faustin with his title as emperor of Haiti while the reverse is formed by his crowned arms. The empire ended in 1858 when Nicole Geffrard became president. A coinage of 5, 10 and 20 centimes in silver shows his portrait head, while the reverse revives the palm-tree and arms design of Pétion. In 1880 a new monetary system was created with, as its unit, the silver gourde divided into 100 centimes. The types of the gourde and divisionary pieces in silver are a Liberty head with the state name and the year of independence on obverse and the now traditional palm-tree and arms reverse (Pl. 822). The issues of 1904–8 in the form of cupro-nickel pieces of 5, 10, 20 and 50 cents value carried the portrait of the president and had the usual palm-tree reverse. Haiti was occupied by the United States between 1915 and 1934 but when coinage was resumed in 1949 the types of presidential portrait and palm-tree and arms were revived. The nickel 20 centimes of 1956 carry the head of President Magliore on obverse and a palm-tree and arms on the reverse. A similar 10 centimes issue in 1958 had the portrait of President Duvalier on the obverse.

DOMINICAN REPUBLIC

The eastern portion of the island of Haiti declared itself an independent republic with the title of the Dominican Republic in 1844. The earliest coinages in 1844 and 1848 are brass cuartillas or quarter-reales with no types on either side but only the inscription *Republica Dominicana* on the obverse and the value on the reverse. A series of nickel coins in 1877 of low centavo values had as types a cross or arms on obverse and value in wreath on reverse. A new system instituted in 1889 was based on the silver dominicano or franc divided into 100 centesimos. The types on the silver franc, its multiple of 5 francs and its half of 50 centesimos were a Liberty head and arms, and, on the copper 5 and 10 centesimos, arms and value in wreath. In 1897 the peso of 100 centavos was adopted as the monetary unit but the types remained essentially the same. The coinage of the Trujillo regime from 1937 on replaced the Liberty head on the 1 centavo bronze with a palm-tree. In 1955 special gold 30 peso and silver peso coins with Trujillo's portrait celebrated the twenty-fifth anniversary of the regime. On peso and centavo coins issued in 1963 to mark the centenary of the republic the obverse is the head of Liberty.

CUBA

The first coinage to be struck by Cuba after it secured its independence from Spain was a series of silver souvenir pesos in 1897. The obverse carries a female head and is inscribed *Patria y Libertad Souvenir* while the reverse carries the arms and title of the new republic. The next coinage issue, which was not till 1915, consisted of the silver peso in silver with multiples up to 20 on which the types were the head of President Marti on obverse and arms and value on the reverse (Pl. 823). The peso was also issued with a different obverse type, a star on a background of rays, the type used on divisionary pieces in silver down to 10 centavos. Lower value pieces in various metals had as obverse the value as a Roman numeral at the centre of a star. New, modernistic designs were used for the peso between 1934 and 1939. On the obverse *Patria y Libertad* is inscribed beside the bust of Liberty and the state name beside the arms on reverse. On the obverse of the centavo coins in 1952, commemorating the fiftieth year of the republic, a flag flies before a view of the city. The portrait of President Marti on a special issue in 1953 honoured the centenary of his birth. Castro issues of 1963 used the motto *Patria o Muerte* and Castro's portrait appeared on the 40 centavo coin.

DANISH WEST INDIES

The Danish possessions in the West Indies consisted of the islands of St. John (1684), St. Thomas (1716) and Ste. Croix (1733) and a special coinage was struck for these colonies until their sale to the United States in 1917. Coinage was first issued in 1740 in the reign of Christian VI in the form of the silver skilling with various multiples. The types on the skilling itself were the crowned monogram of the king with his titles *D. G. Rex Dan. Norv. Van. G.* as inscription on obverse and the value, 1 *skilling danske*, on reverse with inscription *De Dansk. Americ.*

Eyland. Kaab. Mynt. On the higher multiples the reverse type was a three-masted sailing ship (Pl. 824).

These types persisted until the reign of Frederick VII when in 1859 the coinage system was brought into line with that of the United States with the daler of 100 cents as the monetary unit. Silver pieces of 20, 10, 5 and 3 cents now all carried the royal portrait on obverse but the ship reverse was preserved on the 20 and 5 cent coins; a design of sugar-canes appeared on the reverse of the 10 cent piece and the value only on the 3 cent. A copper cent piece had as types the arms and value. The system was slightly modified under Christian IX in 1905 by the introduction of new divisionary denominations of the franc, equal to 20 cents, and the 5 bits, equal to 1 cent. Gold coins of 4 dalers (20 francs) and 10 dalers (50 francs) were struck with royal portrait and seated-female personification. The reverse of the 1 and 2 franc coins in silver showed three native figures standing, while the 50 bit reverse carried only the value and a branch. The lower value coins in nickel and bronze had the crowned monogram on obverse and a design of trident, sickle and Aesculapius' staff on the reverse. These types were retained on subsequent issues, the last of which was a bronze 5 bit piece of Christian X in 1913.

DUTCH WEST INDIES

The Netherlands Antilles group, of which the most important is Curaçao, like most of the Caribbean territories, made use of cut and counter-stamped Spanish silver coinage until the early nineteenth century. The first coinage specially struck for Curaçao was the silver real of 1821 with obverse a stalk of maize and a caduceus in saltire with inscription *Curaçao* (Pl. 825); the reverse carried the value in a wreath. A silver stuiver in 1822 had simply the name of the colony on obverse and the value on reverse.

In the present century small silver pieces of a quarter and a tenth of a guilder were issued in 1900 and 1901 with an obverse portrait of Queen Wilhelmina similar to that of the Dutch coinage and a reverse, crowned arms dividing the value, inscribed *Kolonie Curaçao*. A more extensive coinage was begun in 1944. The major piece was a rijksdaalder similar to that of Holland itself but inscribed on the reverse *Munt van Curaçao*. Lower values of a guilder, a quarter and a tenth of a guilder were also issued in silver. Bronze coins of 1 cent and 2½ cents were also issued with the types of the Dutch denominations but with inscription *Munt van Curaçao*.

From 1952 a coinage in the name of Queen Juliana has been struck for the Netherlands Antilles as a whole. The denominations are the guilder, the quarter and tenth of a guilder in silver and the bronze cent. The types are similar to those of the Dutch coinage but are inscribed on the reverse *Nederlandse Antillen*.

FRENCH WEST INDIES

In addition to the coinage struck by France for general colonial circulation (see p. 416) a special coinage was decreed in 1730 for the Isles du Vent—the Windward Islands—that is Martinique, Guadeloupe, Grenada and St. Lucia. This coinage consisted of two denominations in silver of 12 and 6 sols. The types on both values were the usual royal bust and titles of Louis XV on the obverse and the words *Isles du Vent* disposed across the field of the reverse within three fleur-de-lis and a scroll (Pl. 826). Currency requirements in the French West Indian colonies were supplemented, as they were in the other islands, by the widespread use of cut portions of the Spanish silver dollar as well as countermarked Spanish silver coinage. In the later eighteenth and early nineteenth centuries general colonial issues were again used but in the later nineteenth and on several occasions in the present century token coinages of 1 franc and 50 centimes were issued for Guadeloupe and Martinique. The obverse shows the bust of a native woman on the Martinique issue and the reverse carries the value, expressed as, for instance, *Bon pour 1 franc,* in wreath. For Guadeloupe the obverse type is a native head in local head-dress and the reverse has the token value around a palm-frond (Pl. 827).

BRITISH WEST INDIES

Either countermarked Spanish silver dollars, pieces of eight, or portions cut from silver dollars in a variety of shapes were used in a number of British possessions in the West Indies. The islands which have been identified from the monogram or the name in full on such cut and counter-stamped coins include Dominica, Grenada, Guadeloupe and Martinique (temporarily seized from France), Monserrat, Jamaica, Nevis, St. Lucia, St. Vincent, Tobago, Tortola and Trinidad (Pl. 828). For some of the islands special coinage has been issued at various times. At Antigua a copper farthing was struck in 1836 with types, a palm-tree and name on obverse and value on the reverse. The so-called 'Hog money' struck for the Sommer Islands, the name originally given to Bermuda, is described in the section on North America (p. 420) where this coinage also passed current. A copper penny with types, the bust of George III and a sailing ship, was also produced for Bermuda in 1793 and a similar halfpenny for the Bahamas in 1806–7.

For the Barbados a copper penny was issued in 1788 with a quaint crowned head on obverse with inscription *I serve* and a pineapple on the reverse inscribed *Barbadoes Penny* (Pl. 829). In 1792 a penny and halfpenny copied the obverse but with an inscription *Liberty*, while the reverse showed Neptune on a sea-chariot.

Jamaica as the largest and most important island has since 1869 had a special coinage in denominations of penny, halfpenny and farthing, struck in nickel and later in nickel-brass. The types which have remained constant in the successive reigns are the royal portrait and titles on obverse and the arms of the island on reverse with the name of the island and the denomination as inscription (Pl. 830). The last issue was made in 1955 when it was superseded by the coinage of the new British Caribbean Territories (Eastern Group). The obverse on all denominations carries the crowned portrait of Queen Elizabeth II. The reverse of the 50, 25 and 10 cent pieces in nickel shows Britannia in a sea-chariot above the arms of the component territories and is inscribed with the title of the confederation (Pl. 831). A sailing ship provides the reverse of the 5 cent coin in brass, while the 2, 1 and ½ cent pieces have simply the value between two palm-branches on the reverse.

A special crown issued for Bermuda in 1959 celebrated the 350th anniversary of its founding with a reverse a map showing the group of islands between two sailing ships.

As a consequence of political changes a number of new coinages have come into being in the Caribbean area. A separate coinage for the Bahamas, struck in 1966, has the new portrait of Elizabeth II as obverse type. The picturesque reverses of the dollar and several subsidiary cent denominations include a starfish on the cent, a pineapple on the 5 cents, and a sailing yacht on the 25 cents. A special Jamaican five shilling issue was made in 1966 to mark the holding of the Commonwealth Games. The decimal coinage, a dollar of 100 cents, introduced in 1969, replaces the royal portrait on obverse with the state arms. Independent Trinidad and Tobago issued its first coinage of various cent values in 1966 with the state arms as obverse type and name and value on the reverse.

AUSTRALASIA

★

Australia	457
New Guinea	458
New Zealand	459
Fiji	459
Hawaii	459
Tonga	460
Western Samoa	460

Australasia

ALTHOUGH voyages of exploration in the south Pacific area were begun by several European nations as early as the sixteenth century, systematic emigration and settlement began only in the later eighteenth century. Since the part which coinage had to play in the developing civilizations of Australasia was relatively small, systematic, independent coinages were called into being only in the beginning of the present century.

AUSTRALIA

The coinage requirements of the early settlements from the first at Botany Bay in 1788 onwards were met by the use of the several coins in gold and silver which already had established for themselves a reputation as international currency. Gold pieces included the English guinea, the Portuguese moidore and the Indian mohur, while silver coinage took the form of the ubiquitous Spanish dollar or piece of eight, the Dutch guilder and the English shilling. One of the earliest attempts to set up a regular coinage was made in New South Wales in 1813. From Spanish dollars a circular piece was removed from the centre and stamped with the state name and a crown on one side and the value *Fifteen pence* on the other. Round the hole left in the dollar the state name was stamped on one side and the value *Five shillings* on the other. These dollars are popularly known as ring dollars, the central piece as a bit or dump.

In the nineteenth century, as local settlements developed and spread, a series of token pennies and halfpennies were issued by local traders, both to supply the deficiency of small change and to advertise themselves (Pl. 832). The great gold discoveries in the mid nineteenth century created a crisis in currency supplies and, since the mint machinery required for coinage production was not generally available, roughly shaped gold ingots stamped with their exact weight were recognized as currency in South Australia. The supplies of British coinage in general use were supplemented by the establishment of branches of the Royal Mint at Sydney, Melbourne and Perth for the production of the gold sovereign and half-sovereign. These Australian sovereigns were identical with the British except that they were distinguished by a small initial letter of the mint on the reverse.

When the separate states were federated in 1901 to form the Commonwealth of Australia steps were taken to provide a distinctive Australian coinage but the first issue consisting of the silver florin, shilling, sixpence and threepence did not appear till 1910. On the obverse was the royal portrait in imperial robes and crown, while the reverse bore the Australian arms with kangaroo and emu supporters (Pl. 833). In 1911 the bronze penny and halfpenny were added with value in words as the reverse type. Two special issues of florins were made in the reign of George V to commemorate the opening of the new Parliament House at Canberra in 1927 and the centenary of Victoria and Melbourne in 1935. The former had on the reverse a view of Parliament House, the latter a mounted figure. The coinage of George VI had more picturesque types—ram's head and wheat-ear for shilling and sixpence, and kangaroo on penny and halfpenny. The coronation crown in 1937 had as reverse the imperial crown. The first coinage of Elizabeth II continued the existing types. Special florin issues marked the Commonwealth Jubilee in 1951 and the Queen's visit in 1954. The new 1966 coinage of a dollar of 100 cents has the second royal portrait and the reverses of the cent, 2, 5, 10 and 20 cents picture unusual Australian fauna, notably the platypus on the 20 cents.

NEW GUINEA

The eastern part of New Guinea was a German colony up to 1914 and had a coinage of gold and silver marks with multiples up to 5 and pieces of 10 and 2 pfennig in copper. The types were a bird of paradise and value and name of the territory within a wreath.

Coinage for New Guinea which has been administered by Australia since the first world war was resumed in 1929. All the denominations are struck with a central piercing and are inscribed with the name of the territory and the value on the reverse. The silver shilling and nickel penny of George V have crossed maces, crowned on obverse, while the sixpence and threepence have the royal monogram crowned. New Guinea was one of the few British coinages to be issued in the name of Edward VIII for whom a copper penny was struck in 1936 with type, crowned monogram (Pl. 835). Issues for George VI repeat the earlier types and so far no coinage of Elizabeth II has been issued.

NEW ZEALAND

The early numismatic history of New Zealand during the period of its settlement, chiefly from Britain, in the nineteenth century is closely akin to that of Australia. The great international currencies detailed in the sketch of early Australian coinage also circulated in New Zealand, supplemented by some of the Australian bronze token coins as well as by British coinage. Independent coinage for New Zealand was first issued in 1933. The obverse on this issue, as on the first Australian, was the royal bust in imperial robes and crown. The half-crown had the arms of New Zealand on the reverse but the other denominations carried more interesting local types such as the kiwi (Pl. 836) on the florin or the Maori warrior on the shilling. The 1935 crown commemorating the centenary of the Waitangi Treaty shows a Maori chief shaking hands with a naval officer. The halfpenny and penny with tui bird reverses were added to the George VI coinage. Crowns were issued, with fern badge (Pl. 837) for the proposed royal visit in 1949, and for the Coronation of Elizabeth II. The new 1967 coinage of a dollar of 100 cents with new portrait obverse has a set of special New Zealand reverses such as the kiwi on the 20 cent.

FIJI

The first coinage in 1934 with imperial bust obverse chose mainly local reverses— native vessel on the shilling, turtle on the sixpence (Pl. 838) and hut on the threepence. Pennies and halfpennies with central hole had only inscriptions. These types remained until the introduction of decimal coinage (100 cents= 1 dollar) in 1969. As well as the new portrait obverse there are new native reverses —a dugout on 5 cents, and a club on 10 cents.

HAWAII

Hawaii was annexed by the United States in 1900 and in 1959 became a state of the Union. It was, however, a kingdom from 1791 until 1894 and at times issued its own coinage. Copper cents were struck by King Kamehameha III in 1847 with his facing bust and value in wreath. A more extensive coinage was issued by Kalakauai in 1883, consisting of a silver dollar, its half and quarter and a 10 cent piece. The types were the king's profile portrait and shield of arms (Pl. 839).

459

TONGA

Coinage based on a unit of a pa'anga divided into 100 seniti began only in 1967. The first issue honouring the late Queen Salote had her portrait on obverse. Reverse types include a turtle on the 1 and 2 seniti coins, stars and branches enclosing value on the 10 and 20 coins, and the Kingdom's arms on the higher seniti values and the pa'anga. A similar coinage but with new portrait and titles has been struck for King Taufa'ahau Tupou IV in 1968 and a series with additional coronation inscription appeared in 1967.

WESTERN SAMOA

The coinage of this new independent state since 1967 is based on a tala of 100 sene with types, the ruler's portrait and value in wreath.

AFRICA

★

Abyssinia	463
Egypt	464
Libya	465
Tunisia	465
Morocco	465
Liberia	466
Ghana	466
South Africa	467
British Colonies	468
French Colonies	469
Portuguese Colonies	469
Sudan	469
The Congo	470
New African States	470

Africa

T HIS section is limited to the consideration of the coinages of the modern, independent states of Africa and of the several European colonies. Coinage in the sense in which it is defined for the purpose of this book was confined before the nineteenth century almost entirely to the northern portion of Africa which had connections with the civilization of the Mediterranean area. The currencies of North Africa in the ancient world are dealt with in the sections on Greek and Roman coins, while the coinages current in North Africa throughout most of the mediaeval and modern periods are discussed in relation to the Near Eastern series of which they are off-shoots. The exception to this classification is the coinage of the kingdom of Abyssinia or Ethiopia which has had a history of independence and an individual coinage since the early Middle Ages.

ABYSSINIA

A series of coins of the Axumite kings of Abyssinia has been identified, ranging from the second half of the third century to the tenth century. The coinage initially is in the form mainly of small gold pieces, deriving their inspiration from the Roman series but carrying regal inscriptions in Greek. The types of this series are a profile bust on either side showing the king usually wearing a distinctive high crown. These Axumite kings were pagan until the conversion of Ezanas in A.D. 330. From this time the inscriptions on the coins incorporate a number of crosses between the syllables e.g. + HZA + NAC + BACI + ΛЄYC on the obverse and + AΣω + MITωN + BICI + AΛЄ NЄЄ i.e. Ezanas, King of the Axumites, of the Alene family (Pl. 840). The series of small gold pieces was supplemented by some bronze issues and very rare silver. A number of changes take place in the sixth and seventh centuries. Greek inscriptions are replaced by Amharic and the coinage degenerates into a bronze series only. The types undergo changes also. In the sixth century the reverse which had previously repeated the obverse-bust type was charged with a cross, and for the latter part of the coinage from the seventh century onwards the obverse showed the figure of the king

463

enthroned in profile and holding a long sceptre, surmounted by a cross (Pl. 841).

In Abyssinia, cut off from Western civilization from the seventh century by the interposition of the Islamic caliphates, the use of coinage lapsed and the striking of Abyssinian coinage was not resumed till the late nineteenth century. Internationally acceptable currencies of other lands undoubtedly circulated in Abyssinia. The most famous of these is the Maria Theresa thaler (Pl. 698) which gained such popularity in East Africa generally and in Abyssinia in particular that this particular denomination has been consistently restruck for use there (see p. 377). Revived contact with the outside world led to the issue of an Abyssinian coinage by Menelik II (1889–1913) in 1894. The system consisted of the talari and subdivisions in silver with the crowned bust of the emperor and the lion of Judah (Pl. 842) with smaller denominations the gersh and its portions in copper. Gold coins of 5, 10 and 20 wark with portrait and lion types, though bearing the portrait of Menelik and dates within his reign, were issued after his death and the gold wark was also struck, though rarely, for his successor the empress Zauditu (1916–30). As well as rare gold the emperor Haile Selassie (1930–36) issued several values of the matona in nickel and bronze before Abyssinia was conquered by Italy in 1936. The emperor's coinage since his restoration in 1941 has consisted of values of 50 cents and downwards. The traditional types of portrait and lion of Judah have been retained but have been modernized (Pl. 843).

EGYPT

Egypt, which in the later stages of Turkish rule had enjoyed the special status of a vice-royalty, became independent under Sultan Husein Kamil in 1915. The monetary unit was the piastre (Pl. 844), divided into 10 millièmes of which, as the name indicates, 1000 constituted an Egyptian pound. As with almost all Islamic coinages portraits were not used as coin types, which consisted of inscriptions in Arabic on both sides, the reverse carrying in addition the denomination name in English and the value in Western figures or as an English word. Multiple piastres up to 20 were struck in silver and a rare 100 piastre piece in 1916 in gold. Millième values from 10 downwards were in cupro-nickel or bronze. Similar piastre coins were issued for Fuad I as Sultan between 1917 and 1922 when Egypt was declared a kingdom. The denominational system remained the same but the obverse carried the profile bust of the king wearing a fez (Pl. 845). The reverse no longer showed the value in Western figures and the millième denominations were issued with an octagonal flan. On the coinage of Farouk I (1936–52) his portrait in uniform and fez was shown facing with the head turned to left. The bronze millième pieces were unusual in having a fluted edge. The coinage of the Egyptian republic established in 1952 is a series of piastres and millièmes in aluminium-bronze with a consistent obverse showing the head of the Sphinx (Pl. 846). The silver 50 piastre issue in 1956 had on obverse a symbolic figure breaking its chains. A special issue of 1 and 5 pound pieces in gold in 1957 have a representation of the Aswan Dam on obverse and the value on reverse. A coinage issued in 1958 consists of denominations in gold of ½, 1 and 5 pounds with the Pharaoh Ramses II in a chariot on obverse and an inscription referring to the creation of the United Arab Republic on the reverse. Silver coins of 25 and 50 piastres have an eagle on obverse and the value divided by a sword on the reverse.

LIBYA

Coins of 1 and 2 piastres and a number of millième denominations in 1952 had on obverse the portrait of King Idris in tasselled cap and on reverse the value in Arabic figures between two palms with a crown above and the denomination in English below (Pl. 847). A new series of millième values in 1965 has state arms obverse and value reverse.

TUNISIA

The coinage of the French protectorate in Tunisia between 1882 and 1891 continued to be piastres in gold and silver of Sultan Ali Bey with Arabic inscriptions on both sides encircled by palms. On the coinage of francs and centimes introduced in 1891 the obverse continued to be inscribed in Arabic but the reverse bore the name of Tunisia and the value in French. The standard of the coinage was altered in 1930 but the types underwent only incidental change. Coinage of independent Tunisia in 1950 had on obverse Arabic inscription and date in both Arabic and Christian reckoning, and on reverse the franc value in Western figures and letters (Pl. 848). New coinage begun in 1960 is based on a dinar of 1,000 millièmes.

MOROCCO

The coinage of silver dirhems of the Sharifi sultans of Morocco under Spanish and French protection in the late nineteenth century was replaced by a series of silver rials and their portions and copper mazunas in 1902. These issues have as types distinctive patterns of a six-pointed star or two interlacing trefoils. In 1921 a coinage based on the French franc began issue. The six-pointed star and other geometric types persisted on the franc coinage begun in 1921 inscribed in Arabic and in French *Maroc* and *Empire Cherifien* (Pl. 849). On the new coinage of a dirham of 100 francs in 1959 the dirham bore the portrait of Mohammed V, and in 1965 of Mulai Hassan II.

LIBERIA

The Liberian coinage with its unit of a dollar divided into 100 cents is modelled on that of the United States. The first coinage in 1833 was a series of copper cents with on obverse a naked figure planting a palm-tree by the sea and across the field of the reverse the foundation date 1816. Later nineteenth-century issues of 1 and 2 cent pieces in bronze had types, the head of the republic in cap of Liberty and a palm-tree (Pl. 850). Larger cent values in silver had head of the republic and value in wreath. Current coins in cent values have an elephant on obverse and palm-tree on reverse. On the new coinage of 1960 coins of 25 and 50 cents in silver have the head of a native girl on the obverse and the value on the reverse. The cupro-nickel 5 cents and bronze cent have an elephant obverse and the traditional palm-and-ship reverse.

GHANA

Until it became an independent state in the British Commonwealth in 1957 Ghana comprised the former colonial territory of the Gold Coast in British West Africa. The first coinage of the Gold Coast issued in 1796 consisted of the silver ackey and its parts with the royal monogram on obverse and the arms of the African Company on the reverse. A second issue in 1818 bore the royal portrait. Coinage of British West Africa consisted of a florin (Pl. 851) and shilling with imperial obverse portrait and palm-tree types and the value in wreath on the sixpence and threepence, first in silver, later in brass. The penny, halfpenny and tenth of a penny denominations in nickel and bronze had a central piercing, with royal title and value on one side and the colony's name and two interlocking triangles on the other. This was one of the territories for which coinage in the name of Edward VIII was struck in 1936 (Pl. 852). These types persisted throughout the coinage which still provides the needs of Nigeria and Sierra Leone, though the latter in 1791 had a brief coinage of silver dollars and subdivisions and copper pennies with a crouching lion on obverse and clasped hands on the reverse. Ghana, however, now has a coinage series of its own. The first issue made in 1958 consists of pieces of 10, 2 and 1 shilling values as well as sixpence and threepence, all in cupro-nickel, and the penny and halfpenny in aluminium-bronze. The types are identical on all denominations, the portrait of Ghana's first prime minister, inscribed *Kwame Nkrumah, Civitatis Ghaniensis Conditor* on obverse and a five-pointed star and value on reverse (Pl. 853). The edge of the 10 shilling piece is engraved with *Independence of Ghana* 6 *March* 1956. A special restricted gold coinage of double sovereign weight marked the creation of the Republic in 1960. The obverse has the portrait of Nkrumah as president and on reverse arms and date. The types on the new decimal coinage of a cedi of 100 pesewas were Nkrumah's portrait and star and value. The 1967 coinage replaced Nkrumah's portrait with various local types such as native drums, and on reverse the state arms.

SOUTH AFRICA

Prior to the formation of the Union of South Africa in 1910, apart from some copper tokens issued in Cape Town and East London and some rare coins of the Orange Free State which never passed beyond the pattern stage, the only substantial coinage was that of the Transvaal or, to give it its proper title, the South African Republic. Extremely rare gold pound pieces with the portrait of President Burgers and the republic's arms were struck in 1874 but a complete coinage series was issued under the presidency of Kruger between 1892 and 1900. Kruger's portrait appeared on the obverse of all denominations, never accompanied by his name or title but on the pound, the 5 shilling piece and the penny by the inscription *Zuid Afrikaansche Republiek*. The reverse on most denominations carried the arms of the republic, surmounted by an eagle and flanked by banners on the higher values (Pl. 854). The shilling, sixpence and threepence bore the value in wreath on reverse. An oddity of this coinage is that the denomination is always given in English not Afrikaans.

Though formed in 1910, the Union issued its first coinage in 1923, using the British denomination system. The usual imperial bust was used for the obverse of all denominations and while heraldic shields formed the reverse of the half-crown and florin more imaginative and original designs were adopted for other values. The figure of Hope leans on an anchor on the shilling (Pl. 855), six bundles of four rods (the provinces) surround a veldt flower on the sixpence and a sailing ship on the bronze penny and halfpenny (Pl. 856). The reverse has the bilingual inscription *South Africa Suid-Afrika*. Similar types were used on the coinage of George VI and Elizabeth II. A special crown issue in 1952 celebrating the tercentenary of Jan van Riebeeck's landing shows his ship in Table Bay. In 1961 South Africa became a Republic and adopted a decimal coinage of a rand of 100 cents. The obverse carried the portrait of Jan van Riebeeck and association reverses such as the springbok on the rand and 50 cents and the vootrekker wagon on the cent (Pl. 857). A second issue in 1965 with new floral and animal reserves was inscribed either *South Africa* or *Suid-Afrika*. Special issues in 1967 and 1968 had portraits of Verwoerd and Swart.

BRITISH COLONIES

The coinage issued for the colonies of British West Africa has been described above (p. 466). Another series has been struck since the early years of this century to serve the needs of colonies in East Africa. The system, when fully developed, consisted of silver coins of florin, shilling, 50 cents or half-shilling, 25 cents or quarter-shilling values and nickel—later copper—coins of 10, 5 and 1 cent values. The types on the higher values were the imperial bust and a lion, here a real not an heraldic beast, pacing to the right against a background of mountains (Pl. 858), together with the words East Africa and the value. The lower values which have a central hole carry the imperial title and value in words on the obverse and crossed ivory tusks and value in figures on the reverse (Pl. 859). In 1948 the metals of the two categories were changed to nickel and bronze. A separate coinage for Southern Rhodesia and for Northern Rhodesia and Nyasaland, first issued in 1932, uses the British system of denominations. The obverses show the conventional imperial bust or head but the reverses, apart from an heraldic type on the half-crown, have been chosen for their local significance; for the florin an antelope (Pl. 860), the shilling the Zimbabwe bird, the sixpence native axes, the threepence native spears, while the penny and halfpenny with central hole carry a crowned rose on the obverse. This type is a recollection of the rose, in Greek rhodos, used as a punning type on the coinage of ancient Rhodes and used here as yet a further pun on the name of the founder of the colony, Cecil Rhodes (Pl. 861). Rhodes himself is commemorated on a special issue of a silver crown bearing his portrait above the arms of Rhodesia, struck on the centenary of his birth in 1953. The coinage of the new Central African Federation in 1955 has continued the tradition of local types—a fish-eagle, antelope, leopard and flower. The central hole on the halfpenny is flanked by two giraffes and on the penny by two elephants, portrayed rather unfortunately like circus elephants, erect on their hind-legs with upraised trunks (Pl. 862).

Coinage in 1960 for the new dominion of Nigeria retains the types of the half-penny and penny of British West Africa. Higher denominations carry the portrait of Queen Elizabeth II on obverse and a variety of designs on the reverse; on the florin ground-nuts, on the shilling palm-tree fronds, on the sixpence cocoa pods and on the threepence a cotton-flower.

FRENCH COLONIES

The issues for the French colonies in Africa in low denominations of francs and, until the post-war period, of centimes, struck in aluminium or aluminium-bronze, are much more standardized than the British. The obverse, apart from wartime issues, carries the head of the republic and inscription *République française* with, after the war, the addition of *Union française*. The reverse on pre-war issues bore the name of the particular territory—the Cameroons (Pl. 863), French West Africa and Togoland—together with the value and some local attribute. The post-war coinage has followed a similar pattern but usually has a more prominent type on the reverse such as a facing antelope head. Issues have been made for Somaliland and Madagascar in addition to those already enumerated. Wartime coinage of territories supporting de Gaulle have Gallic cock and cross of Lorraine types.

PORTUGUESE COLONIES

Angola. In various reigns in the nineteenth century from 1814 onwards a coinage of macutas and portions was issued in copper. The obverse carried the *quinas* arms of Portugal on a globe, crowned, together with the royal name and title, while the reverse bore the value and the inscription *Africa Portuguesa*. The issues of the present century are in various centavo denominations with the Portuguese arms on globe and inscription *Angola* on obverse and the value on the reverse. Silver coins of 10 and 20 escudos issued in 1952 have, on the reverse, the broad-ended Portuguese cross with arms on globe at centre.

Mozambique. The nineteenth-century coinage consisted of copper pieces of 20, 40 and 80 reis issued in 1840. The types were the royal arms and title on obverse and on the reverse the value with the inscription *Pecunia totum circumit orbem.* Modern issues in escudo and centavo values have either the arms and name of Mozambique on obverse and the value on reverse or the arms of Portugal on obverse and those of Mozambique and the value on reverse (Pl. 864).

SUDAN

The new republic of the Sudan began coinage in 1956. Denominations of 10 piastres in cupro-nickel and 10, 5, 2 and 1 mille in bronze have as types an Arab on camel, as on Sudanese stamps, and the value on the reverse.

THE CONGO

The Belgian Congo was established initially not as a colony but as a free state by Leopold II in 1885 and the coinage of francs and centimes bore his title as *Roi des Belges et Souverain de l'état independant du Congo*. Silver coins with franc values had Leopold's portrait and the reverse his arms between palm-branches, while the centime pieces with central hole had four double L's back to back, crowned on obverse and a five-pointed star on reverse. By the treaty of 1908 the Congo became a Belgian province and the silver franc of Albert I bears his ordinary title of *Roi des Belges* (Pl. 865). The issues for Leopold III made by the Bank of the Belgian Congo are inscribed with its name and value on the obverse, while the reverse is usually an African elephant. The most recent of several short-lived systems of the new republic is the zaire of 100 makuta.

NEW AFRICAN STATES

Kenya. The coinage unit is the shilling of 100 cents. On the 1966 issue the types are portrait of President Kenyatta and state arms. *Uganda*. The unit here is also the shilling of 100 cents. On the higher values in 1966 the types are state arms and a view of Lake Victoria with value. *Malawi*, has retained the British coinage system and uses the existing Rhodesia and Nyasaland lower values. On higher values the obverse has the portrait of President Banda and reverses local plants and animals. *Tanzania*. On the 1966 coinage of a shillingi of 100 senti the types are the President's portrait and native fauna. *Zambia*. The 1964 coinage of shillings and pence with arms obverse and flora and fauna reverses was replaced in 1966 by a decimal system of a kwacha of 100 ngwee with an obverse of President Kaunda. *Gambia*. The 1966 coinage of shillings and pence retained the royal portrait with inscription *The Gambia* across the field. The reverses represent local plants, animals and birds. *Sierra Leone*. On the 1964 leone and component cent pieces the obverse bore the portrait of President Sir Milton Margai and somewhat more traditional reverses.

A common franc coinage has been issued since 1961 for Dahomey, the Sudanese Republic, Senegal, Upper Volta, Ivory Coast, Mauritania, Togo and Niger. The types are an antelope head and value reverse inscribed *Banque Centrale Etats de l'Afrique de l'Ouest*. Similarly a common franc coinage has been issued since 1961 for the Central African Republic, Cameroon, Congo (Brazzaville), Gabon and Chad. The obverse of three antelope heads is inscribed *Etats de l'Afrique Equatoriale Banque Centrale*. The franc coinage of the Malagasy Republic (Madagascar) in 1965 has a floral obverse and on reverse an ox head. *Burundi* and *Rwanda*, formerly Belgian have issued independent coinages since 1965.

THE NEAR EAST

The Sassanian Empire   473
The Muhammadan coinage   475
Georgia   490
Modern States of the Near East   491

The Near East

THE geographical area with which this section is concerned is basically western Asia, bounded by the Mediterranean in the west, the Indus in the east and by the line of the Black Sea and the Caspian Sea to the north and, finally, by the Red Sea and the Indian Ocean to the south. The historical range of the coinage to be considered and some aspects of its territorial spread require more careful definition. Coinages current in western Asia throughout the centuries of Greek and Roman ascendancy, since they have affinities with the coinages of these civilizations, are included in the first two sections of this book. The present section begins with the consideration of the coinage of the Sassanian empire which was established in the early third century A.D. This was the first important coinage in western Asia to utilize a language of types derived from its own culture and civilization. In tracing the coinage of the various dynasties which eventually divided the widespread conquests of Islam it will be necessary to deal with areas outside western Asia which either conquest or conversion brought under Islamic influence, such as North Africa, Spain, parts of eastern Europe and the steppe lands of Asia. The coinages of the Muhammadan invaders of India, however, are described in the context of the other Indian coinages. A further exception, this time territorial, is that the coinages of the Crusader states in the Levant and of Christian Armenia have been incorporated in the section on European coinage.

THE SASSANIAN EMPIRE

About A.D. 200 Papek revolted against the local dynast of Persis (see p. 95) and secured the recognition of his son Sapor. On the death of Papek his second son, Ardashir, rose against Sapor and put him to death and about 212 revolted against his Parthian overlord, Artabanus V. The defeat and death of Artabanus in 224 ended the Arsacid dynasty and Ardashir proclaimed himself 'King of Kings' and initiated in Persia a new Sassanian line of kings which endured until its overthrow by the rising power of Islam in 651.

The coinage of the Sassanian kings throughout something over four centuries

473

remained remarkably consistent in its essentials. Gold, to judge from surviving examples, was struck with no great frequency and is completely absent for many of the kings. Copper, too, was not commonly struck nor were the smaller divisionary pieces in silver. Silver drachms, however, were struck in all reigns, in some of them in massive issues. Sassanian silver had an extremely wide circulation from the Mediterranean coast to the Indus and from the Persian gulf to the Caucasus and together with contemporary Byzantine gold provided the means of exchange for the whole of the Near East.

There is only one basic set of types on the Sassanian coinage. On the obverse appears the portrait bust of the king, joined occasionally by that of his queen and, more rarely, also by that of his heir. Stylistically the portraiture derives from that of the Parthian issues but undergoes considerable change in detail of costume and head-dress in the course of the centuries. This obverse portrait is accompanied, as on the later Parthian issues, by an inscription in Pehlvi giving the king's name and titles. The obverse shows a fire-altar, similar to that on some of the coinage of Persis (see p. 95). The altar is most often shown flanked by two figures, the king and his son, but occasionally stands on its own.

The coinage of Ardashir I (226–240) in addition to issues in gold, silver and bronze includes tetradrachms in potin, the only instance of the use of this base metal in the Sassanian coinage, though this alloy was commonly used in the later Parthian issues, prior to the rise of the Sassanians. The first coinage of Ardashir shows him on the obverse wearing a domed tiara very similar to that of the Parthian kings and his portrait is accompanied by the Pehlvi inscription *the worshipper of Ormuzd, the divine Ardashir, King of Kings of Iran.* On the reverse the fire-altar stands alone and the inscription reads *the fire of Ardashir* (Pl. 866). On other issues Ardashir is depicted wearing either a crown with three crenellated ornaments surmounted by a circular plume of hair or a species of cap, again surmounted by the circular plume, or a kind of plain diadem. Sapor I (240–271), who defeated and captured the Roman emperor Valerian I in the battle near Edessa in 259, is usually shown wearing the crenellated crown and on the reverse the fire-altar is flanked by two figures, possibly the king and a priest.

Bahram I (272–275) wears an unusual head-dress, consisting of a diadem with fire-rays and still surmounted by the circular plume, while on some issues of Bahram II (275–283) the obverse carries the jugate busts of the king and queen (Pl. 867) and a rare series shows the smaller bust of the heir facing that of his parents. Under Hormuzd II (300–309) the head-dress is ornamented with wings, a feature which recurs on some subsequent issues. On the coinage of Firuz (457–483) there began the practice of indicating the regnal year by means of letter numerals placed on the reverse by the fire-altar and from the time of Bahram V

(420–439) other letters placed on the reverse indicate the mint which struck the coin, but, as only the initials are given, the exact interpretation and location of these mints is frequently a matter of uncertainty.

In the earlier coinage the dies from which the coinage was struck coincided almost exactly, as regards size, with the flan but from about the time of Sapor III (383–388) the flans became thinner and more spread so that an unstamped margin was left around the struck portion. On the coinage of Kavad and most of his successors it became customary to place four crescents, equally spaced, on this blank margin, presumably in an attempt to discourage clipping of the coins. The standard both of design and execution gradually deteriorated, particularly in the later sixth and early seventh centuries, resulting in some rather barbaric, if still extremely effective, portraits such as the facing portrait of Chosroes II (590–627), the Sassanian king who captured Jerusalem and carried off the True Cross in A.D. 614 (Pl. 868). In the last century of Sassanian coinage the only denomination struck was the silver drachm of which the issues of Yezdigird III (632–651) is representative (Pl. 869).

THE MUHAMMADAN COINAGE

The coinages which are described in the earlier sections possess two primary features which facilitate their recognition and arrangement: they are, in most cases, equipped with types in the form of representations or designs and are inscribed in languages which are intelligible to a greater or lesser degree to people of Western civilization. When, however, attention is turned to the coinage of the Eastern world, and in particular to that of the Moslem world, little assistance can be gained from the helpful features of Western coinage just mentioned. The Muhammadan coinage, with some few exceptions, avoids, in accordance with religious tenets, the representation of living objects or indeed of any objects at all and both sides of the coins are devoted to inscriptions in scripts and in languages unfamiliar to the generality. The Muhammadan coins possess a certain interest as examples of calligraphic design but their chief value lies in the remarkably full, continuous and dated record they provide of the successive rulers of the various dynasties of the Moslem world; and, as almost all these coins carry a mention of their place of mintage, they supply some indication of the location and the territorial extent of these kingdoms.

In the circumstances, the present section can attempt to do little more than give a description of the typical coinage of the various Muhammadan dynasties within a framework, as far as possible, chronological; but, since many of the dynasties were co-existent, the chronological arrangement must be compounded with a geographical arrangement. The Muhammadan coinage is dealt with in this way in this first section, from its inception in the seventh century up to the nineteenth century, and the emergence of the national states of the present day. A separate, following, section is devoted to the coinages of these states.

IMITATIVE COINAGE:
ARAB–SASSANIAN ARAB–BYZANTINE

The Muhammadan era dates from the year A.D. 622, the year of the Hegira or flight of Muhammad from Mecca to Medina. From this base the new, militant religion of Islam made rapid conquest of the more settled and civilized nations outside Arabia until, within a few decades, Palestine, Syria, Egypt and Persia had all passed to what became, in effect, a new Islamic empire. In the field of coinage the Arab conquerors were at first content to continue to issue coins of the type current in the various areas which they had overrun. In the east, where by 651 Yezdigird III, the last of the Sassanian kings, had met his death by assassination the coinage issued by the Arab governors of the former Sassanian provinces was a copy, almost exclusively in silver, of the Sassanian coinage with its conventional portrait and its reverse of a Zoroastrian fire-altar with two attendants. The most commonly copied coins were those of the last Sassanian king, Yezdigird III, or the famous Chosroes II and can be distinguished from original coinage by the additional inscription in Arabic appearing on the margin of the obverse (Pl. 870). These imitations continued to be produced in the Western provinces of the former Sassanian empire until in the caliphate of Abd al-Malik a new Islamic coinage was introduced in stages from A.D. 696.* In the east, in the province of Tabaristan, coins in the Sassanian style continued to be issued even after the first or Umaiyad caliphate was replaced by the Abbasid dynasty in 749 and in Bokhara these imitations continued as late as the reign of Harun al-Rashid (786–809).

The Western conquests of Islam were at the expense of the Byzantine empire. Damascus was taken in 635 and in a short space of years the rest of Syria, Palestine, Egypt and later the remaining Byzantine provinces in North Africa fell to the Arabs. As happened in the provinces of the Sassanian empire, the administrative and financial systems of the Byzantine empire were taken over and a coinage imitating a selection of Byzantine coinage was issued. Whereas the Sassanian copies were almost wholly in silver, the Byzantine copies were almost exclusively in copper with a small percentage in gold, but none in silver.

The copper 40 nummia piece of Justin II showing the seated figures of the

* Dates throughout are given in the Christian not the Muhammudan era.

emperor together with his empress, Sophia, on the obverse and the Greek numeral M = 40 on the reverse (see p. 201) when copied received in place of the imperial legend on the obverse an inscription in Graeco-Latin giving the mint of the coin (Pl. 871). The 40 nummia coins of Heraclius with the standing figure of the emperor holding cross and globe on the obverse (see p. 204) were also extensively copied with the substitution of a Graeco-Latin inscription on the obverse giving the mint name and often an inscription in Arabic on the reverse. Other coins of Heraclius with the emperor together with one or two of his sons were also imitated as well as coins with the half-length portrait of Constans II.

The Byzantine gold which was most commonly copied by the Arabs in North Africa and in Spain was the gold solidus of Heraclius minted at Carthage, with the busts of Heraclius and his son on obverse and a cross on steps on the reverse. In the first stage of imitation the cross was transmuted into the form of a pole with a globe on top on the imitations of the solidus, the semissis or half-piece and on the tremissis or third (Pl. 872). The imitation tremisses struck in Spain are further removed from the originals and frequently have an eight-pointed star on the obverse and a Kufic inscription in the centre as well as round the circumference. One further class of Arab-Byzantine coinage, derivative rather than purely imitative, is that on which the standing figure of the caliph is portrayed on the obverse. This type, usually on copper coins, is a derivation from Byzantine copper coins showing the standing figure of Heraclius holding a long cross in his right hand; the Islamic version shows the figure of the caliph with hand on sword, the attitude in which he delivered the Khutba, or Friday Sermon in the mosque. The reverse sometimes copies the cursive M of the Byzantine original but often takes the form of the pillar with circlet on top, derived from the Byzantine cross-on steps type (Pl. 873).

THE UMAIYAD CALIPHATE

The institution of a new, purely Islamic coinage in place of the imitative issues described above took place in the caliphate of Abd al-Malik. Tradition has it that the stimulus to this coinage reform was supplied by the anti-Moslem policy of the Byzantine emperor, Justin II. In brief the story runs that Byzantium which derived its stock of papyrus from Egypt, now in Arab hands, was displeased to discover that the official headings guaranteeing the papyrus included phrases in Arabic of religious character, such as that there was no god but Allah. To the Byzantine threat to retaliate by placing legends abusive of Muhammad on their gold solidi, which still secured wide circulation in Egypt, the caliph replied by issuing his own gold dinars with Islamic legends.

However much truth there may be in the tradition, it is the case that the first Islamic coins to be issued were gold dinars, in the year A.D. 696–697. Most of these gold dinars carry no mint name but were presumably struck at the caliph's mint at Damascus for they carry a fuller form of inscription than do the half- and third-dinars of which some bear the name of the area of their minting, either Ifrikiya (Africa—mint at Kairawan) or al-Andalus (Spain—mint at Cordoba). The obverse inscription, adapted from the Koran, reads 'There is no god but Allah alone (He has no partner). Muhammad is the Apostle of Allah whom He sent with guidance and the religion of truth (that He may make it victorious over every other religion)'. The fuller form, including the bracketed portion, appears on the dinars struck in the east (Pl. 874); the shortened form on the divisionary pieces with or without mint name issued in the west. The reverse inscriptions on gold struck in east and west differ more widely. On Eastern gold the legend reads 'Allah is One, Allah is the Eternal; He begets not, neither is He begotten', while western issues have the form 'In the name of Allah, the merciful, the compassionate'.

The silver dirhem which was first issued in A.D. 698–699 carries inscriptions of similar type and, almost without exception, has an indication of its mint and the date. In the east a whole range of mints struck the silver dirhem (Pl. 875) the most constantly active being Damascus in Syria and, after its foundation in 703, the new city of Wasit, mid-way between Kufa and Basra in Iraq. In the west no mint towns appear on the dirhems, only the names of the two provinces Ifrikiya and al-Andalus. The signed and dated dirhems carry the formula, e.g. 'In the name of Allah this dirhem was struck in Damascus in the year 79' (A.D. 698–699). Copper was also issued as a coin termed the *fals*, a name clearly deriving from the Roman and Byzantine *follis*. The earliest coppers are inscribed only with religious formulae with no indication of mint or date; these were followed by issues bearing the names of mints in various parts of the Islamic empire as well as by issues without mint name but with a date.

THE ABBASID CALIPHATE

The line of Umaiyad caliphs was replaced by that of the Abbasids in 749 but brought little change to the coinage system or to the details of the coins themselves, except for some alteration in the arrangement of the religious formulae. On the reverse the first part of the formula used under the Umaiyads in the marginal inscription 'Muhammad is the Apostle of Allah', now occupied the centre, replacing the 'Allah is One, Allah is the Eternal' of the Umaiyads. Gold dinars continued to carry no overt indication of their mint town until the ninth century but the silver dirhems, as before, were regularly marked with their place of minting.

Under the caliph al-Mansur (754–775) the name of the heir who was responsible for coinage appeared on the coins and shortly afterwards that of the caliph himself. Later other names came to be added, those of the mint master, of governors and so on. The copper fals also continued, as under the Umaiyads, to carry the names of provincial governors. In the east, in Tabaristan, as already mentioned, Arab-Sassanian imitations were produced by the governors for at least a century after the establishment of the Abbasid caliphate. It was under the Abbasid caliph al-Mansur that the new capital of Baghdad was founded and, of the line of Abbasid caliphs, the name most familiar to the west is that of Harun al-Rashid (Pl. 876).

The Abbasid caliphs, however, were not long able to preserve the unity of their empire and in various provinces governors and generals established themselves as more or less independent rulers, owing only a nominal allegiance to the caliph in Baghdad, then called Medinet-es-Salam. In addition foreign conquerors made themselves master of parts of the Islamic empire and all of these arrogated to themselves the right of coinage, exercising it in the beginning in the name of the caliph. Something of the order of a hundred dynasties exercised rule in the Moslem world at various times but here space permits mention only of the more important in the several geographical divisions.

SPAIN

Although the Abbasid dynasty had replaced that of the Umaiyads in the east, the Arab conquests in Spain never came under their authority, for an independent Umaiyad caliphate continued to exercise rule in Spain until its dissolution in 1031 and its replacement by a number of petty, mutually hostile principalities. The coinage of the Umaiyad caliphs in Spain consisted of gold dinars and silver dirhems of the conventional type struck mainly at the mints of al-Andalus—Cordoba and also at the mint of Medinet-ed-Zahra (Pl. 877). Towards the end of the period the dirhems were struck not in pure silver but in a baser alloy. On the break-up of the caliphate of Cordoba smaller kingdoms were established. The dynasty of the Beni Hamud ruled at Cordoba between 1016 and 1017, that of the Beni Idris at Malaga from 1035 to 1055, the Beni Abbad at Seville from 1023 to 1091 and Beni Hud at Saragossa from 1039 to 1145. These were all in turn overwhelmed by the Christian reconquest of Spain, but while they exercised authority they issued both gold and silver coins from mints in the capital cities of their kingdoms. Successively the Moorish dynasties of the Almoravides and the Almohades in Africa (see below) exercised rule in Spain in the eleventh and twelfth centuries and coined at a number of mints in Spain, including Cordoba,

Murcia and Granada. The dynasty of the Beni Nasra maintained their kingdom of Granada from 1238 until 1492 when Moslem power in Spain was finally over-thrown by Ferdinand and Isabella. A change from the hitherto conventional designs is seen on the gold and silver of the kingdom of Granada where the central inscription on both obverse and reverse is enclosed not in a circle but a rectangle (Pl. 878).

NORTH AFRICA

Unlike Spain, North Africa came under the authority of the Abbasid caliphate when it replaced the Umaiyad in 750 but in 800 Ibrahim ben Aghlab who had been appointed governor of the African province by Harun al-Rashid established an independent kingdom which soon comprised Tripoli, Tunis, Algiers and Morocco. The Aghlabite kingdom extended its influence across the Mediterranean, capturing Sicily, Malta and Sardinia in the years between 827 and 866 and in the same period held Bari in Apulia and ravaged Italy. Dinars and dirhems and rarer copper pieces were struck by the several Aghlabite rulers in Africa until the kingdom, already weakened by the establishment of the Idrisid kingdom at Fez in Morocco, was conquered by the Fatimids in 909. Following the Fatimid capture of Egypt in 969 and the removal of their capital from Mahdia on the Gulf of Tunis to Cairo in 972 the former Aghlabite territory was split amongst smaller dynasties, chief of which was that of the Zirids in Tunisia. Sardinia was lost to the Genoese, and Sicily to the Normans in 1061.

A new dynasty, that of the Morabites or Almoravides arose in 1056 and soon controlled the whole of Morocco and, in response to requests for aid from the Moslem kings in Spain, extended their authority over southern Spain. The Morabite coinage is almost entirely of gold dinars struck at mints in Spain such as Cordoba, Seville and Granada and in Africa at Fez and Marrakesh. On the obverse, in addition to the usual profession of faith, is inscribed the name of the ruler with the title Prince of the Moslems, for the Abbasid caliph was still recognized as Prince of the Faithful. The marginal inscription of the reverse gives the mint and date (Pl. 879). The Almoravides were replaced in 1147 by the Muwahids or Almohades who created a kingdom which extended over southern Spain, Morocco, Tunis and Tripoli. The gold dinars of the Almohades are of unusually thin, spread fabric and the central inscription on both sides is contained in a rectangular frame. Marginal inscriptions frequently record not only the name of the reigning monarch but of his ancestors. Silver dirhems which were square in shape are without name of ruler or mint and without date and have no marginal inscriptions (Pl. 880). In Spain the Christian kingdoms, for once united, inflicted a defeat on the

Almohades in 1212 at Las Navas de Tolosa, and in North Africa their kingdom succumbed in 1269 and was divided amongst smaller dynasties, the Marinids in Morocco, the Ziyanids in western Algeria and the Berber Hafsids in eastern Algeria, Tunisia and Tripoli. The coinage of these dynasties was mainly one of gold dinars, usually in the thin spread fabric of previous North African dynasties. On Marinid gold, struck at Fez and Marrakesh, the central area is rectangular and is enclosed by a double frame of two continuous lines. The Ziyanid gold struck at Tlemcen in western Algeria also encloses the central area in a double-lined rectangular frame but on Hafsid dinars struck at Tunis—when a mint can be read—the rectangular central inscription is bounded by a triple frame of which the outer and inner lines are continuous but the central is formed of a row of dots. Rarer silver dirhems of all three dynasties are rectangular in shape and so irregularly cut that it is not always possible to determine the nature of the enclosing frame.

In Morocco the Marinid dynasty was replaced by that of the Wattasids about 1465 and the Hafsids gradually gained the ascendancy over the Ziyanids. In the course of the sixteenth century the whole of North Africa witnessed further changes of rule, this time of greater duration, lasting well down into the nineteenth century. The control of Morocco was disputed between the Wattasids and the Sharifs between 1510 and 1554, the latter finally emerging victorious. To the east, Corsair raiders established smaller kingdoms, nominally vassals of the Ottoman empire of Constantinople, in Algeria in 1556, in Tunis in 1514, in Tripoli in 1551 and in Cyrenaica in 1521. The Sharif coinage of dinars and dirhems begins with types where the central area is enclosed in a rectangular frame but a greater variety of outline makes its way into the coinage—two superimposed squares giving rise to an eight-pointed star design and, much more commonly, two interlinked triangles, making up a six-pointed star. Multiple dinars and dirhems were also issued and, in the eighteenth century, copper mazunas. On these copper coins with their six-pointed star design the date in the Muhammadan era is given frequently in figures, of the type used in the Western world (Pl. 881). French intervention in Morocco began in 1844 and finally in 1912 the country was divided as protectorates under France and Spain (see p. 465). Coinage was struck by the Ottoman empire (see p. 488) for its North African provinces. Algeria was occupied by France in 1830 and Tunisia in 1883 while Tripolitania and Cyrenaica were seized by Italy in 1912.

EGYPT

The Abbasid caliphs controlled Egypt till about 868 from which date, though nominally recognizing the Abbasid caliph, Egypt was in effect controlled by the Tulunids with their capital at al-Fustat in the Delta. The Tulunids also controlled Syria after 899 and disputed with others the control of the Hejaz. The Tulunid coinage, mainly gold dinars, was issued with the mint names of both Misr–Egypt and Filisteen–Palestine. From about 934 the ruling dynasty was that of the Ikshidids. In 969 came the conquest of Cyrenaica and Egypt by the Fatimids who established their first capital at Mahdia on the Gulf of Tunis until the capture of Cairo in 972. Fatimid dinars struck at Cairo and at Mahdia have a distinctive arrangement of the religious formulae which themselves are unusual, since the Fatimids belonged to the unorthodox Shi'a sect. The circular central area is bounded by a plain circular margin which in turn is encircled by the marginal inscription (Pl. 882). On other issues the centre of the coin is plain and is surrounded by three circular inscriptions. An extensive series of rubas or quarter-dinars was also struck, principally in the island of Sicily (Pl. 883). The Fatimids also controlled parts of Syria from 969 until the First Crusade in 1070. Silver was struck much more rarely by the Fatimid caliphs.

In 1171 a new dynasty, that of the Ayyubids, seized control of Egypt and under its first and most famous ruler, Saladin, recovered control of most of Syria in 1183. Gold dinars of Saladin from mints at Cairo and Alexandria have a small central inscription, surrounded by three circles of inscription (Pl. 884). Silver dirhems and halves of the Damascus mint have a square frame enclosing the central inscription and those struck at Halab have a hexagram or six-pointed-star outline for the central area. Copper coins of Saladin show a feature unusual on Islamic coins in the presence of a type on the obverse, either a recumbent lion or a figure seated cross-legged. These copper coins have an affinity with issues of the Urtukids (see p. 484). The square- or star-shaped central area persists on dirhems of later Fatimid caliphs but gold dinars generally return to the more traditional form of a circular central area enclosed by a marginal inscription. Copper coins with an obverse type were also struck in 1200 for El-Awhad of the Mesopotamian branch of the dynasty. The figure on the obverse is shown either as a half-length bust facing, crowned or wearing a cap with tassels, or as a figure seated cross-legged and holding an orb (Pl. 885).

In 1250 the Mamelukes, the Turkish bodyguard of the Ayyubid caliphs, put forward their own candidate and established a new dynasty which shortly added Syria to its dominions. Shejer-ed-durr, the Turkish concubine of El Salih, the last of the Ayyubids, retained the sovereignty for a few months then made the Mameluke Eybek her husband and sultan. A very rare dinar exists in the name of Shejer-ed-durr alone (Pl. 886). The typical gold dinar of the Mameluke sultans eventually abandoned the use of a marginal inscription and has only lines of inscription across the field on both sides of the coin (Pl. 887). Rarer silver follows much the same pattern but copper pieces have the central inscription enclosed in a triangle or other geometric patterns.

The Mamelukes, first the Bahri dynasty till 1382 and then the Burji, ruled till 1517 when Egypt became part of the empire of the Ottoman Turks. Between 1832 and 1882 Egypt, under Muhammad Ali and his heirs, had a special, semi-independent status in the Turkish empire until, after British and French intervention in the late nineteenth century, it became a British protectorate in 1914 (see p. 464).

ASIA

The effective rule of the Abbasid caliphs in the Asian provinces was of comparatively short duration, though the nominal authority of the Abbasid caliph at Baghdad continued until the Mongol conquest in the thirteenth century. The caliphate was divided into a number of independent kingdoms under various dynasties, each of which struck their own coinage. In the east the Samanids who controlled Transoxiana between 874 and 998 struck a coinage at mints at Samarkand, Egh-Shash and Bokhara. Gold dinars and silver dirhems, produced in quantity, found their way in the course of trade across Russia as far as Scandinavia and have been recorded as finds in England as well. The formulae on these coins are arranged in the conventional pattern, a circular central area surrounded by marginal inscription (Pl. 888). For most of the latter half of the ninth century Khorasan, Afghanistan and much of Persia was controlled by the Saffarids but by the middle of the tenth century the Ghaznavid princes had established their supremacy in the whole of this area and extended it to Transoxiana in the early eleventh century. The Ghaznavid coinage, principally of silver but with a considerable amount of gold, was struck at a range of mints—the capital, Ghaznah, at Balkh in Khorasan and at Mahmudpore and Lahore in northern India. Silver issues from these latter mints have bilingual inscriptions, usually in Arabic on the obverse and Sanskrit on the reverse (Pl. 889). On some of the copper coinage from Indian mints a figure of a bull is incorporated in the rude script on the obverse or a horseman on the reverse. In Mesopotamia effective power was seized between 929 and 945 by the Hamdanids who were succeeded by the Buwahids, a dynasty which maintained itself until about 1094. The Buwahid coinage, mainly silver, was struck at a variety of mints including Shiraz, Medinet-es-Salam, Basra and Oman. The central inscription is contained in a circle bounded by either a dotted or a plain-line border and surrounded by one or two lines of marginal inscription

SELJUKS

In the eleventh century the caliphate was increasingly subjected to invasion by non-Arabic peoples, principally of Turkish origin from the great steppe lands. Penetrating south and west the Turkish Seljuks took possession of Transoxiana, Khorasan, the greater part of Persia, Mesopotamia and Syria by about 1037 and maintained their empire till the Mongol conquests in the mid thirteenth century. Control of part of the eastern areas was maintained by the Ghaznavid princes, succeeded later by the Ghurids, and from the mid twelfth century part of Meso-potamia and most of Persia was held by the Khuwarizim shahs but in Mesopotamia, Syria and Asia Minor various branches of the Seljuks exercised effective control. Up to this point the Muhammadan coinages described have maintained with only minor variations of pattern the conventional types of central and marginal inscriptions only, on both obverse and reverse, but the coinage of the Seljuks and the various Atabegs or generals presents a series of figure types on the majority of issues and a great proportion of the coinage is not in the form of the traditional gold dinars and silver dirhems but of thick heavy copper pieces. The Great Seljuks, who under their sultans Tughril-Beg, then Alp-Arslan and their successors reigned in Persia between 1037 and 1157 and became the protectors of the Abbasid nominal caliph, adhered to the old pattern of coinage in their issues from mints at Nisabur, Medinet-es-Salem and Isfahan.

The Seljuks in Rum (1077–1308), the area in Anatolia which they had conquered from the Byzantine empire, produced, perhaps under the influence of Byzantine coin types, a certain amount of coinage with figure types on the obverse. Some early copper pieces show a mounted warrior with drawn sword and silver coins of Suliman II (1199–1203) struck at the mint of Caesarea carry a mounted figure brandishing a mace and with head in nimbus (Pl. 890). Figure types lapsed after Suliman but under Kay Khusru II (1236–45) a lion surmounted by a sun appeared on the obverse of silver coins (Pl. 891). On the coinage of the Urtukids of Diyar-bekr in Mesoptoamia, however, figure types on obverse are the rule and inscriptional types the exception. Though these coins are large, heavy, copper pieces some of them bear the name dirhem and some of them still show traces of silvering. The sources of inspiration of the obverse figure types are as diverse as the great coinage series which had served the area through past ages. A diademed profile portrait is copied from the tetradrachms of the Seleucid kings, a winged Victory shows the influence of Roman coinage (Pl. 892) and a bearded portrait wears the distinctive head-dress of the Sassanian kings. The greatest influence naturally was exerted by the more recent types of Byzantine coins. The two facing busts, one larger and one smaller, stems from the obverses of coins of Heraclius and Constans II while a standing figure of an emperor, crowned by a saint, copies more clearly contemporary Byzantine issues. The facing bust of an enthroned figure (Pl. 893) is a close copy of the bust of the enthroned Christ on many Byzantine issues and the influence of Western coinage, made familiar by contact with the crusaders, is seen in the facing bust wearing trifoliate crown. An unusual figure type which seems to be original as far as coins are concerned is the double-headed eagle (Pl. 894), a type which later found wide popularity in many European coinages. The issues of the Zengids of Mosul include a slightly higher proportion of purely inscriptional coins but thick copper coins with figure obverses were also struck extensively. The choice of obverse figures betrays much the same influences as those noted in the Urtukid coinage but in general the figures are executed in a much cruder style. The coinage of the Begteginids of Arbela is a similar mixture of conventional inscription and figure types.

PERSIA

Roughly contemporary with this unusual figure-type coinage of the Seljuks were the issues of the Khuwarizim shahs who, between 1097 and 1230, controlled part of Mesopotamia and most of Persia. Their coinage in gold and silver followed, in the main, the established inscriptional types but an unusual feature was the introduction of large, spread copper coins with either circular or square central area and marginal inscription.

MONGOLS

In the late twelfth century the Mongol nomads in the steppe lands north of the Gobi desert were forced into union under Temujin, the leader of one of the clans. In 1206 Temujin assumed the title, Genghis Khan 'the Very Great King', and under his leadership the Mongols embarked on a career of conquest which soon brought them control of northern China, of Turkestan, of Khorasan and Afghanistan, the outlying provinces of the Khuwarizim shahs, as well as Azerbaijan, Georgia and south Russia. Genghis Khan died in 1227 but under his successors the Mongol conquest was continued until his grandson Kublai Khan held the whole of China and Korea, and Mongol invaders swept over eastern Europe, penetrating as far west as Hungary. In 1256 the Mongols under Hulagu demolished the kingdoms of the Khuwarizim shahs and the Seljuks in Persia and Mesopotamia and their westward advance was checked only by the Mamelukes in Palestine. It was in the course of the conquest that the last titular Abbasid caliph in Baghdad was murdered.

The coinage of the Great Khans, struck for the areas where their southern conquests impinged on the Islamic world, was issued almost exclusively in silver with inscriptions in Arabic. The silver coins of Ghengis Khan himself (1206–27) are pieces of small module (Pl. 895) but coins of the interregnum under Turakina, the widow of Ogotai (1241–6), have a figure type on the obverse, a horseman drawing his bow and accompanied by small figures of a stork and a dog (Pl. 896). The type, reminiscent of a figure-type on the coins of the Seljuks of Rum, is a familiar theme in earlier Sassanian and Persian art. The issues of Mangu (1248–57) are, however, purely inscriptional.

The great Mongol empire eventually divided into a number of independent kingdoms which, for a time, recognized the nominal supremacy of the Great Khan. Most of western Asia from the Mediterranean to the Indus was ruled from 1256 to 1336 by the dynasty of the Il Khans, set up by Hulagu. The Il Khans, converted to Islam, issued a coinage which included some gold and copper but was mainly in the form of silver dirhems (Pl. 897). Something more than fifty mints have been identified on this coinage. Copper coins in the earlier reigns perpetuated some of the figure types of the Urtukid and Zangid coinages and on some later issues the lion and sun of the silver coins of the Seljuks of Rum was used as a type on copper. Gold and silver, however, preserved the traditional inscription types on both obverse and reverse with the central inscription enclosed in a circle, a square or more elaborate geometric forms. On the early coinage of Hulagu (1256–65) the name of Mangu the Great Khan was also inscribed but after the accession of Kublai in 1257 only the title of Great Khan appeared but not his proper name, and from the beginning of the reign of Ghazan (1295–1304) all mention of the Great Khan as overlord was omitted. In addition to the silver dirhem a half-piece was also struck as well as a double piece and occasional higher multiples. The Mongol dirhems were originally issued at the conventional weight of 2·6 gm. but suffered falls in standard to a weight of 2·1 gm. under Ghazan.

The coinage of the khans of the Kipchak Mongols of the Golden Horde, whose various dynasties controlled southern Russia and parts of eastern Europe between 1224 and the final submission to Russia in 1502, is almost exclusively of silver. The types on obverse and reverse consist of a central inscription, usually in a circular frame but without marginal inscription. These silver dirhems are of small module and correspondingly low weight and in somewhat degenerate script (Pl. 898). The hold of Islam on south Russia was completed by the seizure of Astrakhan by Tatar khans in 1438 and by the conquest of Genoese possessions in the Crimea and the Sea of Azov in 1475 by other Tatars. A coinage in silver was struck by these Krim Tatars for some three centuries till their final subjection by Russia in 1783.

After about a century of rule the Mongol empire suffered the same fate which had overtaken the Abbasid caliphate and the Seljuk kingdom, the splintering of its power and the setting up of smaller, semi-independent kingdoms. Persia was controlled by the Jalayrs from 1336 to 1393, Kurdistan by the Muzaffarids (1345–92) and Khorasan by the Sarbadarids (1335–81), while the Kart Mongols ruled Afghanistan until 1389 and the Jagatai Mongols Transoxiana till 1358. The coinage of these dynasties, mostly silver dirhems with only occasional gold dinars, perpetuated the conventional inscriptional types with the central area enclosed in a variety of geometric outlines.

A fresh wave of Mongol conquest began under Timur, better known in Western history as Tamerlane, of Transoxiana, (1369–1404). His conquering armies swept south and east as far as Delhi and westwards through Persia and Mesopotamia, but on Timur's death the more Western conquests were lost. His descendants succeeded in holding central and southern Persia for half a century and Khorasan for the remainder of the fifteenth century, but when Timur's dynasty was replaced by that of the Sheybanids in 1500 Timur's empire had shrunk to the khanate of Bokhara. The principal mint for the Timurid coinage was at Samarkand and the coinage was mainly of silver with some copper issues. In the reign of Timur some silver issues are of the traditional smaller diameter but the majority of Timur's coinage and that of his successors are of larger type (Pl. 899). The silver coins of the Sheybanids in Bokhara in the sixteenth century are of a similar spread fabric as are those of the Astrakhan dynasty which ruled from 1599 till 1785. Most of the coinage of the Mangit dynasty which reigned until Bokhara became tributary to Russia in 1868 is of gold.

THE OTTOMAN EMPIRE

In Phrygia one of the small kingdoms into which the empire of the Seljuks of Rum had disintegrated began to exercise a supremacy over the others under its chief, Othman, in 1299 and within a century the Ottoman Turks were masters of Asia Minor. Although they suffered some reverse at the time of Timur's westward conquests, Ottoman power revived under Murad II (1421–51) and began to extend. Under Muhammad II (1451–81) the Byzantine empire was finally extinguished and Constantinople captured in 1453. The Balkans fell to the Turks in the fifteenth century and the next century saw further Turkish advances westwards into Hungary, and in the same century Syria, Mesopotamia and part of Persia were absorbed into the Ottoman empire. In the early sixteenth century

Egypt was taken and later Tripoli, Tunis and Algiers became Ottoman vassals. The extreme Turkish conquests in Europe were short-lived but the rest of the Ottoman empire survived, with some losses in Africa, until the first world war.

The Ottoman coinage, like almost all other Islamic coinages, is remarkably conservative and almost completely eschews figure types, both obverse and reverse carrying only lines of inscription, usually only horizontally across the field of the coin. At first a simple religious formula was placed on the coins but this was soon dropped and the inscriptions normally record only the name and style of the sultan, the place of minting and frequently the date. The earlier Ottoman coinage omits mint and date but from the time of Murad II (1421–51) these are consistently present. Of the chain of mints throughout the life of the Ottoman empire the most important and prolific were Adrianople and Constantinople in Europe, Aleppo, Damascus, Baghdad and Tiflis in Asia and, in Africa, Cairo, Tripoli, Tunis and Algiers.

Initially the Turkish coinage consisted solely of silver in a denomination known as the akce (Pl. 900), introduced by Urkhan in 1328. The weight of the silver akce was approximately one-third of the silver dirhem of earlier Islamic coinages and the manghir, a copper coin (Pl. 901), was introduced by the next sultan, Murad I (1360–89). The Turkish gold coin, the altun (Pl. 902), was struck for the first time by Muhammad II in 1478 after the capture of Constantinople. Since the altun replaced the Venetian gold zecchino or sequin, which had previously supplied currency needs in gold, the Turkish gold coin has traditionally been referred to in the west as a sequin. The tughra, the monogram of the sultan's names and titles which is a feature of later Turkish coinage (Pl. 903), appeared for the first time under Suleyman I (1520–66) but did not become common until the issues of Muhammad III (1595–1603).

A new, large silver denomination approximating to the thaler class of coinage in Europe was introduced in 1687 by Suleyman II but the weight of 19·5 gm. at which it was issued was only some two-thirds of the normal weight of this category of coin in most European series. The name given to this new denomination, the ghurush or piastre (Pl. 904), recalls the grosso, groschen, etc., of European coinages. Already in 1655 another smaller silver denomination had been introduced, the para. At first the para was equivalent to 4 akces but later as para and akce deteriorated the para was issued at a rate of 40 to the ghurush and the akce at 3 to the para. The para was also issued in a number of multiples of 5 paras of which the more important were the zolota of 30 paras and its double, a double ghurush of 80 paras and the yuzlik of 100 paras. In the reign of Ahmet III (1703–30) the earlier gold altun of 3·4 gm. was replaced by a new gold coin, the funduk altun, which had only the tughra but no formula on the obverse. Subdivisions of this gold coin

were also struck. In the same reign a lighter gold coin, the zer mabub, was introduced at a weight of 2·6 gm. (Pl. 905). Subdivisions and multiples of this coin
were issued until the coinage reform in the reign of Abdul Mejid (1839–61).
Subsequent Turkish coinage is described below in the section on the coinage of
the modern states of the Near East.

SHAHS OF PERSIA

The Jalayrids who had ruled Persia until the invasion of the Mongol Timur in
1336 survived as vassals of the Timurid Mongols till 1411. For the remainder of
the fifteenth century the control of Persia was disputed between the Timurids
and Black Sheep and White Sheep Turcomans, but in 1502 the Safavids under
Ismail I gained the ascendancy, establishing the state of Persia which, with vicissitudes of dynasty, has persisted into modern times. The Safavid dynasty ruled
until 1736, the final decades being disrupted by the Afghan claimants Mahmud
(1722–5) and Ashraf (1725–30), but in 1736 Nadir established a new dynasty of the
Afsharis. The Zands at Shiraz who came to power under Kerim Khan in 1750 were
finally eclipsed in 1794 by the Kajars at Teheran who had been in revolt since
1779. This last dynasty endured until 1925 when it was replaced by Reza Shah,
the first of the present Pahlavi dynasty.

The unit of the Persian gold coinage was the ashrafi (Pl. 906) of a weight of
3·4 gm., roughly that of the contemporary Venetian ducat and similar European
gold pieces. In silver the coins were the shahi, the mahmudi equal to 2 shahis and
the abbasi (Pl. 907) of 2 mahmudis. The copper kazbegi was tariffed at a tenth
of the shahi. Persian gold and silver coinage has initially, like other Islamic issues,
exclusively inscription types on both obverse and reverse. The language at first is
Arabic. The central area on the obverse is occupied by a religious formula, surrounded, where there is a margin, by the names of the twelve imams, while the
reverse gives the royal name and title, together with the mint and the date.
Under Abbas I (1587–1629) Persian appears on the reverse. A feature of Persian
coinage is the use of a distich or poetic couplet incorporating mention of the shah's
name. Nadir (1736–47) introduced a new gold piece, the mohur, on the heavier
Indian standard alongside the ashrafi which disappeared from the coinage of Kerim
Khan (1750–79) and his successors. A new coinage was instituted by Fath Ali
(1797–1834) with the toman as the gold unit and the karan, equal to a tenth of
the toman, as the main silver piece. Subdivisions and multiples of the gold toman
were also struck.

The next adjustment to the coinage system under Nasr-ed-din in 1877 provides a convenient point to begin the description of the coinage of modern Persia in the section on modern states below. In this reign too the striking of the Persian coinage was restricted to the mint at Teheran, the issues of earlier centuries having been struck at a number of mints of which the most important were Shiraz, Tabriz, Isfahan and Kazvin.

The first departure from the exclusively inscriptional coinage comes only in the early nineteenth century when Fath Ali on double gold tomans of 1823 is depicted on the obverse as a mounted figure and on half-tomans of 1833 as an enthroned figure (Pl. 908). A half-toman of Muhammad in 1846 has on obverse the Persian lion with raised sword, familiar on modern Persian coinage.

Persian copper coinage was issued autonomously until the nineteenth century and differed from the previous metal issues in that the obverse almost always presented a figure type. A common type is the lion surmounted by sun which had originally appeared on coins of the Seljuks of Rum but other issues present a whole menagerie of birds and animals on the obverse (Pl. 909).

GEORGIA

This relatively small mountainous country lying between the Black Sea and the Caspian had a chequered history of successive phases of precarious independence and submission to the empires which rose and fell on its borders, and in the Georgian coinage these vicissitudes of history are reflected. In the classical period the only coinage of the area was that of the Greek colonies on the Black Sea coast (see p. 18) and, later, barbarous imitations of staters of Alexander the Great and Lysimachus and denarii of the early Roman empire.

Georgia became Christian as early as the time of Constantine the Great but it was not the Byzantine empire but the Sassanian which exerted influence on the Georgian coinage which was struck in the seventh century. This took the form of imitations of the Sassanian silver drachm with bust of the Sassanian king on obverse and a version of the fire-altar on the reverse, with, however, the significant addition of a cross above the altar. In 655 Tiflis, the Georgian capital, captured by the Arabs, became a mint for the issue of dirhems of the successive Islamic dynasties until the eleventh century. The growing power of the native Bagratid kings in the south-west from the tenth century is seen in rare silver coins of Bagrat IV (1027–72) and his immediate successors in the early twelfth century. The obverse depicts the facing bust of the Virgin, and the reverse carries an inscription detailing the king's titles (Pl. 910). The decline of Seljuk power gave opportunity for a considerable territorial expansion of the Georgian kingdom. Georgian coinage from

1125 to 1247 consists of copper pieces of thickish fabric. Georgi III (1156–84) appears on the obverse of his coins seated cross-legged and holding a falcon on his right hand but the reverse carries lines of inscription only while from 1184 both sides of the coin have only inscriptions.

The Mongol conquest of 1236 absorbed Georgia, and Mongol dirhems were struck at the mint of Tiflis in the name of the Great Khans and later for the Il Khan dynasty established by Hulagu in 1260. Under the Mongol khan, Abaga (1265–81), and some of his successors, dirhems struck at Tiflis have a Mongol inscription on the obverse but the reverse inscription consists of a Christian formula with a cross at centre (Pl. 911). Georgia came under the control of the Safavid shahs of Persia in the late sixteenth century and Tiflis issued the Persian silver abbasi as well as a series of autonomous copper with figure-type obverse. After a brief Ottoman occupation (1723–35) Georgia was reoccupied by Nadir Shah but in 1744 Georgia was granted independence. The coinage of the last Bagratid kings for the remainder of the eighteenth century are silver abbasis and halves as well as copper pieces in the Persian style. The special coinage after 1800 when Russia took over Georgia was the silver abbasi, its double and half as well as the copper puli. The types are similar on all metals, the mint name of Tiflis with a mural crown above and crossed palm- and olive-branches below on obverse, and a three-line inscription giving value and metal on the reverse (Pl. 912). This coinage was suspended in 1834 in favour of regular Russian issues.

MODERN STATES OF THE NEAR EAST

This section on the coinage of the modern states deal with the issues of states in western Asia since the coinage of other modern Islamic countries in Africa has already been described in the section devoted to Africa. The coinage of the late nineteenth century comes almost entirely from Persia and the Ottoman empire but the division of the latter empire after the first world war created a number of new states, all of which now issue their own coins.

TURKEY

A new Turkish coinage system was instituted in the reign of Abdul Mejid (1839–61) with the piastre as the monetary unit. One hundred piastres made up a lire or pound and the piastre was in turn divided into 40 paras. The types were simple and conservative and practically identical on all metals; the tughra and regnal year above crossed branches on the obverse and on the reverse an inscription stating the mint of the coin—Constantinople for the metropolitan issues—together with the sultan's accession year. Gold was struck in denominations of 5 up to 100 piastres with some exceptional multiples of even higher value. The silver piastre (Pl. 913) was issued in various multiples between 1 and 20 as well as a half-piastre of 20 paras and the copper paras ranged in value from 1 to 40. Succeeding reigns brought little change except in the record of the sultan's accession year while under Muhammad V (1909–18) the para denominations were issued in nickel. The last Turkish sultan, Muhammad VI, struck mostly the gold piastre piece and only the 40 paras denomination in nickel.

The Turkish Republic, set up in 1923, retained the existing monetary system but the details of the types underwent change. On the obverse of gold denominations a large crescent with star between its points enclosed an inscription and the Muhammadan date, while the reverse bore between two branches an inscription and the Christian date. Denominations from 5 to 25 piastres struck in nickel or aluminium-bronze have inscription and date within a spray of wheat-ears on obverse and value flanked by an oak-branch on reverse. The coinage was further modernized in 1933 when a new system of 100 kurus to the lira was adopted. The Latin alphabet was used for inscriptions and Western numerals for the values and the date which was expressed in the Christian reckoning. The obverse of the 25, 50 and 100 kurus carried the portrait of Kemal Ataturk, the founder of the new Turkey. The reverse bore the value, within a crescent and star, for the 100 kurus and divided by a corn-ear for the lower values. Lower value kurus and paras in nickel had crescent-and-star obverse and value reverse. The portrait of the second Turkish president, Ismet Inonu, appeared only on the silver lira of 1940–1. In the post-war coinage, begun in 1947, the only types were crescent and star and value. The coinage begun in 1957 of lira, 50 and 25 kurus in silver, and lower values in brass had types of crescent and star and value. Ataturk's portrait re-appeared on the lira from 1957 and more varied types on lower values such as the peasant woman on the 25 kurus.

SYRIA

The coinage system of Syria which was made a mandated territory of France in 1920 was similar to the Turkish, 100 piastres to the lira. Pieces of 10, 25 and 50 piastres were struck in silver and lower values in nickel and other alloys. Silver coins are inscribed with the value and *Etat de Syrie* on the obverse, while the reverse has an ornate, involved design and the date. Lower values have the state name and date on obverse and value on reverse. Syria, an independent republic from 1944 until its union with Egypt in 1958, adopted as types an eagle with shield on breast on obverse and value at the centre of an ornate design on reverse. In 1958–61 during the union with Egypt similar types were used but with new reverse inscriptions. These were changed again in the 1962 coinage after resumed independence.

LEBANON

The piastre was adopted as the monetary unit for Lebanon, like Syria a French mandate between 1920 and 1944. Coins of 10, 25 and 50 piastres have as their obverse type a cedar of Lebanon with the state name in French and Arabic, while the reverse bears a double cornucopiae and the value. Similar types are used for values from 2 to 5 piastres struck in bronze but lower values have simply name and value in French on the obverse and in Arabic on the reverse. Lebanon also became an independent republic in 1944 but coins were issued only from 1952. The Lebanese cedar remains the obverse type but, though the higher values, 25 and 50 piastres, have only the value on the reverse, the 10 piastre reverse reproduces the facing lion's head of Ancient Greek issues and the 5 piastre piece an ancient galley (Pl. 914).

ISRAEL (PALESTINE)

The coinage of Palestine which became a mandated territory administered by Britain in 1922 was first issued in 1927. The major unit authorised was a gold pound piece equivalent to a sovereign and comprising 1000 mils. The pound was never coined but subsidiary pieces in multiples of 100 mils and lower were issued, the 100 and 50 mils pieces in silver the lower values in cupro-nickel or nickel-bronze, in most years up to 1946. The types, selected in 1927 and never altered, were on the 100 and 50 mils coins an olive-branch and circular inscription giving the name of the country in English, Hebrew and Arabic on obverse and the value in figures in the centre of the reverse, surrounded by an inscription giving the value in words in the three languages. The 20, 10 and 5 mils pieces were similar but since they had a central perforation they lacked the main central types. The 1 and 2 mils pieces in bronze had the name Palestine in the three languages across the field of the obverse and an olive-branch and circular inscription giving the value on the reverse.

In 1948 mandated Palestine was replaced by the independent state of Israel. In the new coinage first issued in 1949 the pound was divided into 1000 prutah and only the 500 prutah was struck in silver, the lower values using cupro-nickel and other alloys. The reverse on all denominations was consistent, the value and date within a wreath, but the obverses inscribed 'Israel' in Hebrew and Arabic had a varying type for each denomination, some, such as the palm-trees on the 100 prutah or the bunch of grapes on the 25 prutah, reproducing types from coins struck in ancient Palestine (Pl. 915). A feature of Israeli coinage is the succession of special issues such as the 1960 5 pound piece with portrait of Theodore Herzl and the 1969 10 pound marking the twenty-fifth anniversary of independence. A new coinage introduced in 1960 is based on a system of 100 agorot to the pound. Obverses revive types from ancient Jewish coins—the palm-tree, lyre and menorah, while the reverse gives the value.

JORDAN

Coinage based on a dinar or pound of 1,000 fils was first issued in 1949. On obverse was the value in Arabic numerals within a crowned wreath and with Arabic inscription; on reverse the value was in Western numerals with inscription *The Hashemite Kingdom of The Jordan*. On issues of 1955–66 this was shortened to *Kingdom of Jordan*. A new coinage begun in 1968 has the portrait of King Hussein on obverse.

IRAQ

Iraq or Mesopotamia, formerly part of the Ottoman empire, was a British mandate after the first world war until it became an independent kingdom in 1932. Its coinage system is similar to that of Jordan, 1000 fils to the dinar. The first Iraqi coinage was struck in 1931, towards the end of the reign of Faisal I (1921–33). The types which are uniform for all denominations and have remained unchanged except for the royal portrait under successive rulers consist of a portrait head accompanied by Arabic inscription on obverse and the value at the centre of the reverse, surrounded by inscriptions and dates arranged in radial segments. The higher fils values were in silver, the lower in nickel or bronze. The first coinage of Faisal II in 1943 had the portrait of the boy king, the next in 1953 a more adult portrait. The coinage of the Republic after Faisal II's assassination in 1958 had mainly inscriptions and value types but the 5 and 10 fils coins of 1967 show a date-palm grove on reverse.

IRAN (PERSIA)

In the reign of Nasr-ed-din (1844–96) the almost exclusively inscriptional types of earlier Persian coinage gave place, under the influence of European coinage, to figure types on the obverse, either the portrait of the shah or the Persian lion with uplifted sword. The major unit in gold was still the toman, divided into 10 karans, each of 20 shahis, which in turn comprised 50 dinars. On some issues of the gold toman the shah's facing portrait occupied the obverse while the traditional inscription type remained on the reverse, but other issues of the toman, its multiples and portions carries the Persian lion type on obverse. The lion obverse with inscription or value reverse supplied the types for the silver karan denominations and the dinar denominations in nickel (Pl. 916). This distribution of types over the denominations remained largely unchanged under succeeding shahs until in 1925 Ahmed, the last of the Kajar shahs, was overthrown by Reza Khan who instituted the new Pahlavi dynasty. In the reign of Reza Shah (1925–41) a new coinage was instituted—100 dinars to a rial and 20 rials to the pahlavi. His first gold pahlavi used the lion-and-inscription types, and later issues a portrait bust and either inscription or lion types. Rial denominations in silver and dinar pieces in nickel had lion-and-value designs. The coinage of the present shah, Mohammed Reza (1942–), has followed much the same pattern and it is only on the gold pahlavis from 1952 onwards that his portrait has appeared.

SAUDI ARABIA

The kingdom of Saudi Arabia which comprises most of the Arabian peninsula has had an independent coinage since 1926. The major pieces are the silver rial and its portions with divisionary coins in cupro-nickel in values of girsh, of which 22 are equivalent to a rial. The types on the silver coins consist of a central and a marginal inscription, the date and value appearing at the foot of the reverse. On the girsh denominations there is only a marginal inscription on the obverse but the reverse with a semi-circular inscription carries also the value and date. An issue of a gold guinea in 1957 has a palm and two crossed sabres on obverse and the value on reverse. Similar types appear on cupro-nickel denominations of 4 and 2 piastres.

HEJAZ

This sultanate is now part of Saudi Arabia but it had an independent coinage issued in 1923 for its last sultan, Hussein ibn Ali (1916–24). As well as the gold dinar, the silver rial and its portions were issued and in bronze the girsh and smaller para denominations. The types on all denominations were purely inscriptional, the marginal inscriptions being sometimes continuous, sometimes divided into segments.

YEMEN

The major unit of this coinage issued since 1923 is the imadi of 40 bogaches, each of 2 halala. The imadi and portions are issued in silver, the bogach and the halala in copper or bronze. Inscriptional types occupy both obverse and reverse and while the reverse has the conventional arrangement of central and marginal inscriptions the inscriptions on the obverse are arranged in an unusual and distinctive pattern. A circular inscription towards the top of obverse is supplemented by two further inscriptions arranged in expanding circles. The coinage of the Republic set up in 1962 has continued the same denomination system. Both obverse and reverse have circular inscriptions with, commonly, the value at centre and a hand holding a torch, or a five-pointed star.

MUSCAT AND OMAN

A copper coinage of portions of the anna was struck in the late nineteenth century by Sultan Fessul ibn Turkee but coinage then lapsed until 1940. The present system is based on the rial of 20 baizahs. So far only the half-rial in silver has been struck with types, crossed Arab swords and inscription on obverse, and inscription within a wreath on reverse. Various baizah denominations have been issued with a similar type on obverse and a simplified inscription on reverse. Those lower value coins are struck in nickel and have either a rectangular or a fluted outline.

KUWAIT

Coinage based on a dinar of 1,000 fils was first issued in 1961. The types, uniform for all values, are an Arab dhowa on obverse, and on reverse the value and circular inscription in Arabic (*Emirate of Kuwait*) and in English *Kuwait*. On the 1962 coinage the Arabic inscription was changed to *Al Kuwait*.

THE INDIAN
SUB-CONTINENT

★

Ancient India   499

Mediaeval India   505

Sultans of Delhi   511

Muhammadan States (thirteenth to sixteenth
      centuries)   515

The Mogul Emperors   518

European coinage in India   521

Independent States (eighteenth to twentieth
      centuries)   526

Republics of India and Pakistan   529

Ceylon   530

The Indian Sub-Continent

THE great Indian peninsula, cut off as it is from the rest of the continent of Asia by the semi-circular sweep of the Himalayas and the Hindu Kush, developed a civilization somewhat different from that of either western or eastern Asia. Although India has never been immune from the incursions and influences of other peoples and civilizations and, by the time that the story of Indian coinage begins, had been subjected to several invasions, particularly through the passes of the north-west, sufficient of the individuality of its civilization had survived to impart a different character to its early coinages, especially in the south. In almost all the periods of its history after the introduction of coinage India has comprised an array of separate states, each with its own characteristic coinage; only in the heyday of the Mogul empire in the late sixteenth and in the seventeenth century did India possess anything at all resembling a universal coinage. Even in modern times British India with its unified control and swifter communications preserved until the end vestiges of local coinages in a number of states. This chapter endeavours to sketch the general sweep of development and change of the plethora of coinage covering more than two thousand years of history and to illustrate the detail of the more interesting and important coinages.

ANCIENT INDIA

'PUNCH-MARKED COINS'

One coinage series in the early history of India has already been mentioned, that of the Greek kings of Bactria in north-west India who issued coinage from the third to the first century B.C. (see pp. 95-6); but what in all probability is the earliest series of coins or coin-like objects in India developed independently of external influences. A series of small silver ingots, marked only by three circular dots, as well as heavier bars of silver with marks punched on one side, seem to have been used as an early form of exchange and it has been suggested that they were in use as early as the beginning of the sixth century B.C. They were, in fact, rather later than the beginnings of Western coinage in Asia Minor. These two series of objects are rather rare but the series of small silver pieces known as 'punch-marked coins' had an extensive output, to judge from the quantities which have survived, and from the find records of these coins they enjoyed a circulation over the whole peninsula. These 'punch-marked coins', also called puranas or dharanas, are flat pieces of silver of irregular weight and of either rectangular or circular outline. The earliest examples appear to be those which have small devices punched on one side only and to this category most of the rectangular pieces belong. The next category includes most of the circular pieces which have stamps or punches on both sides (Pl. 917). On this early form of coinage these punches are presumably the badges or signs of merchants and bankers through whose hands they passed. The punches themselves present a whole range of types—birds, animals, other natural objects as well as human figures and religious symbols. There is archaeological evidence for the existence of these 'punch-marked coins' certainly by the mid third century B.C. alongside coins of Bactrian kings, and in south India at least, mixed hoards of these objects and of silver denarii of the early Roman empire witness to their circulation into the beginning of the first century A.D.

EARLY HINDU

In addition to this unusual form of coinage other series conforming more closely to the usual definition of coinage as objects in metal of approximately standard weight with designs on either side appeared in the smaller kingdoms, chiefly in northern India, after the break-up of the Maurya empire at the end of the third century B.C. The majority of these coins are in copper, though some are of lead and the earliest were cast and not struck from dies. On coins of Ajodhya from about 150 B.C. to A.D. 100 the common types are a humped bull together with the name of the rajah in Brahmi script on obverse and religious or solar symbols on the reverse. On coins of Avanti of about the same period the usual obverse type is a standing figure of the king while the reverse is a design of a cross with a circle at each extremity. A conventional tree design within a railing and a humped bull supply the usual types on coins of Kausambi in the second century B.C. (Pl. 918), while copper coins of Taxila have a lion obverse and commonly a blank reverse. The issues of Malwa which extend from the second century B.C. probably as late as the early fourth century A.D. are of smaller module than those just described. The obverse is commonly an inscription in one or two lines across the field but a variety of types—bull, elephant, symbol or rough portrait head—appear on the reverse. Types on the copper coins of the rajahs and satraps of Mathura in the last two centuries B.C. are commonly a standing figure on obverse and an elephant, elephant's head or horse on the reverse.

The first most extensive coinage of Indian origin is that of the Andhra dynasty whose influence controlled a great area from the Godavari river south into Mysore from the late second century B.C. down to the early third century A.D. Coinage is ascribed to rulers as early as the mid second century but issues are plentiful only in the last century B.C. and the first two centuries A.D. A great proportion of the Andhra coinage is in lead, the remainder in potin, an admixture of lead and copper. The commonest types represent a bow and arrow together with inscription giving the ruler's name on the obverse and a *chaitya* or monastery, roughly depicted as tiers of arches on a base and usually flanked by a tree on the reverse (Pl. 919). Other obverses show an elephant, a poorly drawn horse or a lion and in place of the *chaitya* the 'Ujain' symbol, a cross with balls or circles at its terminals, is frequently placed on the reverse.

Off-shoots of the Sakas, the Scythian conquerors of Bactria who were themselves pushed further into north-west India by another Scythian tribe, the Yueh-chi, replaced the Hindu kings of Mathura in the first century A.D. and another of the Scythian chieftains or western satraps as they are called, Chastana, founded a kingdom in Malwa about A.D. 115 and his successors conquered much of the west coast from the Andhras. Coinage struck by Chastana and successive Western satraps is almost exclusively in the form of imitations of the silver drachm of the Indo-Greek kings with a rough portrait on the obverse and a version of the *chaitya* on the reverse. The coins of Chastana have inscriptions in both Nagari and Kharoshthi but on later issues Kharoshthi disappears (Pl. 920). The coinage of the Western satraps came to an end with the conquest of their territories by the Guptas in 395.

INDO-SCYTHIANS AND INDO-PARTHIANS

The Indo-Scythians, driven out of Bactria by the Yueh-chi towards the end of the second century B.C., settled in Sind and about 75 B.C. under their chief, Maues, captured Pushkalavati (Peshawar) in the Punjab. Silver coins of Maues copy some types of the Indo-Greek kings with figures of standing Zeus and Greek inscription on the obverse and a standing Nike or Victory and Kharoshthi inscription on the reverse. Copper coins have the typical Indian rectangular outline and as well as also reproducing types from Indo-Greek coins present some novelties such as elephant on obverse and figure of the king seated cross-legged on stool on the reverse (Pl. 921). Coins of Maues' successors, Azes I, Azilises and Azes II, follow a similar pattern; a frequent obverse type on silver coins depicts the king as a mounted figure (Pl. 922) while the Dioscuri figure frequently on the reverse. Of the Indo-Parthian kings who ruled west of the Indus the most important was Gondophares who struck billon tetradrachms similar to those of the Indo-Scythic kings and with similar types, and copper coins, which presented on obverse a portrait of Gondophares in the Parthian style with a figure of Nike on the reverse. Later kings—Abdagases, Orthagnes and Pakores—issued a very similar coinage.

KUSHANS

In the early first century A.D. the Kushans, a branch of the Yueh-chi tribe, invaded north-west India and under their chief, Kujula Kadphises, put an end to the kingdom of Hermaeus, the last of the Indo-Greek kings, and subsequently, about the middle of the century, occupied part of the kingdom of the Indo-Parthians. Under successive kings—Kujula Kadphises, a nameless king with the title Soter Megas, Vima Kadphises, Kanishka, Huvishka and Vasu-deva—the Kushan kingdom flourished until A.D. 220 and survived with diminished power until the irruption of the White Huns in the late fifth century. The Kushan coinage (except for that of Kujula and Soter Megas in copper only) is of gold and copper, the principal gold unit being struck on the same standard as the contemporary Roman imperial aureus, though double pieces and quarters are also found. The copper coins of Kujula Kadphises were first issued as a joint coinage with Hermaeus, whose portrait and titles in Greek occupied the obverse, while a Kharoshthi legend with the name of Kujula accompanied a standing figure of Heracles. On a later issue the obverse, though still bearing the bust of Hermaeus, is inscribed with Kujula's name. The coinage without king's name, in copper only, presents a diademed bust of a king on obverse and a horseman on the reverse, accompanied by the inscription in Greek, *Basileus Basileon Soter Megas,* 'King of kings, the great Saviour' (Pl. 923). Since the inscription includes no personal name, the precise attribution of this coinage remains in question.

On copper coins of Vima Kadphises the types are a standing figure of the king with hand outstretched over altar on the obverse and a facing figure of the Hindu deity, Siva, and a bull on the reverse. A similar reverse on a double gold stater has as obverse type the figure of the king squatting on a low couch, while on the obverse of the stater itself Vima is shown as a half-length figure. On the gold coins of Kanishka the king is usually represented on the obverse as a standing figure but the reverses present a variety of deities, both Greek and Iranian (Pl. 924). On the coinage of Kujula and Vima the obverse inscription had been in Greek, the reverse in Kharoshthi, but on the issues of Kanishka and his successors only Greek inscriptions appear. The copper coins of Kanishka largely repeat the types of his gold coinage and these types continue with some variations under his successor, Huvishka, whose portrait on gold coins is a half-length figure or a bust and not a standing figure.

THE GUPTA EMPIRE

One of the most magnificent coinages of ancient India is that of the Gupta empire which flourished from the fourth to the sixth century A.D. The splendour of its coinage, which is preponderantly in gold, reflects the prosperity of a kingdom which at its greatest extent stretched from the Himalayas in the north to the river Narbada in the south and from the Jumna in the west to the Brahmaputra in the east; and the artistry of the coins lends weight to the claim that the Gupta period represents one of the peaks of Hindu civilization. The dynasty was founded by Gupta in the territory around Pataliputra (Patna) in the later third century, as the Kushan power began to decline, but the official Gupta era begins only with the accession of Gupta's grandson, Chandragupta I, in 320 and the great territorial expansion took place under his successor, Samudragupta (335–380). It was also in the reign of Samudragupta that the Gupta coinage began to be issued, for the coinage which bears the portrait of Chandragupta I and his wife Kumaradevi was a posthumous issue in the reign of Samudragupta.

The Gupta gold coin is the direct descendant of the Kushan gold stater, itself modelled on the standard of the Roman imperial aureus and gold was the only metal coined by Samudragupta. From the reign of Chandragupta II (380–414) onwards silver coinage was also struck, principally for the western areas of the empire. These silver coins continue in general terms the tradition of the small silver pieces issued both by the Andhras and by the Western satraps (see p. 501). A more restricted copper coinage was issued by Chandragupta II and his successors. The inscriptions on both obverse and reverse of the Gupta coins are in classical Sanskrit.

In types as well as weight-standard the early Gupta gold declares its descent from the gold coins of the Kushan kings whose most constant types of standing figure of the king on obverse and the goddess Lakshmi seated on reverse are repeated on coins of Samudragupta. The types on Samudragupta's coins are not only infinitely better executed than on the later Kushan coins but are considerably modified. On the obverse Samudragupta is shown as a standing figure with nimbus about his head and stretching out hand over altar, while in the background is a standard surmounted by the sacred Garuda bird. The reverse with the goddess Lakshmi, who is also nimbate, is much more ornate and on some specimens is not dissimilar to the much later Byzantine reverse with a seated figure of Christ (Pl. 925). Lakshmi also figures seated on a recumbent lion with her feet on a lotus on the reverse of the coins honouring Samudragupta's parents, Chandragupta I and Kumaradevi, whose figures, both nimbate, stand side by side on the obverse (Pl. 926). On other varieties of Samudragupta's coins the king appears as a standing figure holding either a bow or a battle-axe in his left hand or as a seated figure playing the lyre. On yet another issue the obverse type is a horse standing by a sacrificial post, while on the reverse stands the chief queen holding a sacrificial spear.

Chandragupta II (375–414) under whom the Gupta territory was considerably expanded, principally at the expense of the Western satraps, has an even more plenteous coinage of gold than Samudragupta. The latter's archer type on which the king is shown holding bow is repeated by Chandragupta II but a whole range of new varieties was added to the gold coinage. The king is shown sacrificing at an altar while a small attendant holds a chattra or parasol above him. Another spirited obverse represents the king, armed with a bow, shooting a lion (Pl. 927) and the mounted figure of the king which was a feature of Saka coins was revived by Chandragupta II. The silver coinage of the Western satraps was continued by Chandragupta but whereas the obverse retained the portrait head, which was one of the distinctive features of the small silver coins of both the Andhras and the Western satraps, the equally typical *chaitya* on the reverse of these latter coins was replaced by the Garuda. Copper coins issued by Chandragupta II also picture the Garuda with outstretched wings on the reverse, while on the obverse is a nimbate portrait of the king in profile as either a three-quarter or a half-length figure.

Of new types introduced on the gold by Kumaragupta (414–455) particularly attractive are those which honour the god Karttikeya and his peacock Paravani. On the obverse the standing king feeds the peacock from a bunch of fruit in his hand, while, on the reverse, the god is shown mounted on the peacock (Pl. 928). The silver coinage of Kumaragupta is much more extensive than that of the previous reign and in addition to the Garuda reverse now also pictured the peacock with outstretched wings. The beginning of decline under Skandagupta (455–480), the last of the great Gupta kings, is apparent in the distinct fall in quantity of gold coinage and in the restriction of types largely to two, the archer type and a new obverse on which the king and the goddess Lakshmi stand on either side of the Garuda standard. Skandagupta introduced two new reverses on the silver coins, Siva's bull, Nandi, and an altar. There is further evidence of decline in the base silver in which these coins were struck and in their irregular flans. After Skandagupta's death in 480 only gold coins of the archer type were struck by the Gupta kings down to 560 with a steady decline in technique and in the literacy of the inscriptions.

The devastations of the Huns probably account for the lack of any direct imitations of the Gupta gold coinage by the kingdoms which came after. Only in Gauda in central Bengal was an imitative gold coinage struck by its king, Sasanka (600–625), with types of Siva reclining on his bull Nandi on the obverse and on the reverse the goddess Lakshmi seated on a lotus.

MEDIAEVAL INDIA

The complete collapse of the Roman imperial system in the West in the early fifth century, the invasions of barbarian peoples and the slow re-creation of civilization in the early Middle Ages has its counterpart in India. In the later fifth century in India it was the great Gupta empire which began to disintegrate under the attacks of the Hephthalites or White Huns, a branch of the same Hunnish people which under Attilla had assisted at the downfall of the Roman empire. Somewhat in the same manner as in western Europe, the early Middle Ages in India was a period in which numerous petty kingdoms flourished but, unlike Europe where historical circumstances permitted the coalescing of small states into great national kingdoms, the later Middle Ages in India brought, in the twelfth century, the first of several waves of new conquerors, the Muhammadans who in time established wide sovereignty over most of the sub-continent. The mediaeval coinage of India between the invasions of the Huns and the Muhammadans, particularly in northern India, mirrors the reduced economic circumstances of the period in its dearth of good silver and the absence of any single unifying power in the diversity of issues of which the most typical and important are outlined in this section.

HEPHTHALITES (WHITE HUNS)

The Hephthalites who had established themselves on the Oxus earlier in the fifth century pushed into north-west India where they were temporarily repulsed by Chandragupta II in 455, but by 500 they were established under their leader Toramana in Malwa and under Mihiragula, who succeeded two years later, the conquest of northern India was extended and the capital fixed at Sakala in the Punjab. A revolt of his Indian tributary princes drove out Mihiragula who seized and held Kashmir till his death in 528. The Hephthalite hold on Transoxiana was finally broken by the Sassanian king Chosroes I with the assistance of the Turks in 565. The coinage of the Hephthalites is an imitation in base silver of the silver drachm of the Sassanian kings. The drawing is crude on both the obverse, which carries a portrait bust in elaborate tunic and head-dress, based on the Sassanian model, and on the reverse, which is a version of the Zoroastrian fire-altar with its two attendants. The obverse portrait is accompanied by a symbol resembling a trident usually to the left of the bust. The heads of both the Hephthalite chiefs, Toramana and Mihiragula, who held rule in India appear on coins of this description (Pl. 929) as well as on copper coins reminiscent of those of Chandragupta II with obverse portrait and reverse with a horizontal bar. In place of the type of the Garuda above the bar on Gupta coins appears a solar symbol or a bull on the Hephthalite coppers with the king's name below.

INDO-SASSANIAN

The coinage of the White Huns in India was not the only series which derived its inspiration from Sassanian prototypes. Other imitations of Sassanian issues with inscriptions in Pahlevi and Nagari were produced by minor dynasties which, in the sixth and early seventh centuries, acknowledged Sassanian suzerainty. Typical of this category is the coinage of flat silver pieces with Sassanian-style portrait and a version of the fire-altar which bears the name Napki Malik (Pl. 930). The Sassanian silver drachm was also the original model for a series of thin flat coins with an extremely degenerate and sketchy version of the Sassanian portrait and fire-altar. Smaller but thicker coins in base silver which circulated for a lengthy period in Gujarat and are known as Gadhiya paisa have types which, though they have become elaborate patterns, still show the elements of the original Sassanian types (Pl. 931).

RAJPUT DYNASTIES OF HINDUSTAN AND CENTRAL INDIA

By far the most common coinage in this period is the bull-and-horseman type struck by most of the Rajput dynasties in gradually degenerating style and an increasingly base metal. The types which were first introduced by the Hindu kings of Kabul and Ohind about the middle of the ninth century represent on the obverse a recumbent humped bull with a trident-like symbol on its flank and a Nagari inscription above; on the reverse is a mounted horseman, probably the king, holding a lance pointing downwards and a further inscription in a cursive Bactrian script. The most prolific issue of this coinage, inscribed with the title Samanta-deva, belongs to the early tenth century (Pl. 932). Later bull and horseman coins of this ruler appear in billon while on another Samanta-deva series the types are elephant on obverse and lion with tail curled over back on the reverse.

The second most widespread coinage was in rather base gold with a reverse depicting the seated goddess Lakshmi who had figured so prominently on the Gupta coinage. Here, however, the goddess is portrayed with four not two arms. The obverse consists solely of a three-line inscription in Nagari giving the king's name. The earliest coinage of this category seems to have been struck by Gangeya-deva of the Kalachuri dynasty of Dahala (Jabalpur) in the early eleventh century (1015–40) and then by the Chandella kings of Bunkelkhand in the last half of the century. Coinage of a similar base gold fabric was issued by the kings of Mahaka-sola in the mid-twelfth century, again with line inscriptions giving the king's name on obverse but with a lion-rampant type on the reverse.

The issues of other Rajput dynasties present an admixture of these two cate-gories of coinage. The Tomara dynasty of Ajmir and Delhi in the late tenth and the eleventh centuries struck mainly the bull-and-horseman coins in billon or copper but Kumara-pala-deva (1019–49) has a coinage in base gold with the seated Lakshmi as on the coins of the Kalachuri kings. The Chauhan dynasty which followed the Tomara at Delhi in the later twelfth century confines its issues to bull-and-horseman coinage. The Rathor dynasty of Kanauj in the eleventh and twelfth centuries also had varied issues of copper bull and horseman and base gold seated-goddess coinage but the billon coins of Malaya-varma of Narwar (1220–32) combine types from both classes and show a three-line inscription on obverse and a horseman on reverse. This combination of types was also a feature of the later copper coinages of the maharajahs of Kangra between 1300 and 1625, though the earliest issues are closer copies of the bull-and-horseman coinage.

A rare copper coinage with types, a portrait bust and a vase have been ascribed to a ruler Khingila in Kashmir in the fifth century and copper coins with the Kushan types of king standing by altar on obverse and seated goddess on the reverse have the name Toramana, who may be the Hephthalite chief of the early sixth century. Extremely crude imitations of the standing-king and seated-goddess types were produced in base gold by kings of the Naga dynasty of the eighth century but under subsequent dynasties from the ninth to the twelfth centuries this coinage was struck in copper only (Pl. 933). The coinage of the kings of Nepal of the sixth to eighth centuries was also of copper but presented some variation from the more usual Hindu mediaeval types. The seated goddess still appeared on the reverse of one issue but was combined with a standing-lion type with lotus in front on the reverse. On the other issues the lion on the obverse is winged and there is a sun-type on the reverse.

The coinage of southern India, which was not subjected to the successive waves of invasion and conquest which northern India suffered, developed along quite different lines. The silver punch-marked coinage disappeared in the early decades of the first century A.D. and the currency requirements of south India, to judge from the numerous hoards, appear to have been served by the widespread use of Roman imperial gold coins in the first two centuries A.D. and of silver denarii in the first half of the first century. The frequency with which such Roman aurei were subjected to test by a chisel cut suggests, however, that these gold coins were used as bullion rather than as pieces of currency. Roman and, later, Byzantine solidi were again imported in mass by south India from the later fourth to the fifth century, and in the extreme south as well as in Ceylon the small bronze coins of the fourth-century Roman emperors were used as small change and even imitated locally. This predilection for these two metals is apparent in the native coinages of the early mediaeval period. Gold was struck in two denominations, the heavier hun or pagoda and the smaller fanam, and copper in a denomination known as the kasu, from which the English word cash is ultimately derived. The earliest gold coins are slightly spherical and since, apart from some tiny punch marks, they are completely blank their attribution to specific dynasties and even areas is uncertain, for, in view of the wide circulation of gold coinage, the evidence of hoards for the localization of issues is not of the same value as in the case of copper coins which had a more restricted circulation. Even the next development on the gold coins, the placing of devices on one or both sides, is of little service in the absence of informative inscriptions. Of gold coins of this category the padma-tankas with an obverse design with an eight-petalled lotus at the centre are attributed to the Kadambas in Mysore.

One of the earliest dynasties to whom coinage is attributed, the Chalukyas, reigned in the Deccan from the mid sixth century till their conquest by the Rashtrakutas in 753. Gold pagodas and fanams with the Chalukya badge of a boar were probably struck by the earlier Chalukya rulers but the earliest coinage of certain attribution, with types of lion and trident flanked by two lamps, from the Telugu inscription on the obverse, was issued by Vishnu-Vardana (615–633). The Chalukya power revived and the rulers of the western Chalukya kingdom with its capital at Kalyani issued gold coins in the eleventh and twelfth centuries similar to the lotus-tankas of the Kadambas but with a temple or a lion as the obverse type. The rulers of the eastern Chalukya kingdom from the mid seventh to the eleventh centuries struck gold coins including a series of large, flat gold pieces with a boar device at the centre (Pl. 934) for Saktivarman (1000–12) and Rajaraja (1012–62). The Hoysalas who overthrew the Chalukyas in 753 retained on their gold the lion type which also features on Chalukya coins and the Cholas who conquered the kingdom of the eastern Chalukyas in 1153 also made use of the temple-and-lion types on Chalukya tankas.

Of the Ganga dynasty which ruled in Kalinga from the sixth to the eleventh centuries Antanavarman Chodaganga issued gold fanams with a recumbent bull on the obverse and a Telugu regnal date on the reverse. The pagodas with ornate elephant on obverse and a floral scroll design on the reverse were struck in the ninth century at Orissa by the Chera kings who had settled there after their expulsion from Kongudesa by the Cholas. The coinage of Kadamba chiefs of Goa had as types an inscriptional obverse and a lion reverse. Issues in the late twelfth century for Vishnu Chitta-deva are in gold, for Jayakesin in silver.

TAMIL STATES

Of the Tamil peoples in the extreme south of India the first to attain a position of ascendancy were the Pallavas who issued pagodas and fanams with a maned lion as the chief type. Silver Pallava coins have this lion type also on the obverse and a vase within a circle of rays on the reverse. The history of the Pandyas in Madura is a succession of periods of independence then of subjection to other peoples, first the Pallavas in the eighth century and then the Cholas in the eleventh and twelfth centuries. In the interim period of independence the Pandyas issued both gold and copper coins with either one or two fish on the obverse and an inscription on the reverse (Pl. 935). This fish symbol is also used particularly on copper coins in the thirteenth century when the Pandyas had risen superior to the Cholas whose specific standing-figure type is sometimes incorporated on the coins of the Pandyas. The coinage struck by the Cholas for their Deccan conquests has been mentioned above but on gold and silver coins issued in their own territory on the Coromandel coast in the earlier tenth century the same type, a tiger seated under a canopy and flanked by the two fish of the Pandya coins, appears on both sides (Pl. 936). In a later period of Chola eminence between the eleventh and thirteenth centuries the coinage which is in copper only has a standing figure and a seated figure on the reverse, types copied on the coinage of Ceylon in the twelfth and thirteenth centuries (see p. 531). The coinage of the Chera rulers in Malabar is represented only by extremely rare silver with inscriptions on both sides.

The Muhammadan invasion of northern India in the twelfth century was followed by the establishment of Muhammadan states whose coinage is reviewed in the next section. By the early fourteenth century Muhammadan penetration of southern India had effected the capture of the Pandya capital, Madura, in 1311 and to counter the threat of further conquest the kingdom of Vijayanagar was founded in 1336. Though its greatness was brought to an end by the battle of Talikota in 1565, it survived in attenuated form until the late seventeenth century. Like other south Indian coinages the issues of Vijayanagar are for the most part in gold in which not only the pagoda but its half and quarter were struck. Copper coinage was also issued but on a more restricted scale. On these pagodas whose small dumpy fabric was perpetuated in the pagoda issues of subsequent centuries, both by native states and by European trading companies, the reverse types mostly derive from the Hindu pantheon, while the obverse inscription in Nagari gives the king's name.

One of the earliest of the Vijayanagar pieces is a half-pagoda of Harihara (c. 1379) with the deities Siva and Parvati seated side by side on the reverse (Pl. 937), a type repeated for Deva Raya II about 1422. On coins of Achuta Raya (1530–42) occurs an unusual type, a double-headed eagle-monster, known as the *Ganda bherunda*, holding up elephants in its beaks and claws. The most popular reverse type is a single seated deity who from his attributes is sometimes Siva, sometimes Vishnu, who also appears standing under a canopy on coins of Rama Raja in the mid sixteenth century. The 'three swami pagoda' which was extensively imitated in later centuries was first issued by Tirumala Raja about 1570 (Pl. 938). The three holy figures of whom the central one stands and the other two are seated have been variously identified as Laksmana with Rama and Sita, or Venkatesvara with his two wives. On copper coins the reverse type is a boar, a device taken over from the Chalukyas.

After the decline of the Vijayanagar kingdom in the sixteenth and seventeenth centuries gold pagodas were issued by the Rajas of Ikkeri. The first of these, Sadasiva Nayaka (1539–75), struck pagodas with the seated figures of Siva and Parvati on the obverse and his name in Nagari script on the reverse, types used by later Nayaka princes until their conquest by Haidar Ali in 1763. On the numerous copper kasu issued by princes in Mysore in this period the most common type was an elephant to left with sun and moon above on the obverse. The reverse consisted of double lines crossing each other at right angles with a circle in the centre (Pl. 939). These 'elephant cash' pieces continued in circulation up until comparatively recent times. The pagodas and fanams struck both by native rulers and by the Dutch and English in south India are described later (see p. 523).

SULTANS OF DELHI

The feature common to Western coinage and to the coinages of ancient India, both of the Hindu states and the successive invaders and conquerors in the north and to the mediaeval coinages of the Rajput dynastes and the states of south India, is the use of a pictorial or heraldic device on at least one side of the coin. The Muhammadan conquest of India which began in the late twelfth century, however, very soon imposed a new pattern on the Indian coinage; for, on the Muhammadan coins of India, just as in the majority of the Islamic coinages of the Near East, the representation of all objects is eschewed and, with some notable exceptions, the types on both sides of the coins consist only of inscriptions composed of religious formulae and details of the ruler, his date and the place of minting. This general pattern of coinage persisted throughout most of the remaining history of Indian coinage under the Muhammadan sultans of Delhi, the Muhammadan states into which that sultanate eventually divided and, later, the Mogul emperors. Only occasional survivals of Hindu coinage break the pattern until the advent of European coinage. The Muhammadan conquest which once again brought India into a relationship with western and central Asia made for easier access to silver supplies and resulted in the eventual return of a widespread use of silver in the Indian coinage.

A Muhammadan kingdom had existed in India in Sind in the north-west since the early eighth century but it was only with the invasions of some three centuries later that a Muhammadan coinage of any importance had currency and was struck in India. In the first quarter of the eleventh century Mahmud of Ghazni invaded and annexed the Punjab (see p. 483) and when, in the middle of the century, the Ghaznavids were ousted from Ghazni by the Ghorids, Lahore became their capital and the mint for small billon coins with the bull, Nandi of the Rajput coinage on the obverse and a Kufic inscription on the reverse. This coinage came to an end with the defeat in 1187 of Khusru Malik, the last of the Ghaznavid rulers of Lahore by the Ghorid prince, Muhammad-ibn-Sam. Muhammad's further advance into India was temporarily halted by his defeat at the battle of Tanesar in 1191 at the hands of Prithviraja of Ajmer and Delhi, but on the same battlefield in the following year Muhammad defeated a confederacy of Indian princes under Prithviraja and the way lay open to the complete conquest of Hindustan.

The replacement of Indian coinage by pure Muhammadan types was, however, not achieved immediately and, indeed, not till after the death of Muhammad. His large silver coins with a small central inscription and three circular inscriptions on both sides are from the Ghazni mint, as are his gold coins with central inscription in square frame and marginal inscriptions in the segments. His Indian coinage consists of imitations of the gold coinage of the Kanauj kings with a degenerate seated Lakshmi type on the obverse and an inscription in Nagari on the reverse. The most prolific of his coinages is the continuation of a version of the Rajput bull and horseman struck in billon or copper, the so-called delhiwalas, with one of the types, more often the horseman, on the obverse and an inscription in Nagari on the reverse (Pl. 940). Muhammad's successor, Kutbu-d-din, who extended and consolidated the Muhammadan conquests in India and established a capital at Delhi, is represented only by a very rare billon coinage of the horseman-and-inscription type. This was also the sole class of coinage for the third sultan, Alam Shah, in 1210.

This derivative bull-and-horseman coinage in base metal was supplemented by Altamsh (1210–35) by issues in silver. The first issue of his silver tankahs showed the sultan on horse-back surrounded by a marginal inscription while the reverse consisted of lines of inscription in Arabic within a dotted circle. Following the receipt of a diploma of investiture from al-Mustansir, the Baghdad caliph in 1228, Altamsh issued a further series of silver tankahs with inscriptions on both sides. The reverse continued to carry the sultan's name and title but the obverse was inscribed 'In the reign of the Imam, al-Mustansir, the commander of the faithful'. These central inscriptions were enclosed in circles with marginal inscriptions giving the mint and the date. The mint calling itself Bilad-al-Hind, 'the cities of Hind', is the first mint to appear in the reign of Altamsh. This form of silver tankah (Pl. 941) was preserved by subsequent sultans down to Balban (1266–86), even though the caliph al-Mustansir died in 1242. The billon or copper coinage which in this reign sometimes carries the name of Delhi as the mint with one of the adaptations of the bull-and-horseman types was also continued with occasional innovations such as on the copper coins of Raziya (1236–9) with bull type on obverse and small central inscription within a circle of rays on the reverse. Of the more usual varieties, that with bull on obverse and horseman on reverse was struck down into the reign of Alau-d-din Mas'aud (1241–6) and that with horseman obverse and inscription reverse till the reign of Nasiru-d-din (1246–65).

A gold coinage with the same types and weight as the silver tankah was first minted by Alau-d-din Mas'aud but his issues and those of his immediate successors were sparse. With the extension of Muhammadan conquest into the rich south,

where gold had always formed the chief metal for coinage, Alau-d-din Muhammad (1296–1316) was enabled to strike a more profuse gold coinage (Pl. 942).
The same sultan finally took the step of omitting from the obverse inscription the
name of the caliph. In its place came a bombastic inscription acclaiming the
sultan as 'the second Alexander, the right hand of the Caliphate'. The arrangement of inscriptions was also altered in this reign. Only the obverse now carried
a marginal inscription and the reverse field was left free for a linear inscription
running from edge to edge of the coin and, since this silver coinage was produced in massive issues, it impresses itself as the typical coinage of the sultans of
Delhi (Pl. 943). The coinage of the next effective sultan, Kutbu-d-din Mubarak
(1316–20), saw the revival on some issues both of precious metals and billon of
the square shape which is a recurrent feature of Indian issues.

The issues of Muhammad-ibn-Tughlaq (1325–51) can claim, on several
grounds, to represent the climax of the coinage of the sultans of Delhi. Not
only is his by far the most plentiful coinage but it was produced on a higher
standard of technical execution and, in addition, it presents a number of features
of unusual interest, both in the matter of variety of inscriptions but also in the
way of experiments in the coinage system itself. After an initial issue of gold and
silver tankahs of the traditional kind, Muhammad-ibn-Tughlaq introduced in
1326 new denominations in gold and silver. In what was evidently an attempt to
establish in the coinage the actual relative values of gold and silver in the free
market he abandoned the old standard weight of about 11 gm. for both metals
and struck a gold dinar at a weight of some 13 gm. and a new silver coin, the adli,
weighing approximately 9 gm. The experiment was not a success and in 1332
coinage of the gold and silver tankahs of the old type was resumed. The second
experiment between 1329 and 1332 represents one of the earliest attempts to
establish a fiduciary coinage. As a substitute for the silver and billon coins, tokens
in brass and copper were issued but, despite the cautionary and reassuring inscriptions such as 'Whoso obeys the Sultan, obeys the Compassionate' (i.e. Allah)
and 'Sealed as a tankah of fifty ganis' which appeared on these tokens (Pl. 944),
the consequence was widespread forgery and lack of confidence. Some idea of
the improbability of the success of such a system in the early fourteenth century
can be gained from the realization that it was only in the last century that such
fiduciary coinages began to gain acceptance in the Western world and only in the
present century have they become of general application. This attempt by
Muhammad-ibn-Tughlaq was a genuine monetary experiment and was not
dictated by a bankrupt economy, for, on the failure of the scheme, the fiduciary
pieces, both genuine and false, were redeemed.

Some of the early issues of Muhammad-ibn-Tughlaq in gold, silver and billon were struck in memory of his father, Ghiyasu-d-din, whose name appears on the inscription with the suffix al-Shahid, 'The Martyr', an ironic addition, since it was by the murder of his father that the sultan secured his accession to the throne. The signature of a variety of mints in addition to Delhi now appeared regularly on the coinage inscriptions and the Kalima, the inscription containing the profession of faith and recording the name of the actual reigning caliph, returns to most of the issues. In addition to a variety of epithets and titles proclaiming his religious adherence Muhammad-ibn-Tughlaq inscribed on some of his issues the names of the first four orthodox caliphs, Abu Bakir, Omar, Usman and Ali.

The extensive billon coinage which present a considerable number of inscriptional varieties appear to have filled the rôle of subsidiary pieces of the silver tankah. In Delhi and the north this denomination was divisible into fifty jaitils and in the south into various values of gani but the weight variations of extant specimens render their assignation to specific denominations a matter of uncertainty.

A steady decline in the political fortunes of the sultans of Delhi took place after the reign of Muhammad-ibn-Tughlaq as, increasingly, the governors of provinces came to regard themselves as independent and to set up their own kingdoms. The shrinkage of precious-metal coinage in the latter half of the fourteenth and in the fifteenth centuries is an index of this decline, for only in the reign of Firoz III (1351–88) was gold coinage issued in any appreciable quantity. These pieces continued to have the somewhat reduced module but thicker fabric which had been introduced under Muhammad-ibn-Tughlaq and which distinguishes such gold issues as were made by the later sultans. Firoz III, like his predecessor, placed on his gold coins the name of the caliph on obverse and on the reverse his own name, accompanied by such titles as 'The deputy of the commander' (i.e. the caliph). In 1359 the name of Fath Khan, his son, is joined with that of Firoz on the gold coins. Silver coinage was struck only in small quantity but billon issues both of Firoz and of Firoz together with Fath Khan were extensive. Silver coinage for the later sultans is practically non-existent and even the billon coinage tended to lose much of its already small silver content, and coinage in copper became more frequent.

In the issues, almost exclusively in billon and copper, of the Lodi dynasty between 1451 and 1526 the only coinage innovation was the introduction of a somewhat larger billon coin by the sultan Bahlol Lodi and hence known as a bahloli (Pl. 945). In 1526 Ibrahim the last of the Lodi dynasty was defeated at Panipat by the Mogul Babar who occupied Hindustan until his death in 1530, when he was succeeded by Humayun.

The coinage of these two Mogul rulers is dealt with in the section on the Mogul coinage below but the story of the coinage of the sultans of Delhi has not yet reached its conclusion, for in 1540, on the expulsion of Humayun, a new dynasty was established by the Afghan Sher Shah (1540–5). The innovations imported into the coinage by this ruler anticipated the system which was later consolidated by the Mogul emperor Akbar. Only rare gold was struck but in silver a new denomination, the rupee, was issued with a broad flan and a weight of 11·5 gm. and some divisionary pieces of the rupee are also found. The obverse retained the Kalima in the central area with the names of the four orthodox caliphs in the marginal segments but the reverse now carried the sultan's name, date and the legend 'May God perpetuate his kingdom', with, below, the sultan's name in Hindi. In the margin was often inscribed the name of one of a whole chain of over twenty mints at which this coinage was struck. The central inscriptions are enclosed on either a circle or a square and frequently incorporate as a mint-mark a small ornament, for instance a four- or five-petalled flower, a swastika or two interlocked triangles (Pl. 946). On occasional issues both of Sher Shah and his successor Islam Shah (1545–52) the coins were struck on a square flan.

A new denomination, the dam, was struck in copper at a weight of 21·5 gm. and of this denomination divisionary pieces down to a sixteenth were also issued. The reverse has a set of inscriptions similar to those on the silver but the obverse inscription abandons the usual Kalima and contents itself with the more general 'In the time of the Commander of the faithful, the protector of the religion of the Requiter' (Pl. 947). Similar silver and copper coinage was struck in the brief reigns of the remaining Suri sultans, Muhammad Adil, Sikandar and Ibrahim in the years between 1552 and the return of Humayun in 1556.

MUHAMMADAN STATES

(THIRTEEN TO SIXTEENTH CENTURIES)

In some of the constituent provinces of the empire of the sultans of Delhi governors began at quite an early date to issue coinage in their own name and, as the central authority of Delhi declined, a number of these provinces became independent kingdoms which were on occasion retaken by the Delhi sultan but which in most instances endured until the establishment of the Mogul empire in the first half of the sixteenth century. The initial issues of these states are based on the pattern of the Delhi coinage but in time local variants assume the ascendancy. The history of the gradual decay of the precious-metal coinage and the survival of a mainly base-metal coinage of billon or copper which is observed in the Delhi coinage repeats itself in the issues of the Muhammadan states of this period.

From 1202 when it was conquered by the sultans of Delhi Bengal was a single province but in 1310 it was divided into east and west Bengal, until finally in 1339 the whole province became an independent kingdom under Shamsu-d--din Iliyas. A number of governors before the division in 1310 and all of them afterwards issued a coinage almost entirely in silver with only some very rare gold issues. The silver coinage follows closely the pattern of the Delhi coins with the usual Kalima or later the name of al-Mustansir, the last caliph of Baghdad, on the obverse and the local ruler's name and title on the reverse. The issues of the first of the independent sultans of Bengal continue this pattern but in the reign of Sikandar (1358–89) begins the local practice of enclosing the central inscription on one or both sides within geometric outlines of various degrees of elaboration. The coinage of Jalalu-d-din Muhammad (1414–31) is notable for the use of tuhgra characters which, with the strokes elongated right to the edge of the coin, impart a peculiar ridged appearance to the sides on which they are employed (Pl. 948). No less than twenty-four rulers reigned in Bengal, though coinage is not recorded for all, between 1338 and 1538 when it was retaken by Sher Shah, the Suri sultan of Delhi. After the fall of the Delhi branch, an off-shoot of the Suri dynasty continued to rule Bengal from 1552 till 1563. The silver coinage struck in this period has the fine broad flan of the new coinage instituted by Sher Shah (see p. 515). A final dynasty, that of the Afghan Kararanis, held Bengal till the defeat of its last ruler, Daud Shah, in 1576 and the incorporation of Bengal into the empire of Akbar.

JAUNPUR

Jaunpur secured its independence under its governor, the eunuch Khwajah-i-Jahun, in 1394 but the earliest coinage was issued by Ibrahim (1400–40). The main Jaunpur coinage consists of billon and copper pieces similar to the Delhi issues, modified by the practice of the last three rulers of this kingdom Mahmud (1440–56) Muhammad (1456–8) and Husen (1458–76) of issuing 'pedigree' coins, that is, coins on which the name of the ruler's predecessors are added to his own name. After the defeat of Husen and the re-incorporation of Jaunpur into the central empire by Bahlol Lodi in 1476 billon coins in the name of Husen continued to be issued for some thirty years. Rare gold coins of the last three rulers use elongated tughra characters similar to those on the Bengal issues of Jalalu-d-din.

DECCAN

An independent kingdom was established in the Deccan in 1347 by Alau-d-din Hasan, the first of the Bahmani dynasty, with its capital at Kulbarga or Hasanabad. After almost two centuries, in the reign of Mahmud Shah (1482–1518), the kingdom splintered into five smaller sultanates which survived into the seventeenth century. As elsewhere the inspiration of the Deccan coinage is to be found in the Delhi issues, particularly in the case of the silver and the much rarer gold pieces which follow closely the style of the tankahs of Alau-d-din Muhammad, the Delhisultan. Later, from the reign of Ahmad Shah II (1435–57), the coins present on both sides inscriptions detailing the high-sounding epithets assumed in the sultan's title.

MADURA

The most southerly province of the sultans of Delhi was transformed into an independent state by its governor Jalalu-d-din Aghan in 1334 but its existence was short-lived, for it was conquered by the kingdom of Vijayanagar in 1371. Only billon and copper coins similar to those of the Delhi coinage and extremely rare gold pieces were issued in the few decades of independent rule.

MALWA

Dilawar Khan Ghori, the governor of Malwa, set himself up as an independent governor in 1401 but it was only under his son and successor, Hoshang (1405–32), that coinage was begun. Issues in gold, silver and copper by Hoshang and Muhammad I (1432–6) are similar to those of Delhi but under Mahmud (1436–68) billon issues were also introduced and the square shape which characterizes the majority of Malwa coins began to be used. In the sixteenth century all coinage was struck on these square flans. The reverse of Mahmud's coins is divided into two bands by a lengthening of the tail of the final letter in the first line of the inscription (Pl. 949), while, from the time of Ghiyas Shah (1468–1500), both obverse and reverse have this distinctive feature. Ghiyas also introduced the practice of inserting a small ornament in the inscriptions in the same manner as on the Suri coins of Delhi. In 1530 Malwa was conquered by Gujarat and finally in 1560 it was seized by Akbar and incorporated into his empire.

Gujarat, closer to the centre than most of the other provinces, emerged as independent only in the early fifteenth century when a new dynasty was founded by the governor, Zafar Khan, in 1403 but coinage is recorded only from the reign of Ahmad I (1411–43). The coins of Gujarat, unlike those of neighbouring Malwa, are almost always round. Gold figures only infrequently in the coinage, and silver, though struck by most rulers, is restricted, but billon and copper were struck in quantity. Initially coinage follows the Delhi pattern but later the copper coinage in particular was produced in a distinctive thick, dumpy fabric (Pl. 950). Bahadur Shah (1526–36) was able to overrun Malwa in 1530 and add it to his kingdom but it was not until 1572 that Gujarat lost its independence to the Moguls.

KASHMIR

Kashmir, although conquered by the Muhammadans in 1334, did not become part of the empire of the sultans of Delhi but remained an independent kingdom under its own rulers, the first of whom was Shams Shah (1334–7). Kashmir was temporarily subject to the Mogul Humayun between 1541 and 1551 when it regained its independence until Akbar in 1589 added it to his empire. Gold coinage of Kashmir of this period is not common but silver was issued in some quantity with the sultan's name, title and date on the obverse and the mint on the reverse. The silver coins are of an unusual, small square fabric with the reverse divided into a distinctive lozenge pattern (Pl. 951). The plentiful copper coinage also has a characteristic obverse for it is divided by a bar with a kind of double loop in the middle (Pl. 952).

THE MOGUL EMPERORS

The Mogul rulers who established a new empire in India in the mid sixteenth century were descendants of the Mongol Timur or Tamarlane who in the fourteenth century had conquered western Asia and even raided India as far as Delhi. Five generations after Timur, his descendant Babar, driven out of Transoxiana, settled in Afghanistan in 1505 and twenty years later began the invasion of India which terminated with the defeat and death of Ibrahim, Sultan of Delhi, at Panipat in 1526. Before he could consolidate his conquest Babar died in 1530 and his son, Humayun, after years of campaigning, was driven out by Sher Shah, the new Afghan sultan of Delhi in 1542. After thirteen years of exile in Sind, Humayun recovered his conquests and captured Delhi again, but was killed in 1556. The coinage of both Babar and Humayun is mainly of silver dirhems, similar in fabric and types to the Timurid coinage in western Asia (see p. 487). Some small gold pieces were also struck by Humayun and coppers by both Babar and Humayun.

The establishment of the Mogul empire proper dates from the accession in 1556 of Akbar, the son of Humayun. In his long reign he extended his rule successively over the provinces of north and central India and the conquest of the Deccan provinces in the early years of the seventeenth century carried Akbar's empire far to the south before his death in 1605. The political and military achievements of Akbar were matched by a coinage which in extent and quality is ranked amongst the great currencies of history. After a brief issue of coinage of the Timurid type of his predecessors Akbar introduced a coinage which, while new in the completeness of its system covering all metals, yet owed much to the coinage instituted by the Suri sultan, Sher Shah, in 1540. The principal silver coin and perhaps the most famous Mogul coin of all was the silver rupee, adopted from Sher Shah's system, and, like it, supplied with supplementary half-pieces and even lower divisions. Almost equally famous is the new gold piece, the mohur, of which multiple pieces were also issued, though only very few have survived. The system was completed by issues of the copper dam which also had been first introduced by Sher Shah.

The early issues of Akbar perpetuate the inscriptional types which had been used on most of the earlier Delhi coinage, namely the Kalima and the names of the four early caliphs on the obverse and the name of Akbar with his title and laudatory epithets on the reverse. These inscriptions are contained in a variety of geometric outlines, and usually the date in the form of the Hegira year and always the mint name are included on the reverse legend. These issues were all of the usual round shape (Pl. 953) but this gave place to the square type of coin which is a recurrent feature throughout Indian coinage. The Ilahi or divine era of Akbar was introduced as a dating formula in 1584 and subsequent coins carry this new regnal date together with the name of the Persian solar month in which the coin was struck. Coin types also were changed and after 1579 have the new inscription *Allahu Akbar* on the obverse (Pl. 954), expanded to *Allahu Akbar jalla jalalahu* on some later silver issues. On the coinage from some mints the inscriptions took the form of a distich or poetic couplet, as on some Persian issues, incorporating mention of the names of the emperor and the mint. A few very rare gold issues are notable for the use of a figure type on the obverse, a hawk on a mohur struck at Asir, a duck on a mohur from Agra and, on a half-mohur of the mint at Lahore, the standing figures of Sita and Rama (Pl. 955).

On earlier Muhammadan coinages in India the name of the mint had not invariably found a place in the inscriptions but in the issues of Akbar and on the Mogul coinage generally the mint is more often recorded than not. The steady territorial extension of Akbar's empire was accompanied by an expansion of the mints for his coinage and something over twenty mints are recorded as active in his reign. The presence on the coinage of a combination of mint name and date on the majority of the coins provides useful supplementary evidence for the history of the expansion of Akbar's empire.

Impressive as is Akbar's coinage in its broad sweep and its vastness, it nevertheless yields pride of place to the issues of his successor, Jahangir (1605–28), on the score of interest and artistic merit. The great amount of copper coinage struck by Akbar and earlier sultans of Delhi presumably were sufficient for currency needs, for copper issues by Jahangir are less common but gold and silver were struck in some profusion, in great variety and in both the round and square forms. The early issues of the gold mohur and the silver rupee and their half-pieces had the traditional Kalima on obverse and the emperor's name and titles on the reverse but these types were soon replaced by a couplet legend. A third variety, introduced about 1611 and continuing at most mints till the end of the reign, placed Jahangir's name on the obverse and the date, including the month, as on Akbar's coinage, and the mint on the reverse. For some years the silver rupees of the mint of Agra were struck in alternate months in the round and square form.

An unusual feature of some of Jahangir's issues is the association in the couplet legend of the name of the empress Nur Jahan with that of the emperor. The best of the ordinary issues of Jahangir are outstanding for the distinction and beauty of their calligraphy (Pl. 956) but they are eclipsed by two special series of mohurs. The first in the years between 1611 and 1614 present, most exceptionally on Islamic coins, a series of portraits, mostly of Jahangir himself. One coin, probably unique, shows a three-quarter facing turbanned bust of Akbar with a sun on the reverse (Pl. 957). Jahangir himself with his head in a sort of nimbus is represented by a profile bust with long moustaches, turbanned head and ornate dress, while the reverse has a lion with sun above, very similar to the type on coins of the Seljuks of Rum some centuries before (Pl. 958). On one variety Jahangir holds up a fruit in his left hand and in another a wine-goblet. Yet another issue portrays the emperor seated cross-legged on his throne and holding up wine-goblet on the obverse with either lion and sun or sun only at the centre of inscriptions on the reverse (Pl. 959). In 1618 Jahangir began the issue of his famous Zodiac coins on which the obverse carried the sign of the Zodiac of the particular month in which the coin was issued (Pl. 960). Mohurs of this class were struck up to 1622, principally at the mint of Agra, and rupees only for a portion of 1618 at the mint of Ahmadabad, though sporadic pieces from a few other mints are also recorded.

Mogul coinage, particularly in the form of the silver rupee, continued to be prolific in the reigns of subsequent rulers whose names, because of their impingement on British history, are many of them familiar, such as Aurangzib and Shah Alam in whose reign the Treaty of Allahabad in 1765 ended the reality of the Mogul empire, though the outward form in the person of a puppet Mogul emperor was maintained until the Indian mutiny in 1857. Mohurs and rupees of the later emperors had either the traditional Kalima and title types or more usually a couplet type (Pl. 961).

The policy of farming out the mints which was adopted by Farrukhsiyar (1713–19) marked the end of the monolithic coinage system of the Moguls. The coinage of states acknowledging the nominal suzerainty of the Mogul emperor, and the Mogul-type coinage struck both by the British East India Company and other Europeans in India requires a separate section for adequate discussion.

EUROPEAN COINAGE IN INDIA

The first European expedition to reach India was that of the Portuguese under Vasco da Gama who in 1497 sailed round the Cape of Good Hope and across the Indian Ocean to Calicut, and by the early sixteenth century the first Portuguese settlement was established at Goa. The Portuguese initiative was followed later in the century by the Dutch, French, English and Danes, but it was only in the seventeenth century that trading companies of these powers set up their factories or trading settlements on Indian territory. The political and commercial rivalries of these powers and the consequent wars in Europe had their repercussions on the trading undertakings in India. The wars of the eighteenth century and the Napoleonic wars brought the elimination of the Dutch and French settlements and with the exception of the small Portuguese possessions in Goa the English were left to exercise complete commercial and, finally, political control of the whole of India until the middle of the present century.

The earliest European coinage in India was that of the Portuguese who in the early sixteenth century, in the reign of Emmanuel (1500–21), struck a coinage of half-cruzados in gold with the inscription *Meia* (half) surmounted by a crown on obverse and a globe on the reverse. Gold coinage of John III (1521–57) has a figure of St. Thomas, the legendary early missionary to India, with the inscription *India Tibi Cessit*, while silver coinage of Sebastian I (1557–78) has a figure of St.

Sebastian. No special coinage was issued for Goa while Portugal was under Spanish rule in the later sixteenth and seventeenth centuries but this Spanish connection made familiar in India the ubiquitous coinage of silver reales, particularly the major piece of eight reales. From the eighteenth century onwards the coinage for Goa has consisted of the silver rupia and its portions with types the royal portrait and arms of Portugal (Pl. 962) as well as coinage in copper and other base alloys of the tanga of 60 reis and smaller divisionary pieces. Since 1910 when Portugal became a republic the rupia types have been the arms of Portugal and the broad-ended cross with globe at centre, and on tanga coins the Portuguese arms and the *quinas* shield.

Two series of coinage are associated with the activities of the Dutch trading settlements in India established at Pulicat, Negapatam and Masulipatam in the seventeenth century. The extensive series struck in the Netherlands for the Dutch East India Company, the *Vereenigde Oost-Indische Compagnie* for general circulation in the East consisted in the eighteenth century of ducatoons, guilder and stuiver denominations in silver with the identical types used on the provincial series in the Netherlands (see p. 274) with a monogram of the initials of the company VOC below the reverse type, as well as copper doits with provincial arms on obverse and the company's monogram on the reverse (Pl. 1038). A second series consisted of coinage of local types. Gold pagodas known as Porto Novo pagodas were struck at Negapatam in the seventeenth century with a four-armed deity with the Garuda bird to left and disk with lotus below to the right on the obverse and a convex reverse with granulated surface (Pl. 963). Various copper cash denominations had the company's monogram on obverse and an inscription in Nagari or Tamil on the reverse. At Masulipatam pagodas in the late seventeenth and early eighteenth centuries were of the 'three swami' type with three crowned, standing deities on the obverse and a finely granulated reverse. Pulicat, the last Dutch possession in India, passed into British hands in 1824.

For the Danish possession of Tranquebar on the Coromandel coast, obtained in 1620, coinage was struck from the later seventeenth century in the form of copper cash with obverse type the royal monogram, crowned, and the trading company's initials DOC in monogram on the reverse. Gold pagodas in the eighteenth century had the usual Hindu deity on obverse and at the centre of a granulated reverse the royal monogram, crowned. The silver royalin and its double with monogram-and-value types was added in the later eighteenth century. These silver coins and copper cash were struck in the nineteenth century also, until the cession of Tranquebar to the British East India Company in 1845.

For the French settlement at Pondicherry silver fanams were struck in the eighteenth century with a crown on obverse and five lis on the reverse, as well as copper cash with lis obverse and the name of Pondicherry in Tamil on the reverse. The last issues made in 1836 consisted of silver fanams with cock and crown types and copper cash with types, the Gallic cock on obverse and the date on the reverse. Gold pagodas copying local types were also struck as well as silver rupees of Mogul type with the name of the mint of Arcot. These Arcot rupees copy issues of Mogul emperors from Muhammad (1719–48) with a crescent as a differential mark. The series extends from 1736 to 1839 except for the periods 1761–3 and 1793–1817 when Pondicherry was in English hands.

The British series, extending as it did from 1600 to 1947, is the most extensive European coinage in India. After the success of the early voyages to India, of which the first was in 1591, a Charter was granted to the East India Company by Elizabeth I in 1600 and a special coinage was produced for the company's trade. Because of the supremacy of the Spanish silver coinage in international commerce this new coinage was struck in silver in denominations equivalent to the Spanish 8, 4, 2 and 1 real pieces. The types were the royal arms crowned and a crowned portcullis (Pl. 964). The issue met with little success and over two centuries elapsed before another regal coinage for general circulation in India was produced. In the intervening years coinage of a variety of types and systems was issued on the initiative of the company in the several 'presidencies' under its control.

The three principal trading centres established by the East India Company in the first half of the seventeenth century were in Bengal, at Masulipatam near the mouth of the Godavari on the east coast and at Surat on the west coast. Masulipatam was replaced by Madras after 1640 and Bombay, acquired from Portugal in 1661 as part of the dowry of Charles II's queen, Catherine of Braganza, took the place of Surat. The coinage of gold pagodas at Madras is recorded about 1661 but the exact south Indian types imitated are not yet accurately identified, while the silver fanams with two interlinked C's as type (Pl. 965), traditionally assigned to the reign of Charles II, are now considered to have continued into the eighteenth century. The mint in Bombay became active only in 1671, striking a coinage with a five-line inscription on the reverse and copper pice with similar types were also struck. Silver rupees with types, on obverse a shield containing three ships and the royal arms above and on reverse *Pax Deo* in the field and *Moneta Bombaiensis* around, followed about 1700.

The coinage of Madras in the eighteenth century included further issues of gold pagodas with Hindu deity on obverse and a granulated reverse with a five-pointed star (Pl. 966). Other pagodas, still with granulated reverse, had on obverse the 'three swami' type, that is three crowned deities, standing. At Bombay a coinage of pice, the double and the half with rough designs depicting a crown with GR above and *Bomb* below on obverse and an inscription *Auspicio Regis et Senatus*

Angliae on the reverse was issued in both an undated and a dated series which runs from 1717 to 1771. There followed a series of copper pice from 1772 to 1783 with crown and *Bomb* on obverse and on reverse the company's bale-mark, a heart-shaped design divided diagonally into compartments containing the company's initials V.E.I.C. and surmounted by a mark like the figure **4** (Pl. 967). At the end of the eighteenth century copper coins of 20, 15, 10 and 5 cash, dated 1791 and 1794 with bale-mark on obverse and scales on the reverse, were machine struck as distinct from the rougher, hammer-struck coins of the preceding series. In the early eighteenth century Bombay also took up the minting of silver rupees of Mogul type.

In addition to these several series which have, most of them, clear indications of their issue by the East India Company a number of issues of Mogul type coinage, mostly silver rupees, was produced by the company. The segregation of these coinages and their attribution to mints is not always immediately obvious and presents some difficulties.

As early as 1691 silver rupees and rarer gold pagodas with the types of the Mogul emperor Aurangzib were struck with the mint signature of Chinapatam, the native name for Madras. Rupees of Chinapatam from 1707, the first year of the emperor Bahadur, carry on the reverse an additional five-pointed star, similar to that on the pagodas attributed to Madras. Another series of rupees with the name of Arcot have the types of Alamgir II (1754–9) but all bear the date of his regnal year 6 and the Hegira date 1172, i.e. 1758–9. This series has on the reverse the lotus-like trisul or trident of Siva and, despite the references contained on the coins, was issued at Madras (Pl. 968). In the presidency of Bombay, Mogul type coinage, again chiefly silver rupees, began to be issued in the reign of Farrukhsiyar (1713–19) whose types are copied. This series continued with copies of coins of succeeding emperors into the reign of Shah Alam, the mint signature in all cases being in the form Mumbai.

In Bengal gold and silver coinage of Mogul type was struck after 1765 at the mint of Calcutta, though the coinage of Shah Alam (1759–1806) which was chosen for copying has the name of the mint of Murshidabad. The coinage of mohurs and rupees struck by the company's mint at Benares presents another variety of the fossilized date such as that noted on the 'Arcot' coins of Madras. The reason for this phenomenon lies in the practice of the moneychangers of deducting a percentage, 'batta', on other than recently issued coins and this 'freezing' was designed to conceal the real date of issue. The Benares coinage copied the coinage of regnal year 26 of Shah Alam but strangely enough, although the regnal year remained fossilized, the Hegira year continued to be changed so that combinations of regnal year and Hegira date range from 6/1203 to 6/1233.

In the early nineteenth century the issue of Mogul-type mohurs and rupees by the company's mints was continued. The 'Arcot' coins from Madras, still with their fossilized date, now had as distinguishing mark the lotus-like trisul or trident of Siva and were struck by machinery in a more Europeanized fabric, complete with milled edge (Pl. 969). An identical issue was made from the mint at Calcutta which had as its differential a rose in place of the trisul. The issues from Bombay replaced the signature Mumbai by that of Surat and used as a differential mark a small crown which was replaced by a four-dot then a five-dot ornament before the introduction of machine-struck coins. The Calcutta coinage with the signature of Murshidabad and marked with the frozen date 19 San of Shah Alam II were also produced in a Europeanized fabric with milled edge from 1793.

In the nineteenth century Madras still issued the pagoda in gold as well as the pagoda and its quarter in silver with an actual pagoda as type and the value in English on obverse and a Hindu deity and inscription in Tamil on the reverse (Pl. 970). A range of silver fanams was also struck. Copper cash of values 20 and lower were issued in 1803 with types the company's arms on obverse and the value in Persian and English on the reverse. Other copper coins in 1807 had the value in Persian script on obverse and in Talugi and Tamil on the reverse. Copper pice at Bombay have the company's arms and scales as types (Pl. 971). The arms of the Company and the value appear on copper pice at Benares and later on divisionary pieces of the anna.

In 1835 the East India Company began a universal coinage for the whole of India with a series of rupees and portions carrying the portrait and titles of William IV on obverse and the value within a wreath accompanied by the Company's name (Pl. 972). A similar issue was struck in the name of Victoria in 1840. The authority of the East India Company was superseded by that of the Crown, following the uprisings of 1857, and thereafter coinage, first issued in 1862, is of purely regal type, the name of the East India Company disappearing from the reverse. In addition to the silver-rupee coinage, copper coins of a quarter-anna and lower were issued with similar portrait-and-value types. The main change in the coinage in Victoria's reign was the use of the title empress after 1877 (Pl. 973). The British imperial coinage in India maintained a conservatism of types under succeeding rulers but the metal of anna pieces was changed to nickel under George VI and some values were issued with a rectangular or a scalloped outline. On the final rupee issues in 1946 and 1947 a new reverse type of a tiger was adopted (Pl. 974).

INDEPENDENT STATES

(EIGHTEENTH TO TWENTIETH CENTURIES)

The authority of the Mogul empire began to decline after the reign of Aurangzib (1659–1707) and the history of India in the eighteenth and nineteenth centuries is one of a multitude of independent states, the majority of which issued their own coinage; and the historical and numismatic picture is further complicated by British intervention which eventually either absorbed these states or permitted their survival as subject allies. The majority of the coinages of these states derive at least their initial inspiration from the Mogul issues, though many subsequently developed more individual types. In this section it will be possible to deal with only some of the more important of these coinages as illustrations of the more general numismatic history of India in this period.

MYSORE

Coinage in Mysore in south India had consisted of gold pagodas with Hindu deity or deities on obverse and inscribed reverse, as well as copper pieces with elephant on obverse and a kind of chequer-board reverse. In 1760 Haidar Ali had usurped Mysore from the Wodeyar dynasty and gold pagodas of local fabric were struck with Haidar Ali's initial on the reverse but this soon became the obverse type with the year and date in Persian on the reverse. The coinage of his son and successor, Tipu Sultan (1782–99), though including gold pagodas of similar type was of an inscriptional character, similar to the Mogul series. Tipu coined the mohur and its half in gold, and in silver the rupee with its double and a whole range of divisionary pieces from a variety of mints of which the most important was Seringapatam. On copper pieces of values from 40 downwards Tipu adopted the elephant device of earlier Mysore coins for the obverse, while the reverse gives the mint and denomination (Pl. 975). With the defeat of Tipu in 1799 Britain was left in supreme control of the Deccan.

OUDH

In 1720 Muhammad Amin, appointed subahdar of Oudh by the Mogul emperor Muhammad Shah, made himself an independent ruler. His descendants, the nawabs of Oudh, controlled the Mogul mint at Benares and its coinage of rupees, still nominally in the name of the emperor. Though Benares was ceded to the East India Company in 1775, coinage with the mint name of Benares continued to be issued by the nawabs. These rupees have as a distinguishing characteristic a small fish and were probably struck in Lucknow the new capital of the nawabs. In 1818 the nawab Ghaziu-d-din Haidar assumed the title of king and began an issue of regal coinage which lasted down to 1856. On mohurs, rupees and copper pieces the obverse is entirely inscriptional but on the reverse at the centre of inscriptions is a figure type in the form of a coat of arms which takes several forms in the various reigns. Under Ghaziu two fish face each other surmounted by a crown, with above two tigers holding pennants, while on coins of the last king, Wajid Ali (1847–56), two mermaids hold clubs and pennants with crown above and crossed swords below (Pl. 976).

BARODA

In western India the Maratha state of Baroda became independent under a ruler with the title of Gaekwar and coinage was struck from the early nineteenth century. The early issues were of silver rupees and copper pice with Persian inscriptions and with a distinctive mark of a scimitar incorporated. Baroda was one of the states permitted to continue coinage after the creation of the British empire in India. Silver rupees had a portrait of the Gaekwar on the obverse and inscription in a wreath on the reverse. Copper pice with inscriptions on both sides still had the distinctive scimitar sign on the obverse.

BIKANIR

The rulers of Bikanir in Rajputana struck coinage of silver rupees and copper from about 1760 of the usual Mogul type with the addition of a series of special distinguishing marks. In 1893 Bikanir was one of the states which issued coinage of silver rupees and copper anna and pice divisionary pieces with portrait of Victoria on the obverse and the name of the local ruler in Nagari and Persian on the reverse.

GWALIOR

Gwalior in central India reached a position or semi-independence in the later eighteenth century and in the reign of Daulat Rao (1794–1824) rupees and pice were issued in the name of the Mogul Muhammad Akbar. On rupees of similar type issued by his successors the reverse inscription is accompanied by a distinguishing symbol like a bow and arrow and copper pice have the trisul or trident of Siva on one side and a spear-head and three-pronged sceptre on the other. In 1893, when coinage in silver by native mints was ended, subsequent issues in

1889–91 of copper half-pice and quarter-annas had as types a coiled cobra with sceptre and trident and the ruler's name and value in Nagari. Quarter-annas from 1913 have had the ruler's portrait on obverse and his arms on reverse with the value in both Nagari and Persian.

INDORE

The Maratha state of Indore came into being under the Holkar dynasty in the mid eighteenth century and a coinage of silver rupees was begun by Ahalya Bai, the queen regent (1765–95). These rupees with the legends of the Mogul emperor Shah Alam were struck at the mint of Maheswar, which has as mark a small leaf, and at Indore or Malharnagar which marked its issues with a sun-face. On copper half-annas of Tukoji Rao II (1844–86) the bull badge of Indore appears on the reverse. Sivaji Rao (1886–1903) issued rupees with his portrait on obverse and on reverse his arms, a rampant horse and bull with sun-face above. The copper half-anna and lower values show the recumbent bull on obverse with the ruler's name and title and the value on the reverse (Pl. 977). Silver coinage was ended in 1902 but small copper denominations continued to be struck in the present century with portrait-and-value types.

HYDERABAD

The nizams of Hyderabad struck silver and gold in the emperor's name with the addition of their own initials but, after 1857, on both the gold ashrafi and the silver rupee the Mogul emperor's name finally was displaced by that of the nizam. Between 1903 and 1911 mohurs and rupees acquired new types, the minareted Char Minar on obverse and a central inscription with elaborate marginal inscription on the reverse (Pl. 978). Copper pice and half-annas had a similar reverse and a tughra obverse. Rupees and coppers of similar types were continued by the nizam, Mir Usman Ali Khan, from 1911 up to 1944.

SIKH LEAGUE

In the north-west a Sikh League was formed to oppose the Persian incursions of Nadir Shah in 1739 and the Afghan Durrani, Shah Ahmad (1748–67), and his successors. Rupees with Persian couplet-type inscription were struck by the League between 1764 and 1777. Silver rupees of the Sikhs in the Punjab issued by mints at Amritsar and Lahore under Ranjit Singh (1799–1839) are of the Persian couplet type but are not inscribed with his name but bear the leaf symbol which distinguishes the Sikh coinage (Pl. 979). Other issues were made from Multan and

Kashmir. Later issues roughly inscribed in Gurmukhi, a Punjabi form of Nagari, were mainly in copper and usually carry the leaf mark. Coinage ended with the annexation of the Punjab in 1849.

NEPAL

Coinage in Nepal in the sixteenth and seventeenth centuries consists of pieces of half-rupee weight with types ultimately derived from the Mogul coinage. The coins have a central square or circle with an elaborately ornamented border. The king's name and title in Nagari appear on the obverse and other formulae and symbols on the reverse. Coinage with similar types was continued after the Gurkha conquest of Nepal in 1768 but included full rupees, and in the nineteenth century gold mohurs and copper coinage with like types were added. In the present century gold and silver coins have been struck with the traditional types (Pl. 980) but on various paisa or pice values in copper a central type, two crossed Gurkha knives, has been adopted. On rupees of Trivhuvana Vira Vikrama in 1953–4 the ruler's portrait appeared for the first time on Nepalese coin. New coinage for Mahendra Vira Vikrama has been issued since 1955.

AFGHANISTAN

Coinage issued in Afghanistan has been touched upon in the chapter on Muhammadan coinage in the Near Eastern section but a modern-type coinage was introduced under Abd-el-Rahman (1879–1901). On silver rupees with multiples of five as well as divisionary pieces and on copper paisa the usual types are a throne-room on obverse and Tughra on reverse (Pl. 981). A gold denomination known as the amani with similar types was added by Amanullah (1919–29). The principal silver coin in the present system is the afghani, presenting still the throne-room and tughra types. Pul values (100 pul=1 afghani) still have the throne-room obverse but an inscription or numeral reverse. The 5 afghani piece of 1961 has the portrait of Muhammad Zahir.

REPUBLICS OF INDIA AND PAKISTAN

When independence was restored by Britain to India in 1947 the sub-continent was divided into two separate states of which the larger, mainly Hindu, retained the name of India, while a smaller state, predominantly Islamic in faith, formed of the north-western provinces together with East Bengal, adopted the name of

Pakistan. The coinage of the Republic of India formed in 1950 had as obverse type the three lion capital of the Asoka column at Sarnath, with inscription *Government of India*. The reverse of the rupee and portions showed the value between corn-ears (Pl. 982), and the bronze anna coins a humped bull or prancing horse. In 1957 a decimal coinage of a rupee of 100 paise was adopted with the same obverse but mainly with value numeral reverses. A special coinage in 1964 bore the portrait of Nehru on obverse on the rupee and 50 paise.

On the coinage of Pakistan the obverse type is a tughra with inscription *Government of Pakistan* in English on all denominations. The reverse of the nickel rupee, its half and quarter is the value in words, surmounted by a crescent and star (Pl. 983). The same reverse was used on the copper-nickel 2 annas and 1 anna coins, the former with a square outline, the latter with fluted edges. The bronze pice, because of its central piercing, had only inscriptions on either side. On new anna, half-anna and pice coins introduced in 1953 the Tughra and crescent and star are combined on the obverse, while the reverse carries the value within a wreath or between two corn-ears. A decimal coinage based on a rupee of 100 paisa was issued in 1961. From 1964 the inscriptions in English have been dropped.

CEYLON

Considerations both of geography and history commend placing the sketch of the coinage of Ceylon in this section; for the island lies off the south-east coast of the sub-continent, its history is closely linked with that of south India and its coinage, in almost all periods, follows a pattern not unlike that of India, with the notable exception that the Muhammadan invasions and conquests, which play such a great rôle in India from the thirteenth century onwards, did not extend to Ceylon.

The earliest form of coinage in ancient Ceylon is the purana or flat silver piece stamped with a varying number of small punches representing a whole range of objects. The antiquity of these 'punch-marked' coins remains the subject of dispute but, as in the mainland of India, they may have begun to circulate about the same time as coinage began in the Mediterranean area and certainly were current in the last three centuries B.C. and into the first century A.D. From this class of coinage developed coins on which the various symbols on the punch-marked pieces are united into a single design and small silver pieces, both rectangular and round, are found with such a type struck from a die on one side of the coin only. Some examples of this coinage are in copper also but the more common ancient copper pieces are large, circular coins with a type on both sides. On the obverse the main type is an elephant with symbols above, usually a swastika on a staff surrounded by a railing, a three-branched tree in an enclosure and a *chaitya* or temple. The reverse repeats the swastika and the *chaitya* of the obverse and adds other smaller symbols (Pl. 984). Other less common, smaller copper pieces have a maneless lion on obverse and four dots in a circle on the reverse. A series of roughly rectangular plaques, both cast and struck, with a standing figure of the goddess Lakshmi on one side and the swastika within railing of the coins just described on the other, may also possibly have been used as currency. These several bronze coinages were in use in parallel with the silver 'punch-marked' coins and probably continued to be current till about the sixth or seventh century.

The widespread use of Roman imperial aurei and denarii as either currency or bullion in south India finds a parallel in Ceylon, though on a much reduced scale; and then almost entirely restricted to the earlier period of emperors from Augustus to Nero. Roman and Byzantine gold from the later fourth to the sixth centuries, noted in south India, is found only rarely in Ceylon but small Roman bronze coins from the time of Constantine the Great to the later fifth century are probably more numerous in finds in Ceylon. These types of Roman bronze coins were also widely imitated in the island (Pl. 985) up to the seventh century.

Little is known of the sixth and seventh centuries, the 'Dark Ages' of Ceylon, and the record thereafter for many centuries is of successive invasions by Pandyan and Chola kings of south India, interspersed by occasional successful invasions of south India on the part of Singhalese rulers. In any event, the earliest coinage of mediaeval Ceylon is placed no earlier than the later years of the ninth century and in the tenth century. This is a coinage in gold of which the major piece is the kahavanu with, as fractional pieces, the deka or pala and the even smaller aka. These coins generally carry no regal names or titles. The obverse of the kahavanu shows the figure of Vishnu standing on a lotus plant, holding a flower before his face in the left hand and stretching out the right over a fire-altar or lamp. A similar figure on the reverse squats on a bed-like throne and holds a flower-like object in the left hand (Pl. 986). On the deka or pala a standing figure, possibly Lakshmi, holds in her left hand a vase from which springs a plant but the reverse has only an inscription. The figure on the obverse sometimes holds a lotus in the left hand. Similar types also appear on the smaller aka.

During the Tamil occupation of the northern part of the island in the first part of the eleventh century Singhalese coinage appears to have ceased but gold kahavanus inscribed *Sri Vijaya Bahu* are ascribed to Vijaya Bahu I (1055–1111) as well as similar pieces in base gold or white metal. Under subsequent rulers down to Parakrama Bahu VI (1415–67) the principal coinage takes the form of a development of the kahavanu with steadily degenerating types and in base metal only (Pl. 987). One other series of bronze coins which circulated in Ceylon was that of the kingdom of Jaffna. These coins, dating to the late thirteenth and early fourteenth centuries, have on obverse a recumbent bull surmounted by a crescent and dot and a very crude version of the standing figure on contemporary Singhalese coins.

The first Europeans to secure possessions in Ceylon were the Portuguese who first landed there in 1506, and the whole of the island was under Portuguese control by the end of the century. About the middle of the century the Dutch began to wrest possession of the ports from the Portuguese who were finally driven out in 1658. In the period of Portuguese domination no coinage was struck by the Singhalese. The currencies in use in the sixteenth century were silver larins, the small, thin bars of silver, sometimes turned up at the end like a fish-hook (Pl. 988). The use of this type of coin, originally produced and used in the Persian gulf area and taking its name from the town of Lar, had spread to the eastern sea-board of India and to the Maldive Islands and become one of the chief trading currencies in the Indian Ocean. Gold and silver fanams from south India also had currency as well as European coinages such as the Spanish piece of eight and the Venetian sequin. The silver tangas or double tangas, struck in or for Ceylon by the Portuguese, date from the last few decades of Portuguese domination. The obverse is consistently the crowned arms of Portugal dividing the letters of the mint, e.g. C – L for Colombo, while the common reverse types are the gridiron of St. Lawrence or the standing figure of John the Baptist between the letters S – I (Pl. 989).

The Dutch held Ceylon from 1658 until it was seized in 1795–6 by Britain, whose possession of the island was confirmed by the Treaty of Amiens in 1802. The same admixture of south Indian and European coinages as under the Portuguese continued to pass current, together with the more recent Portuguese tangas, many of which were countermarked with the initials of the Dutch East India Company, the Vereenigde Oost-Indische Compagnie, VOC in monogram (Pl. 989). Towards the end of the seventeenth century a series of thick copper coins of 1 and 2 stuivers in value was struck at Colombo and Jaffna. The type was identical on both sides, a wreath enclosing the abbreviated value, e.g. 1 ST. The next issue of Dutch coinage for Ceylon took place almost a century later. In 1784 an exceptional coinage of silver rupees was struck with inscriptions in Malay Arabic on either side and the date in Western numerals. The earliest of several issues in copper was that in 1783 of the doit or quarter-stuiver with types, the Company's monogram, surmounted by the mint letter C for Colombo on obverse and the value $\frac{1}{4}$ ST on reverse. A series of copper stuivers and double stuivers between 1783 and 1795 has similar types to those of the doit, except that the denomination on the reverse is written in full, e.g. 1 STUIVER and is accompanied by the date (Pl. 990). These coins carry on obverse the initial letters of mints at Colombo, Galle, Trincomalee and Jaffna. The doit was also struck in lead with monogram obverse and a tree dividing the value or the value only on the reverse.

The Dutch monetary system of a rix-dollar or rijksdaalder of 48 stuivers was continued by the British in the early nineteenth century. The types were identical on all denominations, an elephant with date below on the obverse and on the reverse the value expressed in stuivers with a circular inscription *Government of Ceylon* (Pl. 991). Pieces of 96, 48 and 24 stuivers were struck in silver and of 48, 24 and 12 stuivers in copper. These copper coins are of a thick, dumpy fabric and fluctuate greatly in weight. The silver rix-dollar of George IV in 1821, the first British regal coinage struck for Ceylon, had the royal portrait and titles on the obverse and the elephant and value on the reverse. In the reign of William IV and the first decades of Victoria's reign the small silver three-halfpenny was produced for circulation in Ceylon. The types were similar to the Maundy coins, the royal portrait on obverse and the value crowned within a wreath on the reverse (Pl. 992). The half- and quarter-farthing with the same types as the English farthing were also struck for Ceylon in these reigns (Pl. 993).

In 1892 a new coinage with royal portrait obverse and a palm-tree and value reverse was introduced with denominations of 50, 25 and 10 cents in silver (Pl. 994) and values from 5 cents to a quarter-cent in copper. These types were continued under Edward VII and George V but the palm-tree disappeared from the higher values of George VI. The title emperor was omitted from the royal style on coins struck for Ceylon after its independence was restored in 1947. The last coinage of Ceylon with the portrait of a British monarch was the brass 2 cents issue with scalloped edge in 1955 with the portrait of Elizabeth II. New types were adopted in 1963. The obverse on the rupee and the various cent denominations is the Singhalese arms, a lion with sword within a crowned wreath. The reverse carries a value numeral and inscriptions in Singhalese and Tamil.

THE FAR EAST

★

China   537
Tibet   544
Japan   545
Korea   548
Burma   549
Siam   550
Malaya   551
Indo-China   553
East Indies   554
Hong Kong   557
The Philippines   558

The Far East

THE coinage considered in this section is that of the land-mass of Asia east of India, together with the islands of the Indian Archipelago and Japan. Only one series, the Chinese, is commensurate in its historical duration with the coinages of India, western Asia and Europe, for early currency in most other areas of the Far East takes a primitive form and coinage, in the accepted definition of the term, begins much later and tends to be sporadic. A number of Far Eastern coinages have certain characteristics in common: until relatively modern times they usually were cast from moulds and not struck from dies and were provided with a round or square hole at the centre to permit of their being strung together; certain series, particularly the Chinese, Japanese, Korean and Annamese, are notable for the conservatism of their basic types over long periods of centuries. In the islands of the East Indies and the several states of Farther India and Malaya the establishment of European colonies brought, at various dates from the seventeenth century onwards, coinages of European type and even in the countries of the Farther East which were never subject to European control coinage of European pattern finally displaced the age-old forms of coinage in the late nineteenth century.

CHINA

The well-known claim that the Chinese anticipated by many centuries the invention in the Western world of such things as gunpowder and printing has its parallel in the history of coinage; for ancient Chinese authorities have placed the use of a metallic coinage in China as early as the twentieth century B.C. Whatever the justice of the claims may be in other fields, modern research has not been able to to confirm the existence of true coinage in Chinese civilization earlier than the seventh century B.C. The invention of coinage, then, would seem to be of almost equal antiquity in the West, in India and in the Far East. Coinage in China in the first few centuries is remarkable for the variety of its shapes, but in the course of the third century B.C. Chinese coinage, which, with rare exceptions, is always in copper, acquired its characteristic circular shape with

537

a square hole in the centre which it maintained in essentials for over two thousand years until the late nineteenth century. The development of this, the most homogeneous coinage in the world, is traced mainly in the changing fashion of the inscription on obverse and reverse. Coinage, Westernized both in respect of its system and its fabric, has, since the late nineteenth century, introduced some greater variety into the Chinese issues.

SPADE, WEIGHT OR PU MONEY

China is unique in having preserved in its coinage a stage of monetary development of which only vestiges have survived in other civilizations. The intermediate stage between the barter system of primitive civilization and the general acceptance of metal coins of standard weight stamped with a guaranteeing device produced a coinage—if the term can here be properly used—which consisted of replicas in bronze of the actual agricultural spades which in the earlier period were used for barter. The use of these objects as money has been dated to the early part of the seventh century B.C. and their circulation continued down to the fourth century B.C. These copies of spades have a hollow handle and the shoulders of the spade are square. The most primitive examples have only three lines on either side but more developed specimens are inscribed on the obverse with characters which represent place names or serial signs. Although the place names are of doubtful identification the use of this spade money is associated with northern China.

The pu money, to some examples of which the description weight money is sometimes applied since the characters it bears indicate its weight, is in general terms similar to the spade money, though differing in detail. Pu money is much smaller; it has a flat handle and the shoulders of the spade are sometimes round, sometimes angular and the foot of the spade is indented by either a curve or an angular nick. Like the spade money, pu money usually has characters inscribed on the face only and where these characters represent identifiable place names the area where this form of money was in use is again seen to be north China and more specifically the modern provinces of Shantung, Shansi and Honan. The reverses are frequently plain but sometimes carry the three straight lines as on the spade money or characters representing serial numbers (Pl. 995). Despite the seemingly more developed form which the pu money takes, it too has been ascribed to the period between the seventh and fourth centuries B.C.

Of equal antiquity, that is of the period between the seventh and fourth centuries B.C., is another series of money again small copies of objects used in barter, this time knives. This knife money of cast bronze consists of a slightly curved blade and handle with a ring at the end. The very earliest examples are, like the earliest spade money, uninscribed but most have, on both front and back, characters which indicate the place or province in which they were current and sometimes the value. The areas of currency were again provinces in northern China, principally Shantung and Chihli. The earlier series of knife money was about seven inches long, the later series only about five inches or less. Of the smaller variety a very extensive series bears the name of the city of Ming in the province of Shansi, the modern Chihli (Pl. 996).

Of early coinage of unusual shape mention must be made of the copy in metal of the cowrie which, according to tradition, was issued by the prime minister of the king of Tsu (south Honan) about 600 B.C.

ANCIENT ROUND MONEY

Both the antiquity and the identification of the most ancient forms of round money is debatable. It is questionable whether the most primitive forms, consisting merely of a copper ring with a round hole in the centre, can be classed as coins at all and, since some are completely devoid of inscription or have, at best, only an indication of weight, their attribution to locality and era must be dubious. The series of pieces with round hole which have a place name in addition to the weight in characters on the obverse only (Pl. 997) has more of an air of true coinage and where names have been identified they prove to be in the same area as the spade and knife money already discussed. Traditionally, however, this ancient round money with circular hole is said to have been current from the twelfth to the sixth centuries B.C., thus ante-dating the other ancient types of money.

The next stage in the development of this round money in bronze is represented by the series with a square hole at the centre in place of the circular hole. Some changes in fabric were to take place in the next few centuries but the form this developed in the sixth century B.C. remained the basic form of the bronze round money (Ch'ien or Tsien) until less than a century ago. The earliest examples of this form of round money in the sixth century B.C. have characters indicating value on the obverse only. On one series with the name of the city of Ming on obverse there still appears the word *tao*, 'knife', and presumably it is to be dated to the third century B.C. when the knife money of Ming was being replaced by the new round money.

The definite adoption of round money as the standard coinage dates from the establishment of the new Ch'in dynasty which overthrew the old Chou dynasty about the middle of the third century. The 'First Emperor' Shih Huang Ti (221–209) who built the Great Wall issued bronze coins inscribed with the weight *Pan Liang*, half an ounce or 12 shu (Pl. 998). This coinage of *Pan Liang*, continued under the Han dynasty which succeeded in 206 B.C., but suffered a gradual reduction and debasement. Under the empress Kao in 187 B.C. the weight had fallen to 8 shu, under Wen in 179 B.C. to 4 shu and finally to 3 shu under the emperor Wu in 140.

A coinage reform by the emperor Wu Ti in 118 B.C. demonetized the earlier coinage and substituted a piece of 5 shu, equipped now with a raised rim to prevent filing (Pl. 999). This Wu shu or 5 shu coinage remained the standard currency for some 8 centuries and the chronological arrangement of this series depends on calligraphic criteria. This coinage was issued by some nine regular and twenty-three irregular dynasties which ruled over the whole or parts of China successively or contemporaneously. Exceptions to the usual run of 5 shu coins were the large pieces struck by rulers of the Wu kingdom about A.D. 236 with nominal values of 500 and 1000 shu, and, in A.D. 256, the pieces with nominal value of 100 shu.

The only interruption in this series was the attempt by the usurper Wang Mang (A.D. 7–22) to revive pu and knife money. Both these classes of money are distinguishable from the ancient categories, for they are very much smaller, the pu money measuring only some inch-and-a-half, and the knife money about three inches (Pl. 1000).

NEW ROUND MONEY

Under the emperor Kao Tsu (618–627), the first emperor of the Tang dynasty (618–907), a new type of round money was introduced which gave the coinage of China the form it retained down to the end of the nineteenth century. This new coin, still known as the ch'ien or cash, continued to be cast in bronze. For transactions involving the use of a quantity of these coins, the coins were strung together through their central hole, a string of cash amounting, theoretically, to 100 ch'ien. In practice the number was usually 98 and the slightly lower total of 95 was known as a titsz. Ten strings of cash together made up a tiao, but in no bundle of ten strings might there be included more than two titsz (strings amounting only to 95 cash). The relation of the ch'ien to the tael or silver ounce varied in relation to the market price and the fineness of the silver, with the consequence that the tael might be worth anything from 700 to 2000 cash.

The new round money introduced by Kao Tsu was issued at a standard of ten coins to the liang or ounce of bronze. The inscription on the obverse consisted of four characters which are normally read in the order top, bottom, right and left. The top and bottom characters give the *nien hao* or regnal period, a practice which had been used earlier on the 100 ch'ien in 256 but had not been continued. The characters to right and left read *tung pao* or current money so that the full inscription reads 'the current money of the Kai Yuan period' and this is the formula which, with the requisite alteration of the regnal period, continued in use till the nineteenth century. The reverse of the early tung pao coins was frequently plain but sometimes carried a symbol such as a crescent (Pl. 1001). Tradition has it that on the first wax mould for this coinage the empress Wen Te placed her nail-mark which was later continued as a new moon or crescent. Later issues of Kai Yuan tung pao of the Tang dynasty sometimes have an additional character on the reverse indicating the mint, usually the capital, Layang in Honan.

Complete uniformity, however, was not maintained on the coinage throughout all the centuries, for most dynasties introduced some modification. The issues of the Sung dynasty (960–1280) were produced with three styles of writing, the orthodox, the running hand and the grass character. The coinage of the emperor Hsiao Tsung (1163–89) of the southern Sung dynasty has on the reverse, from the year 1180 to the end of the reign, numerals from seven to sixteen representing the emperor's regnal years. By the early twelfth century the empire of the Sung dynasty was reduced to southern China and the north which, from the early tenth century had been subject to Tatar invasions, was in the hands of the Tatar Chin dynasty with its capital in Peking. In 1213 the Mongols under Ghengis Khan captured Peking and north China and under his successors, notably Kublai Khan, the Mongol empire was extended over south China and Korea. The Mongol dynasty of Yuan issued very little copper money but such issues as there were, were inscribed with Mongol characters. Transactions in this period, as we learn from Marco Polo's account, were conducted with paper money which was extensively used.

Under the Ming dynasty (1368–1644) new heights of literary and artistic achievement were attained, territorial expansion resulted in the conquest of Assam and the sixteenth century saw the first European establishment in China, that of the Portuguese at Macao. The coinage, however, continued its conservative course. A kuan or string of cash now was made up of 400 cash and the coins themselves, with the traditional formula on the obverse, frequently had additional characters on the reverse indicating the place of minting and the value for in addition to the ordinary cash, pieces of value 2, 4, 5 and 10 were issued. The issues of the Ching dynasty (1644–1912) were, until 1900, mainly of the ordinary tung pao coins and, following the practice of the Ming coinage, bore on the reverse the name of the mint. The reverse character is in Manchu script while the obverse characters continue to be orthodox Chinese. In place of the ordinary names of places where coinage was struck the reverse of the coin frequently bears the character Hu, the Board of Revenue, or Kung, the Board of Works. In 1653 additional characters for 1 li or a thousandth part of the tael or ounce, indicating the value of the coin in silver, were added to the obverse and from about this time the reverse frequently gives the name of the mint in both Chinese and Manchu (Pl. 1002). In the financial straits caused by the Tai Ping rebellion between 1812 and 1864 recourse was had from 1851 to the issue of coins with nominal values of 5, 10, 50, 100, 200, 300, 400, 500 and even 1000 cash but the inevitable widespread forgery of these coins led to the abandonment of these large-value pieces under the emperor Kuang Hsu (1875–1900). The Tai Ping rebels who for a time occupied Nanking issued their own copper cash with characters indicating 'the celestial state' on one side and 'sacred currency' on the other and occasionally the character for Ming, the restoration of which dynasty was the professed object of the rebellion.

MODERN TYPE COINS OF THE EMPIRE

The centuries-old cash coinage made of cast bronze with a square hole at the centre was finally replaced in 1900 by a series of cash denominations in struck copper without any central piercing. This modernization of the copper cash coinage was in fact anticipated by a series of machine-struck coins in silver earlier in the nineteenth century. The earliest of the Chinese silver dollars so-called was not an imperial issue but was issued in Formosa during the revolution begun by Chang Wen in 1837. The types were the bust of the long-bearded god of longevity on obverse with characters indicating the reign of the emperor Tao Kwang and the value 7 mace and 2 candareens, while the reverse showed a sacrificial vase on three legs and Manchu characters giving the place of minting. A series of imperial silver coins struck at provincial mints for a range of provinces began issue in the last decade of the nineteenth century. In addition to the major piece the dollar of 7 mace and 3 candareens there were divisionary pieces of 50, 20, 10 and 5 cash. The types were uniform for all denominations apart from the state-ment of value. On the obverse in the centre four Chinese characters denote 'Valuable coin of the Kuang Hsu régime' and at the very centre are four smaller Manchu characters with the same meaning, while the circular inscription gives the province name and the value of the denomination. The reverse carries the imperial emblem, a flying dragon and a circular inscription in English giving the name of the province and the value (Pl. 1003). The first provincial series was struck for Kwantung (Canton) in 1889 and was followed by issues in other provinces in the next ten years.

This imperial provincial series in silver was accompanied by copper cash in denominations of 20, 10, 5 and 1 with similar types to those of the copper, usually incorporating at the centre of the obverse the provincial symbol. In the early years of the present century an issue of imperial coins by the central authority was produced in modern style. On the silver tael and denominations of 5, 2 and 1½ mace between 1903 and 1906 the obverse carried Chinese and Manchu characters as on the provincial silver, while the circular characters are the equivalent of the empire of China and the value. The reverse with flying-dragon type has inscription in Chinese and in English *Tai-Ching-Ti-Kuo Silver Coin*, i.e. imperial Chinese silver coin. A rare tael in gold was also struck in this issue. A silver dollar with like types but inscribed in English *One dollar* on the obverse was issued in 1907 and divisionary pieces of 50, 20 and 10 cents between 1907 and 1911. The issue was completed by coins of 20, 10, 5 and 1 cash in copper (Pl. 1004). A second series of copper cash with inscription *Hu Poo* and the cash denomination in English was issued by the authority of the Board of Revenue.

REPUBLIC OF CHINA

Revolution broke out in China in 1911; China was declared a republic in January 1912 and in February Hsuen Tung, the last Manchu emperor, abdicated. Despite the part played in the republican movement by Sun Yat Sen, the assembly at Peking elected Yuan Shih Kai the first president. The attempt of Yuan Shih Kai to have himself elevated to the position of emperor in 1915 miscarried but caused the revolt of Yunan and other southern provinces. Sun Yat Sen became president in 1921 and after his death in 1925 Chiang Kai Shek, as leader of the Kuomintang party, headed affairs until the Communist régime came to power in 1948. The coinage system remained much as it had been with the dollar and subsidiary pieces issued in silver and cash denominations in copper. The portrait of Sun Yat Sen was placed on the obverse of silver dollars and lower values in 1912 with a reverse inscribed in English *The Republic of China One Dollar*. The types on the copper cash in 1912 had the appropriate inscription in English on the reverse and crossed flags on the obverse; these types persisted on the 20 cash piece till 1922.

The first issue of the silver dollar for Yuan Shih Kai in 1912 showing his uniformed bust facing on obverse, and characters indicating the value 1 yuan at centre and a circular inscription giving the value, 1 dollar, in English. The issues for Yuan Shih Kai from 1914 on the dollar and lower values showed his profile bust on obverse and an open wreath enclosing characters on the reverse (Pl. 1005). The various changes of régime and separatist movements in the provinces have also found representation on coinage issues in modern China. The use of pictorial types on the reverse is seen on issues shortly before the last war. Silver dollars with portrait of Sun Yat Sen have a Chinese junk with spread sails on the reverse and other dollars and half-pieces have a representation of the ancient pu money as reverse type. Lower-value coins of cent denominations also use this reverse between 1935 and 1941 (Pl. 1006).

The Communist régimes in Hupeh, Anhwei and Honan in 1932 and in Szechuan and Shensi provinces in 1934 issued some silver dollars with hammer and sickle on globe as obverse type and propaganda inscription on the reverse. Copper coins in denominations of 500 and 200 cash had a hammer and sickle in a five-pointed star on obverse and value on reverse. The currency of Communist China consisted of paper money until the issue in 1955 of aluminium coins of 1, 2 and 5 fen with types five stars above a mausoleum on obverse and the value on the reverse.

The coinage (10 chio=1 yuan) of Nationalist China since 1949 has had obverses of Sun Yat-sen and pictorial types including a map of Formosa. A special coinage with portrait of Chiang Kai-shek marked his eightieth birthday in 1966.

TIBET

China and, later on, Nepal have always provided for the wants of Tibet in regard to coinage and even from the eighteenth century when coins were struck in Tibet itself the influence of Nepalese and Chinese coinage is obvious. It had been the practice for bullion to be sent from Tibet to Nepal in exchange for coinage but after the advent of the Ghurka dynasty in Nepal (see p. 529) its currency proved not so acceptable and in the later eighteenth century silver coins were struck in Tibet itself. The types on these were derived from the Nepalese and had an eight-petalled flower at the centre surrounded by eight fleurets containing Buddhist emblems on the obverse and on the reverse a leaf-scroll design also surrounded by eight fleurets containing emblems. Between 1788 and 1793 degenerate copies of this coinage were issued. Resumed Chinese intervention in Tibet in 1793 was followed by a coinage of cast-silver pieces, copying the basic elements of the Tibeto-Nepalese coinage but with square at centre of the obverse surrounded by four fleurets and four Chinese characters. The reverse was of similar design but with Tibetan characters.

In the early years of the present century silver rupees and portions struck in the province of Szechuan for Tibet had the portrait of a mandarin on obverse and characters within a scroll wreath on the reverse. In 1909 new types appeared on the silver srang and on copper pieces of 2½ and 7½ skar. At the centre of the obverse was a Chinese lion surrounded by eight fleurets containing symbols, while the reverse, with a symbol at the centre, had a surround of inscription and outside this, on the silver only, fleurets with symbols. These remained basically the types in later issues which included a 20 srang piece in gold, the 5 sho in silver as well as the sho and skar values in copper (Pl. 1007). Since 1935 on various srang values in silver and sho pieces in copper the central type on obverse has been the lion with a background of mountains.

JAPAN

The history of Japanese coinage is much briefer than that of the Chinese series, for no regular issues of coins were made before the early eighth century A.D. This first coinage was a cast-bronze series similar to the contemporary Chinese, but after only some two-and-a-half centuries official coinage came to an end. The coinage, resumed again in the sixteenth century, consisted not only of cast-bronze pieces but of gold and silver, differing in fabric and shape from the almost universal round coins. In the later nineteenth century when Japan adopted a general Westernizing policy the traditional coinage forms were replaced from 1869 by a new system of Western type and fabric.

EARLY ISSUES (c. 708–958)

The first coins to be cast in a uniform pattern consisted of both silver and bronze but the silver was produced only for one year, while the copper issues continued for half a century. The bronze coin, produced in the reign of the empress Genmyo in the first year of Wado, is termed the wado kaiko after the four-character inscription on the obverse. This Japanese coinage bears a close resemblance to tung pao coins introduced in China by the emperor Kao Tsu (618–627) of the Tang dynasty. The characters on the Japanese coin, however, are read clockwise and are interpreted as 'Japanese copper initial treasure'. The denomination of this early coin is the sen, a term which has survived in the Japanese coinage till the present day. This wado kaiko coinage falls into two groups: an early class of rougher execution and a second category of better workmanship and quality dating from the use of Chinese craftsmen in 720 (Pl. 1008).

In 760 coins were issued in gold, silver and bronze but no certainly genuine examples of the silver taihei genpo have survived and only a unique specimen of the gold kaiki shoho in the imperial collection. The bronze issue with characters mannen tsuho were tariffed at the rate of 1 to 10 of the earlier copper pieces. All in all, no less than twelve varieties of bronze coinage were produced between 708 and 958, successive issues showing a progressive deterioration both in execution and in metallic content down to the small kengen daiho of 958 (Pl. 1009). Between the mid tenth century and the mid sixteenth century no official coinage was produced in Japan. Currency needs in this period were met by the continued circulation of some of the bronze sen of the twelve dynastic types mentioned above and by counterfeits of this coinage as well as by the acceptance and use of bronze coinage from China and Korea.

SHOGUNATE (SIXTEENTH TO NINETEENTH CENTURIES)

In this period when imperial authority was eclipsed and real power was in the hands of a succession of powerful semi-feudal military overlords, Japanese coinage resumed and developed along most individual lines. The beginnings of the coinage system which developed and persisted in the Tokugawa shogunate from 1599 to 1867 can be discerned in the issues under the military dictatorship of Toyotomi Hideyoshi (1582–98). Cast copper or bronze coins of the traditional type and known as eiraku sen had been issued from about 1570 and were continued under Toyotomi and in fact were minted in China for export to Japan till as late as about 1640 (Pl. 1010). The innovation of the reign, however, was the issue of gold coinage. Gold had for long been used in currency in the form of thin gold plates, but only as bullion. Under Toyotomi these gold plates were developed into a coinage by marking oval-shaped, flat gold pieces with the kiri-flower crest on the edge at top and bottom and inscribing them in Indian ink with their value and the signature of the mint superintendent. The first recorded date of issue of these gold obans is 1586. Extremely rare rudimentary silver coins also appeared in the form of small slabs of silver known as chogin.

Under the Tokugawa shogunate (1599–1867) several denominations of gold in the form of flat oval plates were used. Nominally the major piece contained ten of the standard units of value, the gold ryo, and were stamped as of this value but the gold content was always considerably lower. Of the obans of the various periods the Keicho (1600–95), the Genroku (1095–1710) and the Tempo (1838–60) passed current only at 8 ryo and 2 bu (the bu was a fourth part of the ryo), while the rare Kyoho oban (1725–1838) was current at 7 ryo and 2 bu; but in the economic circumstances which pertained just before the nineteenth-century currency reform the mannen oban (1860–2) reached an exchange value of 25 ryo. These obans followed much the same pattern as the original issue of Toyotomi with inscription in Indian ink but usually had four stamps, one at the centre of each edge, and three stamps on the reverse. The goryoban or half-oban was issued only in 1837 in the Tempo period. The koban or tenth of the oban, of which there were nine issues between 1601 and 1860, carries no guaranteeing inscription in ink and the arrangement of the stamps or seals is different. The kiri stamp was placed at the edge at top and bottom only inside a fan-shaped frame and not a circular one as on the oban; two rectangular stamps were placed one below the top, the other above the bottom kiri stamp. The reverse also carried a central stamp and a second smaller stamp indicating the era of issue (Pl. 1011). On smaller rectangular gold pieces of 2 bu and 1 bu the stamps cover most of the surface area.

The silver used as currency in this period partook even more of the nature of bullion than did the gold and scarcely qualifies to be considered as coinage. One category, the chogin, was in the form of oval-shaped blocks of silver some two to three inches long with guaranteeing stamps on the obverse or face and stamps indicating the era of issue at each end of the obverse. A second category consisted of bean-shaped silver pieces, called mameita gin, stamped with a representation of Diakokusama, the God of Plenty, on obverse and, frequently, a stamp designating the era on the reverse. Of the rectangular silver pieces issued in the later eighteenth and in the nineteenth century the most common is the ichibu gin or 1 bu in silver (Pl. 1012) issued in 1837, 1859 and finally in 1868.

The bronze eiraku tsuho which was already in issue in the time of Toyotomi continued in circulation till about 1640 but the basic bronze coin throughout most of the period was the kanei tsuho (Pl. 1013) which was produced from 1626 until 1863 with four characters on the obverse and wave-like lines on the reverse. Some of the later issues of this coin were in brass or iron. The copper bunkyu eiho, again with characters on obverse and wave-like reverse, of value 4 mon, was cast from 1863 up to the coinage reform of 1869.

MODERN COINAGE (1868–1960)

The fall of the Tokugawa shogunate and the restoration of imperial authority in the person of the emperor Mutsuhito in 1868 opened the new Meiji (enlightened government) era and brought the introduction of a new decimal coinage of European pattern. The new monetary unit was the ycn, divisible into 100 sen, each of 10 rin. The first issue of the new coinage was made in 1870 and consisted of the yen and pieces of 50, 20, 10 and 5 sen in silver with a dragon-type obverse with circular character inscription rendering the country, era and value, and a chrysanthemum in an open wreath on the reverse (Pl. 1014). In 1872 the gold yen with multiples up to 20 was produced, with similar dragon obverse but with the sun-in-wreath reverse type flanked by pennants. In 1873–4 the silver denominations were reduced in size and the rayed sun cn reverse was replaced by three characters indicating the value. Copper pieces of 2, 1 and ½ sen with similar types were now also added to the system at this time as well as the 1 rin piece with chrysanthemum obverse and character reverse indicating the value. The types on the gold were changed in 1891 to a sun on obverse and on reverse value in wreath closed by chrysanthemum. On sen values in silver from 1907 the obverse type became a sun in a circle of cherry-blossom.

In the reign of emperor Yoshihito (1912–26) gold denominations, restricted to 5 and 20 yen, continued the existing types but ceased issue, the 20 yen in 1920 and the 5 yen in 1924. Divisionary sen values in silver returned to the dragon-type obverse between 1912 and 1917, as did the yen in silver in its last year of issue in 1912. The only silver coin later in the reign was the 50 sen piece with sun obverse and value between two mythical birds of longevity on the reverse (Pl. 1015). The bronze sen and 5 rin pieces of this reign had as obverse type the kiri-flower crest which had appeared on the gold obans and kobans of the shogunate. The coins of emperor Hirohito (1926–) included a short issue of gold 5 and 20 yen with traditional types in 1929–31. The silver 50 sen also remained unchanged as did the bronze sen whose types were now repeated on 5 and 10 sen denominations. Coinage in silver and bronze ended in 1937, and from 1938 until the end of the war coinage consisted mainly of 5 and 1 sen denominations in aluminium and even in tin in 1944–5. On the 1 sen piece of 1941–3 the types were Mount Fujiyama and value. The post-war coinage has introduced two new features, the indication of value in Western numerals and the use of pictorial types (Pl. 1016).

KOREA

The great peninsula of Korea under the name of Chao-hsien was a fief of the Chinese empire until the early fourth century A.D. when the Kao clan took possession of it. No Korean coinage was produced until the eleventh century when cast copper or bronze pieces with fabric and types similar to those of the contemporary Sung dynasty in China were issued. Early issues have plain reverse and four characters on the obverse reading *San han tung pao*, 'Currency of the Three Han', that is the three provinces of Korai, Petsi and Shinra which were united into one kingdom of Korea by Ouang in the eleventh century. Li Chengkuei who usurped the throne and acknowledged the sovereignty of Hung Wu, the first emperor of the Ming dynasty of China (1368–98), restored the old territorial designation Chao-hsien which reappears in the four-character inscription *Chao-hsien tung pao* on cast-bronze coins which had an extended circulation (Pl. 1017). For most of the seventeenth and eighteenth centuries the Korean kings were tributary to Japan. From the end of the eighteenth century a regular bronze coinage was issued with four-character inscription *Chang ping tung pao*, 'Currency of the Chang ping', the new dynastic style now adopted. This coinage was produced by a number of mints which placed on the reverse of the coins numerals indicating the sequence of issues and a series of elaborate mint-marks (Pl. 1018).

In the late nineteenth century in the reign of the emperor Tai (1863–97) a modern, Europeanized coinage was introduced. The first issue in 1891 consisted of the rare silver whan and copper pieces of 5 and 10 mun, all with types similar to contemporary Japanese issues, namely a dragon on obverse and value in an open wreath on the reverse. The inscription on the obverse included a statement of the value in English. The 1894 issue was of 1 and 5 yang pieces in silver and 1 and 5 fun coins in copper with types the same as before but for the new denomination names. A new unit, the won, divisible into 100 chon was introduced in the coinage of 1905–6. Gold denominations of 10 and 20 won as well as the half-won and coins of 5, 10 and 20 chon continued to have the same types but the bronze chon and its half had a phoenix as obverse type (Pl. 1019). A final issue of reduced weight was produced before the annexation of Korea by Japan in 1910. On coins of South Korea in 1959 the 100 hwan in cupro-nickel carried the portrait of Singman Rhee on obverse and two peacocks and value on the reverse. War galley and rose types on the 50 and 10 hwan coins continued on the new 5 and 1 won coins in 1966, with a pagoda on the 10 won. In North Korea the types of the 1, 5 and 10 chon coins were arms in wreath and value.

BURMA

Coinage in Burma was not issued with any frequency or regularity until comparatively modern times but some relatively common series of coins are attributed to earlier periods of Burmese history. Perhaps the earliest is a series of flat silver pieces produced by late mediaeval dynasties in Arakan in west Burma. On the obverse is a recumbent humped bull with an inscription above in Nagari and on the reverse the trisul or trident of Siva. Both types are enclosed in a circle of dots (Pl. 1020). Silver coins with the Kalima on obverse and ruler's name and title on the reverse in Kufic script are attributed to rulers of Arakan who in the sixteenth century were tributary to the Muhammadan kings of Bengal. A third series of silver coins of rulers of Arakan was issued from the early seventeenth to the late eighteenth century. These large, flat silver pieces only have inscriptions on both sides giving the date and title in Burmese on obverse and the ruler's name on the reverse in Persian and Nagari. From about 1638 the coins have the same inscription, indicating date and title in Burmese on both sides.

To Pegu and Tenasserim in southern Burma is attributed a series of coin-like pieces some two inches in diameter, made of a mixture of lead and tin. On the obverse is the fabulous animal, a mixture of horse and deer, known in Burmese as *To*. The reverse has a wheel at the centre, surmounted by an inscription in Pali, using Burmese letters. On another series of like pieces the obverse carries the hansa or sacred bird. Metal weights in use in Arakan up to the nineteenth century were in the shape of this bird. A series of smaller coins in silver with the sankh or shell of Vishnu on the obverse and the trisul of Siva on the reverse have been attributed to Pegu as early as the eighth century.

The coinage of the kings of Burma proper begins only in the later nineteenth century and has a Western fabric. The first issue in 1852 for Mindon Ming (1852–78) consisted of the silver rupee with divisionary pieces down to the sixteenth. The common appellation of peacock rupees for these coins is inspired by the obverse type of a peacock with tail in splendour, while the reverse is simply the value in wreath (Pl. 1021). A copper quarter-anna in 1865 had similar types but on the obverse of the half-anna in 1869 appeared the Burmese lion which also formed the obverse for the $2\frac{1}{2}$ mu in gold in 1866. The issue of the gold rupee and multiples of 2 and 5 rupees in 1880 for Thebaw (1878–85) used the peacock type on obverse. Burma, incorporated in Britain's Indian empire in the late nineteenth century, had no individual coinage until the restoration of Burmese independence in 1948. The Republic of Burma adopted for its first coinage of nickel pieces from 8 annas down to half-anna in 1949, the traditional Burmese lion on obverse and value in wreath on the reverse. The types were retained on the new coinage of 1952 based on the kyat (rupee), divisible into 100 pyas. Some of the lower values were struck on a square flan or with a scalloped edge (Pl. 1022). The new coinage in 1966 has the portrait of Ne Win on obverse.

SIAM

The earliest currency of Siam is not a true coinage within the terms of our definition for it was in the form of silver bracelets which are assigned to the period of the seventh to the ninth century. An even more unusual currency is the silver *ka'kim*, conical in shape but with a piercing. Silver bars or *lats* with stamps on the upper surface also were used as currency. Yet another category of silver currency in Siam is the bat or tical, a bullet-shaped piece with turned-in ends (Pl. 1023). The bat, however, qualifies to be rated as a coin as pieces of this kind carry a number of guaranteeing stamps, have consistent weight standards and some issues are furnished with divisionary pieces. It is thought that the introduction of this class of coinage may have taken place as early as the beginning of the fourteenth century and a classification of this coinage has been made, attributing various of the marks stamped on the coins to specific kings. This 'bullet' coinage continued to be produced up to the late nineteenth century and overlapped the introduction of a European-type coinage by the Siamese king, Mongkut (1851–68).

The unit of the new coinage retained the name of tical or bat and was divided into 8 fuang, each of 8 att. The types on the first issue were identical for all denominations, on the obverse the tall Siamese crown flanked by ornate umbrellas and leaf-scrolls and on the reverse an elephant at the centre of a *chakram* or wheel design (Pl. 1024). Coins of 8, 4 and 2 bat were struck in gold, the bat and portions down to a sixteenth in silver and 2 and 4 att in copper. Similar coinage was issued for Chulalongkorn (1868–1910) at the outset of the reign, except that the leaf-scrolls disappeared from the obverse; but a new coinage in 1888 placed the king's portrait with his name and titles on the obverse and Siamese royal arms on the reverse on the silver denominations. A subsidiary nickel coinage in values of 20 down to 2½ satang, a hundred of which now formed a bat, had a facing elephant on obverse and value in wreath on the reverse. The facing elephant was also adopted on this ruler's final issue of the silver bat and on the silver of his successor Rama VI (1910–25). Satang pieces, now with a central piercing, had inscription on obverse and *chakra* design on the reverse. Only slight modifications were effected on the issues of Prajadhipok (1925–33) but the coinage of Ananda Mahidol (1933–46), in satang values only, showed, on the issues of 1946, the portrait of the young king on obverse and a facing winged deity on the reverse. The satang coins in aluminium-bronze of the present sovereign, Phumiphol, show his portrait on obverse and the royal arms on the reverse (Pl. 1025).

MALAYA

Indigenous coinage of the Malay peninsula is somewhat scanty or perhaps it would be more true to say that knowledge of this coinage is still very imperfect. A coinage has been identified of the sultans of Kedah, consisting of base silver pieces with Malay and Arabic inscriptions with dates ranging from the seventeenth to the eighteenth century. A further series from Kedah is in the form of tin coins with a central hole with Malay and Arabic inscriptions on the obverse and dates in the early nineteenth century on the reverse. Coins of the sultans of Johore of much the same period are of an unusual octagonal shape (Pl. 1026). Another coinage in tin was issued by the rajahs of Patani in the first half of the nineteenth century. These coins are pieces of about an inch in diameter with a large hole at the centre with a Malay inscription giving the place name on the obverse and an Arabic inscription with date on the reverse. Tin coins of similar fabric were also issued at Sanggora with inscription in Chinese characters on the obverse and in Malay and Arabic on the reverse. The most unusual coinage in Malaya is the 'tin-hat' money of Pahang, also in the earlier nineteenth century. These pieces, in shape like a square-sided hat with sloping sides and a broad brim, were produced in three denominations with inscriptions stamped on the brim. The ampat or 4 cent piece measures some three inches across, the dua or 2 cent piece an inch-and-a-half and the satu or 1 cent piece one inch.

The next phase of coinage in Malaya is that of the East India Company and of the British domination of the peninsula. For the island of Pulu Penang just off the western coast, secured as a trading settlement in the later eighteenth century, the East India Company issued a coinage in 1788. This consisted of the half, quarter and tenth of a dollar in silver and the cent, quarter and tenth of a cent in copper. The types were similar on all denominations; on the obverse was the company's bale-mark, a heart-shaped frame, divided diagonally into compartments containing the initials of the company, the whole surmounted by a symbol like the figure 4, while the reverse carried an inscription in Persian (Pl. 1027). The company's arms and inscription in wreath formed the types of the copper cent in 1810 and the 2, 1 and ½ pice in 1825 and 1828. Only one issue of copper coins of 1 and 2 kapangs was made for Malacca in 1831 with types a cock on obverse and inscription on reverse.

For Malaya generally an issue of the copper cent and its portions in 1845 carried the portrait of Victoria on obverse and the name of the East India Company and the value on the reverse. On a similar issue in 1862 the name of the East India Company had disappeared and was replaced by that of the India Straits in a circular inscription around the value figure. Later in Victoria's reign the name was again altered to the Straits Settlements but the types otherwise remained unchanged in an issue in silver of coins of 50, 20, 10 and 5 cents (Pl. 1028). This pattern of types continued under Edward VII on copper and silver except for the dollar which had a leaf-and-scroll reverse. Another silver dollar may be mentioned here, although it was issued not specifically for the Straits Settlements but for all Far

Eastern trade. This 'British dollar' has a standing Britannia on obverse with the words *One Dollar* as the sole inscription, while the reverse has leaf-and-scroll design similar to that of the Straits Settlements dollar. This dollar, first issued in 1895, was struck at intervals up to 1935 (Pl. 1029). Apart from the obverse portrait there was little change in succeeding reigns. From 1939 the reverse inscription was altered to *Commissioners of Currency Malaya* and the coinage with portrait of Elizabeth II was inscribed *Malaya and British Borneo* on the reverse (Pl. 1030). The coinage of the Federation of Malaysia formed in 1963 has a dollar unit of 100 sen. Denominations from 50 sen downwards have a value reverse inscribed *Malaysia*.

INDO-CHINA

This territorial designation includes, in terms of modern states, the kingdoms of Cambodia and Laos and the Republic of Vietnam which, since 1954, has been partitioned into South Vietnam and Communist North Vietnam. The numismatic history of Indo-China falls into three phases, indigenous coinage, principally of the Annamese kingdom, the coinage of Indo-China as a French colony and finally the issues of the new independent states.

Since Annam from its earliest history was a tributary of the Chinese empire its coinage for many centuries was similar to the Chinese, namely a series of copper or bronze cast coins of cash denomination with character inscriptions on the obverse and sometimes on the reverse and with a square central hole (Pl. 1031). The earliest series of these copper cash are ascribed to the later tenth century and, with changes of the characters inscribed on the obverse, similar coins were issued up to the time of French colonization in the nineteenth century. A further category of coinage, mainly of nineteenth-century date, is that of the silver taels and portions of Europeanized fabric with types, a rayed sun at the centre of the obverse with four characters around and a dragon on the reverse. This class of silver money was used as presentation money by the Annamese kings. Another unusual coinage in later Annam consists of silver bars inscribed with characters on both back and front (Pl. 1032). The kingdom of Cambodia issued a modern-type coinage in 1860 with the portrait of King Norodom I and his title in French on the obverse, and the royal arms and a native-script legend with the value in French also on the reverse. The franc with multiples up to 5 francs (piastre) and divisionary pieces were struck in silver and 5 and 10 centimes in bronze, all with the same types (Pl. 1033).

A French colonial coinage was issued from 1879 to 1885 for Cochin China with a piastre and fractions expressed in centimes in silver as well as a bronze centime piece. The types were the seated figure of the republic and the value, the inscriptions all being in French. A bronze sapeque or cash was also issued with obverse inscription in French and reverse inscription in Chinese. A zinc sapeque of like types was produced for Tonkin in 1905 and the sapeque, cast in copper or brass, continued to be issued with traditional Annamese types at intervals up to 1926 in the reign of the French puppet ruler, Bao Dai. From 1885 a French colonial coinage was produced for the whole area with types similar to those described for Cochin China but now with the name of Indo-China on the reverse (Pl. 1034). The issues for Indo-China by the Vichy government were confined to centime values struck in zinc. The post-war coinage with obverse bust of the republic and rice-shoots on the reverse was in cupro-nickel for the piastre and aluminium for the centime values.

The first coinage of modern Cambodia in 1953 revived types from the rare coins of ancient Cambodia such as the mythical bird on the 10 centime. All reverses bore the state name in French and value in French and local script. The Laotian coinage begun in 1952 used such local types as the monument consisting of the fore-parts of three elephants on the 20 centime. In South Vietnam, with a dong unit divided into 100 su or xu, the obverse on various xu values showed three portraits representing the provinces of Cochin China, Annam and Tonkin. The obverse on dong values from 1964 pictured a rice plant. On North Vietnamese issues the 20 xu bore the communist star and dong values or the portrait of Ho Chi Minh.

EAST INDIES

Coinage native to the islands of the Indian Archipelago, now mostly grouped in the state of Indonesia, is comparatively rare, and substantive issues of coinage associated with the islands first make their appearance with the spread of the activities of the Dutch East India Company. After the issues produced by the company, there followed the coinage of the colony of the Dutch East Indies and finally the issues of the independent state of Indonesia from 1950.

The most ancient coinage of the islands is a series of small gold pieces, similar in fabric to the fanams of south India but stamped with characters in an incuse. These pieces have been identified as coins of the Hindu period in Java as early as the tenth century. Another series of similar fabric but slightly larger in module and struck in silver is placed after the gold coins and certainly had ceased by about the thirteenth century when the currency commonly in use was the bronze Chinese cash. A series of coin-like pieces in brass with a square hole at the centre have as the general type two 'deities' with a tree above on the one side and a collection of symbols on the other. These pieces were used as temple money not as regular coinage and, though some are of a certain antiquity, they continued to be produced until comparatively modern times. Coins known as pitis were issued in tin with a round hole at centre by some of the small constituent states of Java (Pl. 1035). Coins of this category in Bantam in the eighteenth century have an inscription on obverse and a blank reverse. Similar coins from Cheribon, also in the eighteenth century, have either an inscription formed by four Chinese characters or the name *Cheribon* in Western script.

In the island of Sumatra small gold and silver pagoda-like pieces similar to those described above in Java are attributed to Fantsour. A somewhat more substantial series of coins is that of the sultans of Atjih who struck a coinage in gold from the sixteenth to the eighteenth centuries with inscriptions in local script on the obverse and in Arabic on the reverse (Pl. 1036). Other coinage in Sumatra is mainly in the form of tin pitis. Those issued by Siyak in the seventeenth and eighteenth centuries have a large circular hole at the centre and resemble washers, as do those of Djambi, though some of the latter have an octagonal outline. The tin pitis of Palembang, some round, some octagonal, have a much smaller central hole. On all the piti coinage only the obverse carries an inscription.

The islands further to the east have even fewer coinage series. Copper or bronze cash of Chinese type were issued in Borneo in the seventeenth century and in the late eighteenth and early nineteenth centuries there was a coinage imitating the copper doits of the East India Company. The obverse usually retained a fair copy of the company's monogram but the shield on the reverse, in place of displaying the arms of one of the provinces of the Netherlands, as on the originals, bears an Arabic inscription. The only coinage of any consequence in the Celebes is that of the sultans of Macassar who in the sixteenth and seventeenth centuries struck a gold coinage with inscriptions on both sides.

The beginnings of Dutch coinage for trade in the East are remarkably similar to the English 'portcullis' silver (see p. 523). The issue, made like the English in 1601, also consisted of silver coins equivalent to the Spanish 8, 4, 2 and 1 real coins, with fractional pieces of a $\frac{1}{2}$ and a $\frac{1}{4}$. The coins issued by the United Amsterdam Company had the arms of the province of Holland and inscription *Insignia Hollandiae* and the value on obverse, and the arms of Amsterdam and inscription *Et Civitatis Amstelredamensis* on the reverse. Like the similar English coinage this issue was not long continued. The next coinage, produced in 1645, consisted of silver pieces of 48, 24 and 12 stuivers with wreath and sword on obverse and the initials of the East India Company, the Vereenigde Oost-Indische Compagnie, VOC, in monogram on the reverse. In the eighteenth century coinage of silver ducatoons, 3 and 1 guilder pieces was struck with the identical types of the provincial issues in the Netherlands but with the VOC monogram placed below the provincial arms on the reverse (Pl. 1037). A parallel series of copper doits had the company's monogram on obverse and the provincial arms on the reverse (Pl. 1038).

In addition to such coinages produced in the Netherlands for use in the East Indies rupees in silver and gold coins struck from silver-rupee dies were issued in Java with Arabic and Javanese inscriptions in the later eighteenth century. In the last years of the eighteenth century an emergency coinage of copper 'bonks' was struck. These were rough lumps cut from rods of copper and stamped with the value 1 S (1 stuiver) or 2 S (2 stuivers) on the obverse and the date, ranging from 1796 to 1799, on the reverse (Pl. 1039). In the same period doits were issued in tin with VOC on obverse and the value 1 doit on the reverse.

The decline of the company coincided approximately with the establishment of the Batavian Republic in the Netherlands and the next coinage for the East Indies struck in 1802 bears the inscriptions of the republican period. Denominations in silver ranged from the guilder down to the sixteenth of the guilder and had as types a sailing ship on obverse with the inscription *Indiae Batavorum* and on the reverse the arms of Holland with legend *Mo Arg Ord Foed Belg Hol* (Pl. 1040). Copper doits and half-doits of this issue replaced the traditional VOC monogram on the reverse by *Indiae Batav* and the date, while the provincial arms of the obverse were flanked by the figures $5-\frac{1}{16}$ G or $5-\frac{1}{32}$ G, indicating that 5 doits or 10 half-doits equalled one sixteenth of a guilder. This was an error, for the guilder of this issue was current at 24 stuivers (96 doits) not 20 (80 doits) as indicated on the coins; the value should have read $6-\frac{1}{16}$ G. In the early years of the 1800's rupees and halves with inscriptional types were also issued and copper 'bonks' of 1 and 2 stuiver values. In the reign of Napoleon's brother Louis as King of Holland copper doits were issued with his initials LN in monogram on the obverse and Java and the date 1810 on the reverse. The stuiver and half had similar types with the value, e.g. 1–St., flanking the monogram on the obverse and 'bonks' of 1 and 2 stuivers were also issued in the same year.

During the British occupation of the Dutch East Indies from 1811 to 1816 gold rupees and halves were struck with the inscription 'Money of the English Coy' in Javanese on the obverse and Arabic on the reverse. On the copper stuiver, its half and quarter the obverse carried the East India Company's bale-mark containing the letters VEIC and surmounted by B on the obverse and *Java* and date on the reverse (Pl. 1042). Lead doits in 1813–14 were marked with the company's initials on the obverse and the value and *Java* on the reverse.

From the recovery of the East Indies possessions in 1816 a regal coinage was issued for use in the islands. Under William I (1815–40) the types on the guilder and its divisions were similar to those of the Netherlands itself but with *Nederlandsch Indie* added under the arms on the reverse. The copper cent altered its types to arms and value on obverse and *Nederl. Indie* on the reverse. For William III (1849–90) further standardization of types and values took place. In silver the ¼, ¹⁄₁₀ and ¹⁄₂₀ guilder were issued and the 2½, 1 and ½ cent in copper; on all, the types were arms, *Nederlandsch Indie* and value on obverse, and inscriptions in Javanese, Malay and Arabic on the reverse with no mention of the ruler's name. A similar coinage was issued in the reign of Queen Wilhelmina (Pl. 1041) from 1890 until the capture of the Dutch East Indies by the Japanese in 1941 and then briefly after the liberation of the islands in 1945.

The islands became the independent republic of Indonesia in 1950. The unit of the new coinage is the rupiah of 100 sen. On aluminium coins of 10 and 25 sen issued in 1952 the types are an heraldic eagle with shield of arms obverse and the state name, value and date on the reverse. Sen coinage for the Riau Archipelago and West Irian in 1962 and 1963 carried the portrait of President Sukarno.

Coinage has also been issued for various British possessions in the East Indies. In Sumatra where the British East India Company had been established since 1686, copper coins of 3, 2 and 1 kapang in 1786 had as types the bale-mark on obverse and value and date in Arabic on the reverse. On a later issue in 1810 the obverse was changed to the company's arms. Copper kapangs for the island of Labuan off the north coast of Borneo had similar types except that the company's arms on obverse were accompanied by *Island of Sultana* and not the company's name. A cock and a many-pointed star were the types on the copper kapang of Celebes in 1834. The British North Borneo Company issued copper cents in 1891 with the company's arms on obverse and the value in wreath on the reverse. Later, when North Borneo became a British colony, the arms were retained as obverse type but the company's name was replaced by *State of North Borneo* accompanying the value on the reverse. Various cent values were issued between 1903 and 1941. Sarawak, ruled by the Brooke family as rajahs, had a coinage with the rajah's portrait and name on the obverse and value in wreath on the reverse. The cent and its portions in copper and higher values in silver were issued for three successive Brooke rajahs between 1863 and 1937 (Pl. 1043).

HONG KONG

Coinage has been issued for the British colony since 1863. The types on various cent values 5 to 50 in silver and on the cent in copper were the royal portrait and the colony's name and value in English and Chinese (Pl. 1044). A silver dollar and its half were struck between 1865 and 1868 with regal-portrait obverse and a scroll design enclosing Chinese characters on the reverse, together with the inscription, e.g. *One Dollar Hong Kong*. In later reigns the silver dollar was not issued. The simple inscribed reverses have remained unchanged in successive reigns but in 1960 the dollar with crowned lion type was re-issued in cupro-nickel.

THE PHILIPPINES

For the Spanish colony of the Philippine Islands, the earliest coinage was issued under Charles III in 1766 in the form of copper quartos with a castle and inscription *Cuidad de Man(ila)* on obverse and the arms of the Philippines on the reverse. In the first half of the nineteenth century coinage continued to be of copper quartos, the usual types being a crowned lion on obverse and arms of Spain on the reverse. For Isabel II (1833–70) this copper-quarto coinage was reinforced by issues in gold of the peso and multiples up to 4 and of silver coins of 50, 20 and 10 centimos values. The types on all were the royal portrait on obverse and on reverse the Spanish arms with an additional inscription, *Filippinas*, below the shield. Similar silver coins and the gold 4 pesos were struck for Alfonso XII (1875–85) and in 1897 the last Spanish coinage for the Philippines was the silver peso of Alfonso XIII.

Following the Spanish-American war, the Philippines were bought by the United States in 1898. On the peso and centavo values from 50 down to 10 in silver the obverse showed a standing female figure with a volcano in the background, while the reverse carried the arms and title of the United States of America. A seated male figure and the volcano appeared on the nickel 5 centavos and the bronze centavo and its half, all of which had the same reverse as the silver coins (Pl. 1045). The issues after the creation of the Commonwealth of the Philippines in 1935 continued the denominations, less the peso, and the types of the earlier coinage, but the arms of the United States on the reverse were replaced by those of the Commonwealth. A special issue of the silver peso in 1935 had on its obverse the jugate busts of President Roosevelt and President Quezon of the Philippines. In 1936 the silver peso and its half bore the busts of Governor-General Murphy and President Quezon. After the liberation of the islands from the Japanese the Philippines became an independent republic in 1946. The first coinage of silver peso and 50 centavos in silver in 1947 with arms-and-value reverse carried on the obverse the portrait of General MacArthur inscribed *Defender and Liberator of the Philippines*.

A new cupro-nickel coinage was issued in 1958. The 25 and 50 centavos pieces repeated the types of female figure and volcano on reverse and the 1, 5 and 10 centavos coins the seated male figure and volcano which had appeared on earlier coins. The obverse, the usual shield of arms, now has an inscription *Central Bank of the Philippines*. Issues of special peso coins include one in 1967 commemorating the Bataan and Corregidor campaigns. On the new coinage of 1967, a peso unit of 100 sentimos, the arms obverse is inscribed *Republic of The Philippines*, and the various sentimo reverses present a series of portrait types.

SINGAPORE

The first coinage of this new state in 1967 consists of the dollar and various cent denominations. The obverses represent local flora and fauna with value and name on the reverse.

Select Bibliography

GENERAL

COMENCINI, M. *Coins of the modern world, 1870–1936*. London, 1937.

FORRER, L. S. *The art of collecting coins*. London, 1955.

FREY, A. R. *Dictionary of numismatic names*. New York, 1947.

FRIEDBERG, R. *Gold coins of the world, A.D. 600–1958*. New York, 1958.

FRIEDENSBURG, F. *Die Münzen in der Kulturgeschichte*. Berlin, 1926.

GRIERSON, P. *Bibliographie numismatique*. Brussels, 1966.

LAGERQUIST, L. O. and NATHOORST-BÖÖS, E. *Mynt och medaljer och annam numismatik*. Stockholm, 1960.

LANE-POOLE, S. *Coins and medals: their place in history*. London, 1894.

LINECAR, H. W. A. *Beginner's guide to coin collecting*. London, 1966.

MACDONALD, G. *The evolution of coinage*. London, 1935.

MARTINORI, R. *La Moneta*. Rome, 1915.

MILNE, J. G., SUTHERLAND, C. H. V. and THOMPSON, J. D. A. *Coin collecting*. Oxford, 1951.

PORTEOUS, J. *Coins in history*. London, 1969.

RAWLINGS, G. B. *Coins and how to know them*. London, 1935.

RAYMOND, W. *Coins of the world—Nineteenth-century issues*. New York, 1953.

RAYMOND, W. *Coins of the world—Twentieth-century issues*. New York, 1952.

RENTZMANN, W. *Numismatisches Legenden-Lexicon des Mittelalters und der Neuzeit*. Berlin, 1865–6.

SALLET, A. VON. *Münzen und Medaillen*. Berlin, 1898.

SCHLICKEYSEN, F. W. A. *Erklärung der Abkürzungen auf Münzen der neueren Zeit, des Mittelalters und des Alterthums*. Berlin, 1896.

SCHRÖTTER, F. VON. *Wörterbuch der Münzkunde*. Berlin-Leipzig, 1930.

SUTHERLAND, C. H. V. *Art in coinage*. London, 1955.

YEOMAN, R. S. *A catalogue of modern world coins*. 8th edition. Racine, 1968.

YEOMAN, R. S. *Current coins of the world*. 3rd edition. Racine, 1969.

PARTICULAR

NEW WORLD
General

ADAMS, E. H. *Catalogue of the collection of Julius Guttag, comprising the coinage of Mexico, Central America, South America and the West Indies.* New York, 1929.

RAYMOND, W. *Spanish-American gold coins.* New York, 1936.

RAYMOND, W. *The gold coins of North and South America.* New York, 1937.

RAYMOND, W. *The silver dollars of North and South America.* New York, 1939.

WEYL, A. *Katalog der Jules Fonrobert'schen Sammlung überseeischer Münzen und Medaillen.* vols. 1–3. Berlin, 1878–9.

Particular

NORTH AMERICA
Canada

CHARLTON, J. E. 1970 *Standard catalogue of Canadian coins, tokens and paper money.* Racine, 1970.

TAYLOR, H. C. and JAMES, S. *A guide book of Canadian coins, currency and tokens.* 2nd edition. Winnipeg, 1960.

United States

CROSBY, S. S. *The early coins of America.* Boston, 1878.

NOE, S. P. *The New England and Willow Tree coinage of Massachusetts.* New York, 1943.

NOE, S. P. *The Oak Tree coinage of Massachusetts.* New York, 1947.

NOE, S. P. *The Pine Tree coinage of Massachusetts.* New York, 1952.

YEOMAN, R. S. *A guide book of United States coins.* 23rd edition. Racine, 1970.

Mexico

MEEK, W. T. *The exchange media of colonial Mexico.* New York, 1948.

PRADEAU, F. *Historia numismatica de Mexico desde la epoca precortesiana hasta 1823.* Mexico City, 1950.

CENTRAL AMERICA

GURDIAN, R. *Contribucion al estudio de las monedas de Costa Rica.* San José, 1958.

PROBER, K. *Historia numismatica de Guatemala.* Sao Paulo, 1954.

SOUTH AMERICA

LEITAO, S. *Catalogo de moedas brasileiros de 1643–1967*. Rio de Janeiro, 1967.

MEDINA, J. T. *Las monedas chilenas*. Santiago, 1902.

MEILI, J. *Das brazilianische Geldwesen*. 3 vols. Zürich, 1897–1905.

ROSA, A. *Medallas y monedas de la republica Argentina*. Buenos Aires, 1898.

SALLES OLIVIERA, A. DE. *Moedas do Brasil*. vol. I. *Moedas y barras de ouro*. Sao Paulo, 1944.

TAULLARD, A. *Monedas de la republica Argentina*. Buenos Aires, 1924.

WEST INDIES

LISMORE, T. *The coinage of Cuba*. Havana, 1955.

WOOD, H. *The coinage of the West Indies with special reference to the cut and counter-stamped pieces*. New York, 1914.

AUSTRALASIA
General

ANDREW, A. *Australasian tokens and coins*. Sydney, 1921.

SUTHERLAND, A. *Numismatic history of New Zealand*. New Plymouth, 1939–41.

WEYL, A. *Katalog der Jules Fonrobert'schen Sammlung überseeischer Münzen und Medaillen*. Vol. 4. Berlin, 1879.

AFRICA
General

WEYL, A. *Katalog der Jules Fonrobert'schen Sammlung überseeischer Münzen und Medaillen*. Vol. 4. Berlin, 1879.

Special

ANZANI, A. *Numismatica Auxumita*. Reprinted from *Rivista Italiana di Numismatica*. Milan, 1926.

KAPLAN, A. *Catalogue of the coins of South Africa*. Germiston, 1950.

PARSONS, H. A. *The colonial coinages of British Africa with the adjacent islands*. London, 1950.

NEAR EAST

GÖBL, R. *Aufbau der Münzprägung*. (Sassanian coinage) in *Ein Asiatischer Staat* by F. Altheim and R. Stiehl. Wiesbaden, 1954.

HAZARD, H. W. *The numismatic history of late mediaeval North Africa*. New York, 1952.

LANE POOLE, S. *Catalogue of Oriental coins in the British Museum*. 10 vols. London: I. The Eastern Khaleefehs, 1875; II. Amawee Khaleefehs of Spain and lesser Spanish dynasties; Ghaznawees, Buweyhees, etc., 1876; III. The Turkuman houses of the Seljook, Urtuk, Zengee, etc., 1877; IV. The Fatimee Khaleefehs, the Ayyoobees and the Memlook Sultans, 1879; V. The Moors of Africa and Spain; Kings and Imams of the Yemen, 1880; VI. The Mongols, 1881; VII. Bukhara (Transoxiana), 1882; VIII. Othmanlee Sultans, 1883; IX. Additions to vols. I-IV, 1889; X. Additions to vols. V-VIII, 1890.

LANE POOLE, S. *Catalogue of the coins of the Shahs of Persia in the British Museum*. London, 1877.

LANG, D. M. *Studies in the numismatic history of Georgia in Transcaucasia*. New York, 1955.

LAVOIX, H. *Catalogue des monnaies musulmanes de la Bibliothèque Nationale*. 3 vols. Paris, 1887–96. I. *The Eastern Caliphs;* II. *Spain and Africa;* III. *Egypt and Syria.*

MAYER, L. A. *Bibliography of Moslem numismatics, India excluded*. London, 1939.

NÜTZEL, H. *Katalog der orientalischen Münzen (Königliche Museen zu Berlin)*. 2 vols. Berlin, 1898–1902. I. *The Eastern Caliphs;* II. *Spain and Western North Africa.*

PARUCK, F. D. J. *Sassanian coins*. Bombay, 1924.

RABINO DI BORGOMALE, H. L. *Coins, medals and seals of the Shahs of Iran, 1500–1941*. Hertford, 1941.

RIVERO, C. M. DEL. *La moneda arabigo-española*. Madrid, 1933.

VALENTINE, W. E. *Modern copper coins of the Muhammadan states*. London, 1911.

WALKER, J. *Catalogue of the Muhammadan coins in the British Museum*. 2 vols. London: I. *A catalogue of the Arab-Sassanian coins*. 1941; II. *A catalogue of the Arab-Byzantine and post-reform Umaiyad coins*. 1956.

INDIA

BROWN, C. J. *The Coins of India*. Calcutta, 1922.

CODRINGTON, H. W. *Ceylon coins and currency*. Colombo, 1924.

ELLIOTT, W. *Coins of southern India*. London, 1886.

SINGHAL, C. R. *Bibliography of Indian coins.* Part I. *Non-Muhammadan series;* Part II. *Muhammadan and later series.* Bombay, 1950–2.

VALENTINE, W. H. *The copper coins of India.* 2 vols. London, 1914–20.

Catalogues

Catalogue of Indian coins in the British Museum. 7 vols. London: P. Gardner, *The coins of the Greek and Scythic kings of Bactria and India,* 1886; J. Allan, *The coins of ancient India,* 1936; E. J. Rapson, *The coins of the Andhra dynasty, the Western Ksatrapas,* etc., 1908; J. Allan, *The coins of the Gupta dynasties and of Sasanka, king of Gauda,* 1914; S. Lane Poole, *The coins of the sultans of Delhi,* 1894; do., *The coins of the Mohammadan states of India,* 1885; do., *The coins of the Moghul emperors,* 1892.

Catalogue of the coins in the Indian Museum, Calcutta, 4 vols. Oxford: V. A. Smith, *The early foreign dynasties and the Guptas,* etc. 1906; H. N. Wright, *The sultans of Delhi and contemporary dynasties in India,* 1907; do., *The Mughal emperors of India,* 1908; J. Allan, ed., *Coins of the Native States of India,* (i) *Coins of Awadh* (C. J. Brown), (ii) *Coins of Mysore and South India,* (J. R. Henderson), (iii) *Bombay, Rajputana and Central India* (W. H. Valentine), 1928.

Catalogue of the coins in the Punjab Museum, Lahore. 3 vols. Oxford; 1914–34: R. B. Whitehead, I. *Indo-Greek coins*; II. *Coins of the Moghul emperors*; III. *Coins of Nadir Shah and the Durrani dynasty.*

Catalogue of coins in the Central Museum, Madras. 4 vols. Madras, 1888–90. E. Thurston, I. *Mysore*; II. *Roman, Indo-Portuguese and Ceylon*; III. *Sultans of Delhi*; IV. *East India Company.*

Catalogue of coins in the Provincial Museum, Lucknow. I. C. J. Brown, *Coins of the Guptas,* etc., Allahabad, 1920; II. P. Dyal, *Coins of the Sultans of Delhi,* Allahabad 1925; III. C. J. Brown, *Coins of the Mughal emperors,* Oxford, 1920.

FAR EAST

COUPERIE, A. T. DE LA. *Catalogue of Chinese coins from the seventh century* B.C. *to* A.D. 621 *included in the collection in the British Museum.* London, 1892.

JACOBS, N. and VERMEULE, C. C. *Japanese coinage.* New York, 1953.

KANN, E. *Illustrated catalog of Chinese coins.* Los Angeles, 1954.

LE MAY, R. *The Coinage of Siam.* Bangkok, 1932.

LOCKHART, J. H. S. *The currency of the Far East from the earliest times up to the present day.* 3 vols. Hong Kong, 1895–8.

SELECT BIBLIOGRAPHY

LOCKHART, J. H. S. *The Stewart Lockhart collection of Chinese coins*. Shanghai, 1915.

MILLIES, H. C. *Recherches sur les monnaies des indigènes de l'archipel Indien et de la peninsule malaie*. The Hague, 1871.

MUNRO, N. G. *Coins of Japan*. Yokohama, 1904.

PHAYRE, A. P. *Coins of Arakan, of Pegu, and of Burma*. (*Numismata Orientalia*. vol. 3. Part I.). London, 1882.

SCHJOTH, F. *The currency of the Far East*. London, 1929.

SCHROEDER, A. *Annam, Etudes numismatiques*. Paris, 1905.

Illustrations

(The coins are illustrated by courtesy of the Trustees of the British Museum.)
The metal of each coin is indicated by the following abbreviations:

N=gold   Al.br.=aluminium-   El.=electrum
R=silver   bronze   N=nickel
Æ=bronze   Bill.=billon   P=lead
Al.=aluminium   CN=Cupro-nickel   Pot.=potin

COINS OF THE NEW WORLD, PLATES 48–51

772. Canada; Louis XV, Æ 9 deniers, 1721.	417
773. Canada; Quebec, Æ token halfpenny, 1837.	417
774. Canada; Victoria; R 20 cents, 1858.	417
775. Canada; Ontario, Æ token halfpenny, 1852.	417
776. Canada; Nova Scotia, Æ token halfpenny, 1832.	418
777. Canada; Victoria; R 25 cents, 1874.	418
778. Canada; George V, R dollar, 1935.	418
779. Newfoundland; George VI, R dollar, 1949.	419
780. United States; 'Hog money', Æ sixpence, 1616.	420
781. United States; Massachusetts, R shilling, 1652.	420
782. United States; Maryland, R shilling, 1659.	420
783. United States; George II, Æ twopence, 1722–4.	420
784. United States; R dollar, 1799.	423
785. United States; Æ cent, 1812.	423
786. United States; Æ cent, 1864.	425
787. United States; N dollar, 1862.	425
788. United States; N 5 cents, 1913.	426
789. United States; Æ cent, 1955.	426
790. Mexico; Charles I and Johanna, R 4 reales, 1521–56.	428
791. Mexico; Philip V, N 2 escudos, 1735.	429
792. Mexico; Philip V, R 8 reales, 1732.	429
793. Mexico; Republic, R real, 1826.	431
794. Mexico; Emperor Maximilian, R 50 centavos, 1866.	431
795. Guatemala; R real, 1824.	432

page

796. Guatemala; ℞ 10 centavos, 1928.   433
797. British Honduras; Elizabeth II, brass 5 cents, 1956.   433
798. Honduras; ℞ ½ real, 1869.   433
799. Nicaragua; ℞ 25 centavos, 1939.   434
800. Salvador; ₦ 20 colones, 1925.   435
801. Costa Rica; ℞ ¼ peso, 1850.   435
802. Panama; ℞ 10 centesimos, 1904.   436
803. Colombia (New Granada); ℞ real, 1813.   438
804. Colombia; Æ cuartino, 1830.   438
805. Colombia; ₦ 5 pesos, 1919.   438
806. Venezuela; ℞ ½ bolivar, 1903.   439
807. Ecuador; ℞ 2 decimos, 1895.   440
808. Peru; Philip II, ℞ 8 reales, 1575–98.   440
809. Peru; Æ ¼ peso, 1823.   440
810. Bolivia; ℞ sueldo, 1856.   441
811. Chile; ℞ real, 1834.   442
812. Argentina; ℞ 2 reales, 1825.   443
813. Uruguay; ₦ 10 centimos, 1953.   443
814. Paraguay; Brass 15 centimos, 1953.   444
815. Brasil; Peter II, ℞ ½ pataca, 1696.   445
816. Brasil; John V, Æ 10 reis, 1749.   445
817. Brasil; Emperor Peter II, Æ 40 reis, 1832.   445
818. British Guiana; George III, Æ ½ stiver, 1813.   447
819. French Guiana (Cayenne); Louis XVI, Æ 2 sous, 1782.   447
820. Dutch Guiana; Æ stuiver, 1679.   447
821. Haiti; Henri Christophe, Æ centième, 1807.   448
822. Haiti; ℞ 20 centimes, 1890.   449
823. Cuba; ₦ 5 pesos, 1915.   450
824. Danish West Indies; Frederick V, ℞ skilling, 1748.   451
825. Curaçao; ℞ real, 1821.   451
826. French West Indies; Louis XV, ℞ 12 sols, 1731.   452
827. Guadeloupe; ₦ franc, 1903.   452
828. British West Indies; Trinidad, ℞ cut Spanish real, 18th cent.   452
829. British West Indies; Barbados, Æ penny, 1788.   453
830. British West Indies; Jamaica, brass penny, 1937.   453
831. British Caribbean Territories; C₦ 10 cents, 1955.   453

COINS OF AUSTRALASIA, PLATE 52

    page

832. Australia; Æ token halfpenny, Melbourne, 1860.   457
833. Australia; Edward VII, ℞ florin, 1910.   458
834. Australia; George VI, Æ penny, 1951.   458
835. New Guinea; Edward VIII, Æ penny, 1936.   458
836. New Zealand; George V, ℞ florin, 1933.   459
837. New Zealand; George VI, ℞ crown, 1949.   459
838. Fiji; George VI, ℞ sixpence, 1941.   459
839. Hawaii; Kalakauai, ℞ ¼ dollar, 1883.   459

COINS OF AFRICA, PLATES 52–53

840. Abyssinia; Ezanas, N, c. 330.   463
841. Abyssinia; Armah, Æ, c. 7th century.   464
842. Abyssinia; Menelik II, ℞ ¼ talari, 1894.   464
843. Abyssinia; Haile Selassie, ℞ 50 cents, 1944.   464
844. Egypt, Sultan Husein Kamil, ℞ 2 piastres, 1917.   464
845. Egypt; Fuad 1, CN 10 milliemes, 1924.   464
846. Egypt; Republic, Al.br. 10 milliemes, 1954.   465
847. Libya; Idris I, CN 1 piastre, 1952.   465
848. Tunisia; Republic, CN 20 francs, 1949.   465
849. Morocco; Sultan Muhammad Ben Yussuf, CN 20 francs, 1947.   466
850. Liberia; Æ 1 cent, 1866.   466
851. British West Africa; George V, ℞ florin, 1913.   466
852. British West Africa; Edward VIII, N penny, 1936.   466
853. Ghana; Nkruma, CN shilling, 1958.   467
854. South Africa; Kruger, N pond, 1896.   467
855. South Africa; George V, ℞ shilling, 1936.   467
856. South Africa; George VI, Æ halfpenny, 1938.   467
857. South Africa; Republic, Æ 1 cent, 1961.   468
858. East Africa; George VI, ℞ shilling, 1946.   468
859. East Africa; George VI, Æ 5 cents, 1952.   468
860. Southern Rhodesia; George V, ℞ florin, 1935.   468
861. Southern Rhodesia; George VI, Æ halfpenny, 1944.   468
862. Rhodesia and Nyasaland; Elizabeth II, Æ penny, 1955.   468

page

863. French Cameroons; Brass 50 centimes, 1925. 469
864. Mozambique; Ⓝ br. 1 escudo, 1950. 469
865. The Congo; Albert, Ⓡ 50 centimes, 1921. 470

NEAR EASTERN COINS, PLATES 54–56

866. Sassanian Empire; Ardashir I, Ⓡ drachm, A.D. 226–240. 474
867. Sassanian Empire; Bahram II, Ⓡ drachm, A.D. 275–283. 474
868. Sassanian Empire; Chosroes II, Ⓡ drachm, A.D. 590–627. 475
869. Sassanian Empire; Yezdigird III, Ⓡ drachm, A.D. 632–651. 475
870. Arab-Sassanian; Ⓡ drachm, *c.* A.D. 650. 476
871. Arab-Byzantine; Æ 40 nummia piece, later 7th cent. 477
872. Arab-Byzantine; Ⓝ semissis, or ½ dinar, later 7th cent. 477
873. Arab-Byzantine; Æ 40 nummia, later 7th cent. 477
874. Umaiyad Caliphate; Ⓝ dinar, A.D. 696–697. 478
875. Umaiyad Caliphate; Ⓡ dirhem, A.D. 698–699. 478
876. Abbasid Caliphate; Harun-al-Rashid, Ⓝ dinar, A.D. 801. 479
877. Umaiyads in Spain; Ⓡ dirhem, A.D. 772. 479
878. Beni Nasr, Granada; Muhammad IV, Ⓝ dinar, A.D. 1325–33. 480
879. Almoravides; Ali-ibn-Yusuf, Granada, Ⓝ dinar, A.D. 1128–9. 480
880. Almohades; Abd-el-Mumin, Ⓡ dirhem, A.D. 1130–63. 480
881. Sharifi Sultans; Muhammad, Æ mazuna, A.D. 1871–2. 481
882. Fatimid Caliphate; el-Mansur, Ⓝ dinar, A.D. 947–948. 482
883. Fatimid Caliphate; el-Hakim, Ⓝ ¼ dinar or ruba, Sicily, A.D. 1002–3. 482
884. Ayyubids; Saladin, Ⓝ dinar, A.D. 1175–6. 482
885. Ayyubids; el-Awhad, Æ, A.D. 1202–3. 482
886. Bahri Mamelukes; Shejer-ed-durr, Ⓝ dinar, A.D. 1250. 482
887. Bahri Mamelukes; en-Nasir Hasan, Ⓝ dinar, A.D. 1358–9. 482
888. Samanids; Nasr II ibn-Ahmad, Ⓝ dinar, A.D. 915–916. 483
889. Ghaznavids; Mahmud, Ⓡ dirhem, A.D. 998–1030. 483
890. Seljuks of Rum; Suleiman II, Ⓡ dirhem, A.D. 1200–1. 484
891. Seljuks of Rum; Kay Khusru II, Ⓡ dirhem, A.D. 1243–4. 484
892. Urtukids; Æ, *rev.* Victory, mid 12th cent. 484
893. Urtukids; Æ, *rev.* Half-length facing bust, A.D. 1143–4. 485
894. Urtukids; Æ, *rev.* Double-headed eagle, A.D. 1220–1. 485
895. Mongols; Genghis Khan, Ⓡ dirhem, A.D. 1206–27. 486
896. Mongols; Turakina, Ⓡ dirhem, A.D. 1241–6. 486

		page
897.	Mongols; Ghazan, AR dirhem, A.D. 1295–1304.	486
898.	Golden Horde Mongols; Toktamish Khan, AR dirhem, A.D. 1384–5.	486
899.	Timurids; Timur, AR dirhem, A.D. 1376–7.	487
900.	Ottoman Empire; Urkhan, AR akce, A.D. 1326–60.	488
901.	Ottoman Empire; Muhammad II, Æ manghur, A.D. 1460–1.	488
902.	Ottoman Empire; Bayezid II, AV altun, A.D. 1481.	488
903.	Ottoman Empire; Ahmad III, AR onlik, A.D. 1703.	488
904.	Ottoman Empire; Suleiman II, AR piastre, A.D. 1687.	488
905.	Ottoman Empire; Ahmad III, AV zer mabub, A.D. 1711–2.	489
906.	Persia; Suleiman I, AV ashrafi, A.D. 1666–94.	489
907.	Persia; Tahmasp I, AR abbasi, A.D. 1524–76.	489
908.	Persia; Fath Ali, AV $\frac{1}{2}$ toman, A.D. 1797–1834.	490
909.	Persia; Anonymous, Æ fals, A.D. 1708.	490
910.	Georgia; Bagrat IV, AR dirhem, A.D. 1027–72.	490
911.	Georgia; Davit V and Kuyuk Khan, AR dirhem, A.D. 1247–53.	491
912.	Georgia; Russian protectorate, AR abbasi, A.D. 1804.	491
913.	Turkey; Abdul Hamid, AR 20 piastres, A.D. 1839–61.	492
914.	Lebanon; al.br. 5 piastres, A.D. 1925.	493
915.	Israel; NK 25 prutah, A.D. 1950.	494
916.	Iran; Muzhaffar-al-din. NK 50 dinars, A.D. 1903–4.	495

COINS OF INDIA, PLATES 57–60

917.	AR 'punch-marked', *c.* 3rd cent. B.C.	500
918.	Kausambi, Æ, 2nd cent. B.C.	500
919.	Andhras; Pot., 1st cent. A.D.	501
920.	Western Satraps; AR hemidrachm, *c.* A.D. 200.	501
921.	Indo-Scythian; Maues, Æ, *c.* 75 B.C.	501
922.	Indo-Scythian; Azes I, AR hemidrachm, *c.* 50 B.C.	502
923.	Kushans; Soter Megas, Æ, mid 1st cent. A.D.	502
924.	Kushans; Kanishka, AV, late 1st cent. A.D.	502
925.	Gupta; Samudragupta, AV, A.D. 335–380.	504
926.	Gupta; Samudragupta, AV, A.D. 335–380.	504
927.	Gupta; Chandragupta II, AV, A.D. 380–414.	504
928.	Gupta; Kumaragupta; AV, A.D. 414–455.	504
929.	Hephthalites; Mihiragula, Pot., *c.* 520.	506
930.	Indo-Sassanian; Napki Malik, Pot., 6th cent.	506

page

931. Gujarat; Æ Gadhiya paisa, 6th cent. — 506
932. Ohind; Samanta-deva, R, early 10th cent. — 506
933. Kashmir; Yasovarman, base N, c. 730. — 507
934. Chalukyas; Saktivarman, N, 1000–12. — 509
935. Pandyas; N, 10th cent. — 509
936. Cholas; R, 10th cent. — 509
937. Vijayanagar; Harihara, N ½ pagoda, c. 1379. — 510
938. Vijayanagar; Tirumala Raja, N pagoda, c. 1570. — 510
939. Mysore; Æ elephant cash, 16th cent. — 510
940. Sultans of Delhi; Mahmud, bill. delhiwala, c. 1200. — 512
941. Sultans of Delhi; Altamsh, R tankah, 1210–35. — 512
942. Sultans of Delhi; Alau-d-din Muhammad, N, 1296–1316. — 513
943. Sultans of Delhi; Alau-d-din Muhammad, R tankah, 1296–1316. — 513
944. Sultans of Delhi; Muhammad-ibn-Tuglaq, Æ token, 1329–32. — 513
945. Sultans of Delhi; Bahlol Lodi, bill. bahlodi, 1455. — 514
946. Sultans of Delhi; Sher Shah, R rupee, 1540–5. — 515
947. Sultans of Delhi; Sher Shah, Æ dam, 1540–5. — 515
948. Bengal; Jalalu-d-din Muhammad, N, 1414–31. — 516
949. Malwa; Ghiyas Shah, N, 1468–1500. — 517
950. Gujarat; Mahmud III, Æ, 1536–53. — 518
951. Kashmir; Muhammad, R, 1481–3. — 518
952. Kashmir; Muhammad, Æ, 1481–3. — 518
953. Mogul Empire; Akbar, N mohur, 1556–84. — 519
954. Mogul Empire; Akbar, N mohur (Ilahi class), 1584–1605. — 519
955. Mogul Empire; Akbar, N ½ mohur, 1604. — 519
956. Mogul Empire; Jahangir, N mohur, 1606. — 520
957. Mogul Empire; Jahangir, N mohur (Akbar), 1605. — 520
958. Mogul Empire; Jahangir, N mohur, 1611. — 520
959. Mogul Empire; Jahangir, N mohur, 1614. — 520
960. Mogul Empire; Jahangir, N mohur, 1619. — 520
961. Mogul Empire; Alamgir II, R rupee, 1758. — 521
962. Portuguese; Goa, Maria II, R rupia, 1840. — 522
963. Dutch; Negapatam, N pagoda, 17th cent. — 522
964. British; Elizabeth I, R 4 reales, 1600. — 523
965. British; Madras, R fanam, 17–18th cents. — 523
966. British; Madras, N pagoda, 18th cent. — 523
967. British; Bombay, Æ pice, c. 1780. — 524
968. British; Madras, R 'Arcot' rupee, late 18th cent. — 524

page

969. British; Madras, ℞ 'Arcot' rupee, early 19th cent. — 525
970. British; Madras, N pagoda, early 19th cent. — 525
971. British; Bombay, Æ pice, 1804. — 525
972. British; William IV, ℞ rupee, 1834. — 525
973. British; Victoria, ℞ ½ rupee, 1877. — 525
974. British; George VI, ℞ rupee, 1947. — 525
975. Mysore; Æ elephant cash, 1806. — 526
976. Oudh; Wajid Ali, ℞ rupee, 1847–56. — 527
977. Indore; Shivaji Rao, Æ ¼ anna, 1886–1902. — 528
978. Hyderabad; Mir Usman Ali, ℞ rupee, 1911. — 528
979. Sikh League; ℞ rupee, 1885. — 528
980. Nepal; Tribhuvana Viravikrama, ℞ mohar, 1912. — 529
981. Afghanistan; Abd-el-Rahman, ℞ ½ rupee, 1879–1901. — 529
982. India; Republic, CN 10 paisa, 1959. — 530
983. Pakistan; Republic, CN ¼ rupee, 1948. — 530
984. Ceylon; Æ *c.* 3rd cent. B.C.–3rd cent. A.D. — 531
985. Ceylon; imitation Roman Æ, 4th cent. A.D. — 531
986. Ceylon; N kahavanu, 10th cent. — 531
987. Ceylon; Lilavati, Æ kahavanu, 1197–1200. — 531
988. Ceylon; ℞ larin, 16th cent. — 532
989. Ceylon; Portuguese, ℞ double tanga (counter-marked VOC), *c.* 1650. — 532
990. Ceylon; Dutch, Æ 1 stuiver, 1784. — 532
991. Ceylon; British, ℞ 96 stuivers, 1803. — 533
992. Ceylon; British, Victoria, ℞ penny halfpenny, 1840. — 533
993. Ceylon; British, Æ ¼ farthing, 1868. — 533
994. Ceylon; British, George V, Æ ½ cent, 1912. — 533

COINS OF THE FAR EAST, PLATES 61–63

995. China; Æ pu money, 4th cent. B.C. — 538
996. China; Æ knife money, 4th cent. B.C. — 539
997. China; Æ 'round money', *c.* 300 B.C. — 539
998. China; Æ Pan Liang, *c.* 220 B.C. — 540
999. China; Æ 5 shu, *c.* 118 B.C. — 540
1000. China; Wang Mang, Æ knife money, A.D. 7–22. — 540
1001. China; Kao Tsu, Æ tung pao, 618–627. — 541
1002. China; Kao Tsung, Æ cash, 1735. — 542

page

1003. China; Kiang Nan Province, Æ 1 mace 44 candareens, 1898.   543
1004. China; Tai-ching-ti-kuo, Æ 10 cash, 1907.   543
1005. China; Republic, Yuan Shi Kai, Æ 20 cents, 1914.   544
1006. China; Republic, Sun Yat Sen, Ν 10 fen, 1936.   544
1007. Tibet; Æ 5 sho, 1916.   545
1008. Japan; Æ wado kaiko, *c.* 720.   545
1009. Japan; Æ kingen daiho, *c.* 980.   546
1010. Japan; Æ eiraku sen, *c.* 1600.   546
1011. Japan; Ν koban, *c.* 1860.   547
1012. Japan; Æ 1 bu gin, *c.* 1837.   547
1013. Japan; Æ kanei tsuho, 1769.   547
1014. Japan; Æ 50 sen, 1874.   548
1015. Japan; Æ 50 sen, 1912.   548
1016. Japan; Æ 10 sen, 1951.   548
1017. Korea; Æ cash, 1397.   549
1018. Korea; Æ cash, 1790–1830.   549
1019. Korea; Æ 1 chon, 1905–6.   549
1020. Burma; Arakan, Darma Candra, Æ, 15th cent.   549
1021. Burma; Mindon Ming, Æ rupee, 1852.   550
1022. Burma; Republic, Ν 5 pyas, 1952.   550
1023. Siam; Mongkut, Æ ½ tical, *c.* 1851.   551
1024. Siam; Mongkut, Æ ¼ bat, 1863–8.   551
1025. Siam; Phumiphol, tin 10 satangs, 1950.   551
1026. Johore; Sulaiman, Ν, 18th cent.   552
1027. Pulu Penang; Æ cent, 1787.   552
1028. Straits Settlements; Victoria, Æ 20 cents, 1896.   552
1029. Malaya; Æ dollar, 1895.   553
1030. Malaya and British Borneo; Elizabeth II, Æ 5 cents, 1958.   553
1031. Annam; Æ cash, 1365.   553
1032. Annam; Æ ½ tael, 1847–83.   553
1033. Cambodia; Norodom, Æ 1 franc, 1860.   553
1034. Indo-China; Æ 10 cents, 1889.   554
1035. East Indies; Bantam, tin piti, 18th cent.   555
1036. East Indies; Atjih, Sultan Safiyat-al-din, Ν, 1641–75.   555
1037. Dutch East Indies; Æ 10 stuivers VOC, 1786.   556
1038. Dutch East Indies; Æ 1 doit VOC, 1745.   556
1039. Dutch East Indies; Æ 'bonk'-1 stuiver, 1798.   556
1040. Dutch East Indies; Æ ¼ guilder, 1802.   556

		page
1041.	Dutch East Indies; British in Java, Æ ¼ stuiver, 1811.	556
1042.	Dutch East Indies; Wilhelmina, ℞ ¼ guilder, 1904.	557
1043.	Sarawak; Rajah C. Brooke, ℞ 10 cents, 1900.	557
1044.	Hong Kong; Victoria, ℞ 20 cents, 1896.	557
1045.	Philippines; ℕ 5 centavos, 1918.	558

Index

A

Abaga, Mongol Khan in Georgia, 491
Abbas, Shah of Persia, 489
abbasi, 489, 491
Abbasid Caliphate, 478–9
Abbey tokens, 567
Abdagases, 502
Abd-al-Malik, Caliph, 476–7
Abd-al-Rahman, amir of Afghanistan, 529
Abdul Mejid, sultan of Turkey, 491–2
Abyssinia, 463–4
Achuta Raya, king of Vijayanagar, 510
adli, 513
Adrianople, 488
afghani, 529
Afghanistan, mediaeval coinage of, 483, 485
    modern coinage of, 529
Africa, 463–70
Afshari dynasty, 489
Aghlabite kingdom in N. Africa, 480
Agra, 519–21
agura, 494
Ahalya Baia, sultan of Indore, 528
Ahmad I, sultan of Gujarat, 518
Ahmad Shah, sultan of Deccan, 517
Ahmadabad, 521
Ahmet III, sultan of Turkey, 488
Ajmir, 507, 511
Ajodhya, 500
aka, 531
Akbar, Mogul emperor, 516–19
    portrait of, 520
akce, 488
Alamgir II, Mogul emperor, E.I.C. rupees of, 524
Alam Shah, sultan of Delhi, 512
al-Andalus, 478
Alau-d-din Hasan, sultan of Deccan, 517
Alau-d-din Mas'aud, sultan of Delhi, 512
Alau-d-din Muhammad, sultan of Delhi, 513
Aleppo, 488
Alexander VI, Pope, 415, 444

Alfonso XII, king of Spain, Philippine coins of, 558
Alfonso XIII, king of Spain, Philippine coins of, 558
Algiers, 488
al-Mansur, Caliph, 479
Almohades, 479–80
Almoravides, 479–80
Alp Arslan, Seljuk sultan, 484
Altamsh, sultan of Delhi, 512
altun, 488
amani, 529
Amanullah, amir of Afghanistan, 529
Amharic script, 463
ampat, 552
Amritsar, 528
amulets, 564
Ananda Mahidol, king of Siam, 551
Antanavarman Chodaganga, king of Kalinga, 509
Andhras, 501, 504
Angola, 469
anna, 530, 550
anna, half, 528
anna, quarter, 528
anna, Muscat, 496
Annam, 553
Antilles, 451
Arab-Byzantine coinage, 476
Arab-Sassanian coinage, 476
Arakan, 549–50
Arcot, 523–4
Ardashir, Sassanian king, 473–4
Argentina, 442–3
Artigas, liberator of Uruguay, 443
ashrafi, Hyderabad, 528
ashrafi, Persia, 489
Asir, 519
Atabegs, 484
Ataturk, Kemal, portrait of, 492
Atjih, 555
att, 551
Aurangzib, Mogul emperor, 521
    E.I.C. rupees of, 524
Australia, 457–8
Axumite kings of Abyssinia, 463–4
Ayyubid dynasty, 482
Azerbaijan, 485
Azes I, Indo-Scythic, king, 501–2
Azes II, Indo-Scythic king, 501–2
Azilises, Indo-Scythic king, 501–2

B

Babar, Mogul emperor, 514, 518–19
Bactria, 499
Baghdad, 488
Bagrat IV, king of Georgia, 490
Bahamas, 452
Bahia, 445
Bahlol Lodi, sultan of Delhi, 514, 516
bahloli, 514
Bahmani dynasty, 517
Bahram I, Sassanian king, 474
Bahram II, Sassanian king, 474
Bahram V, Sassanian king, 474
Bahri Mamelukes, 483
baizah, 496
Balboa, conquistador, portrait of, 436
balboa, 435–6
Balkh, 483
Baltimore, Lord, 421
Bantam, 555
Barbados, 453
Baroda, 527
Basra, 551
Begteginid dynasty, 485
Benares, 524
Bengal, 516
Beni Abbad dynasty, 479
Beni Hamud dynasty, 479
Beni Idris dynasty, 479
Beni Nasr dynasty, 480
Bermuda, 452
Bikanir, 527
billon, 513–14
Bilud-al-Hind, 512
bit, 446, 457
Board of Revenue, Chinese, 542–3
Board of Works, Chinese, 542
bogache, 496
Bogota, 437–8
Bolivar, Simon, portrait of, 438–9, 441
bolivar, 439
Bolivia, 441
boliviano, 441
Bonaparte, Louis, King of Netherlands, Javanese coins of, 556
Bokhara, 473, 487
Bombay, 523–5
bonk, 556
Borneo, 557

Bouquet tokens, 417
Boyer, J. P., president of Haiti, 449
bu, 546–7
bull and horseman coins, 506–7, 512
Bunkelkhand, 507
bunkyu eiho, 547
Burgers, president of South African Republic, 467
Burji Mamelukes, 483
Burma, 549–50
Buwaihid dynasty, 483
Brahmi script, 500
Brasil, 444–6
British Caribbean Territories, 453
British Columbia, gold coins of, 418
British Honduras, 433
British West Africa, 466
Brooke, James, Rajah of Sarawak, 557
Byzantine coinage, in Ceylon, 531
In India, 508

C

Cabot, John, 416, 418–19
Cairo, 482, 488
Calcutta, 525
Cambodia, 553–4
Canada, 416–19
dominion of, 418–19
province of, 417
Canada, Lower, bank tokens of, 417
Canada, Upper, bank tokens of, 417
candareen, 542
Canton, 543
card counters, 568
Carolina, token halfpennies of, 421
Carrera, Rafael, president of Guatemala, 432–3
Carson City, 425
Cartier, Jacques, 416
cash, Annamese, 553
Chinese, 540, 542–3
Indian, 522–5
Castro Fidel, portrait of, 450
Cayenne, 447
cedi, 467
Celebes, 557
cent, Abyssinia, 464
British Honduras, 433
Canada, 417–19
Ceylon, 533
China, 542–4
Danish West Indies, 451
Haiti, 448
Hong Kong, 557
Java, 556
Kenya, 470

Liberia, 466
Malaya, 552–3
South Africa, 468
United States, 422–6
two, United States, 425
three, United States, 425
centavo, Angola, 469
Argentina, 443
Bolivia, 441
Brasil, 446
Chile, 442
Colombia, 438
Cuba, 450
Dominican Republic, 449
Honduras, 433
Mexico, 431
Mozambique, 469
Nicaragua, 434
Peru, 441
Philippines, 558–9
Venezuela, 439
centesimo, Dominican Republic, 449–50
Paraguay, 444
Uruguay, 443
centime, Cambodia, 554
Congo, 470
Guiana, French, 448
Haiti, 449
Indo-China, 553
Tunisia, 465
centimo, Colombia, 438
Panama, 435
Paraguay, 448
Philippines, 558
Central African Federation, 468
Ceylon, 530–33
chaitya, 501, 504, 531
chakram, 551
Chalukyas, 508–9
Chandella kings, 507
Chandragupta I, Gupta king, 503
Chandragupta II, Gupta king, 503–4
Charles I, king of Spain, New World coins of, 428
Charles II, King of Spain, New World coins of, 429
Charles III, king of Spain, 430
Philippine coins of, 558
Cherles IV, King of Spain, New World coins of, 430
Charlotte, mint of, 423
char minar, 528
Chera kings, 509
Cheribon, 555
chiao, 544
ch'ien, 540
Chihuahua, 430–1
Chile, 441–2
China, 537–44
Communist coins of, 544
Nationalist coins of, 544

Republican coins of, 543–4
Chinapatam (Madras), 524
Ch'in dynasty, 540
Ching dynasty, 542
chogin, 546–7
Chola kings in S. India, 509
in Ceylon, 531
chon, 549
Chosroes II, Sassanian king, 475–6
Christian VI, king of Denmark, 450
Christian IX, king of Denmark, 451
Christian X, king of Denmark, 451
Christophe, Henri, president of Haiti, 448
Chulalongkorn, king of Siam, 551
Cisplatine Republic, 443
cob real, 429, 432
Cochin China, 553–4
coin weights, 568
Colombia, 437–8
Colombo, 532–3
Columbus, Christopher, 415, 434
colon, 435
communion tokens, 566
condor, 442
Confederate States, U.S.A., 425
Congo, 470
Connecticut, 422
Costantinople, capture of, 487
Turkish mint of, 488, 491
contorniate, 563
Cordoba, 434, 479, 480
Cortes, conquest of Mexico by 428
Costa Rica, 435
counters, 567
cowrie, metal, 538
cruzado, 521
cruzeiro, 446
cuartino, 431
cuartillo, 430, 438, 449
Cuauhtec, Aztec king, portrait of, 432
Cuba, 450
Curaçao, 447, 451

D

Dahlonega, 423
daler, 451
dam, 515, 519
Damascus, mediaeval mint of, 478, 482, 488
Daud Shah, sultan of Bengal, 516
Daulat Rao, Sindhia of Gwalior, 527
Deccan, 508–9, 517
decimal coinage, 422, 431, 440, 441, 443, 458–9, 468, 530, 547

decimo, 439, 442
Declaration of Independence, United States, 421
deka, 531
Delhi, 507, 511, 512
  sultans of, 511–15
Demerary, 446–7
denier, French colonial, 416–17
Dessalines, Jacques, emperor of Haiti, 448
Deva Raya II, king of Vijayan-agar, 510
dharana, 500
dime, 423–6
dinar, 477–8, 495–6, 498
dinero, 440
dirhem, 465, 478
disme, see dime
Djambi, 555
DOC, 522
doit, 447, 532, 555–6
dollar, gold, British Columbia, 418
  United States, 425
dollar, ring, 457
dollar, silver, British trade, 552–3
  Australia, 458
  Bahamas, 453
  Canada, 418–19
  China, 542–4
  Hong Kong, 558
  Liberia, 466
  Malaysia, 533
  New Zealand, 459
  Straits Settlement, 552
  United States, 422–6
Dominican Republic, 449–50
dominicano, 449
dong, 554
drachm, Sassanian, 474, 490, 506
dua, 552
ducaton, 521, 566
dump, 457
Durango, 430–1
Dutch coinage in East Indies, 555–7
  in Ceylon, 532
  in India, 522

E

eagle, gold, 423–5
eagle, gold, double, 425–6
East Africa, 468
East India Company, British, coinage of,
  Borneo, 557
  Celebes, 557
  India, 521–6
  Java, 556
  Labuan, 557
  Malaya, 552
  Sumatra, 557

East India Company, Danish, 522
East India Company, Dutch, coinage of,
  Ceylon, 532–3
  India, 522
  Java, 555–6
East Indies, 554–7
Ecuador, 439–40
Edward VII, king of Great Britain, Canadian coins of, 418–19
Edward VIII, king of Great Britain, British West African coins of, 466
  New Guinea coins of, 458
Egypt, modern coinage of, 464–5
  Republic of, 465
  under Turks, 488
EIC, 524
eiraku sen, 546
eiraku tsuho, 547
Elizabeth II, queen of Great Britain, Australian coins of, 458
  British Caribbean Territories coins of, 453
  Canadian coins of, 418–19
  Central African Fed. coins of, 468
  Ceylon coins of, 533
  New Zealand coins of, 459
  Nigerian coins of, 468
  South African coins of, 468
Emergency coinage, 430, 565
Emmanuel I, king of Portugal, Indian coins of, 521
Ericsson, Lief, Viking explorer, 416
escalin, 448
escudo, gold, Argentina, 442
  Bolivia, 441
  Chile, 442
  Colombia, 437–8
  Costa Rica, 435
  Ecuador, 439
  Mexico, 429–31
  Peru, 440
escudo, silver, Angola, 469
Essequibo, 446–7
Ethiopia, see Abyssinia
Ezanas, Axumite king, 463

F

Faisal I, king of Iraq, 494
Faisal II, king of Iraq, 494
fals, 478–9
fanam, 509, 511, 522–3, 532
Fantsour, 555
Farouk I, king of Egypt, 464–5
Farrukhshiyar, Mogul emperor, 521
  EIC rupees of, 524

farthing, half (Ceylon), 533
  quarter (Ceylon), 533
Fath Ali, shah of Persia, 489–90
Fath Khan, shah of Persia, 514
Fatimid caliphate, 480, 482
Faustin, emperor of Haiti, 449
fen, 544
Ferdinand V, king of Spain, 442
Ferdinand VI, king of Spain, 437
Ferdinand VII, king of Spain, New World coins of, 430, 437
Fez, 480
Fiji, 459
Filisteen (Palestine), 482
fils, 494
fire-altar, 474, 476
Firoz III, sultan of Delhi, 514
Firuz, Sassanian king, 474
fourpence, silver, Br. Guiana, 477
franc, Cambodia, 553
  Congo, 470
  Danish West Indies, 451
  Morocco, 466
  Tunisia, 465
Franklin cent, 422
Frederick VII, king of Denmark, 451
French coinage, colonial,
  in Africa, 469
  in Canada, 415–16
  in Guiana, 447
  in India, 522–3
  in Indo-China, 534
  in West Indies, 452
fruit tokens, 566
Fuad I, king of Egypt, 464
fuang, 551
fun, 549
funduk altun, 488

G

Gadhiya paisa, 506
Galle, 533
Gambia, 470
Ganda bherunda, 510
Ganga dynasty, 509
Gangeya-deva, king of Dahala, 507
gani, 513
Garuda, 503–4
Gauda, 505
Genroku era, 546
George III, king of Georgia, 491
George IV, king of Great Britain, Canadian coinage of, 417
George V, king of Great Britain, Australian coins of, 458
  Canadian coins of, 418
  Hong Kong coins of, 558
  New Guinea coins of, 458
  New Zealand coins of, 459

Rhodesian coins of, 468
South African coins of, 467
George VI, king of Great Britain,
Australian coins of, 458
Canadian coins of, 418–9
Indian coins of, 525
New Guinea coins of, 458
New Zealand coins of, 459
Rhodesian coins of, 468
South African coins of, 467
Georgia, 490–1
gersh, 464
Ghana, 466–7
Ghazan, Mongol khan, 486
Ghaziu-d-din Haidar, nawab of
Oudh, 527
Ghaznah, 483
Ghaznavid dynasty, 483–4
Ghengis Khan, 486, 514
Ghiyas Shah, sultan of Malwa, 517
Ghurid dynasty, 484, 511
ghurush, 488
girsh, 495
glass-weights, Arab, 564
Goa, 509
Gold Coast, 466
Golden Horde Mongols, 486
Gondophares, Indo-Scythian king,
502
Good Samaritan shilling, 421
goryoban, 547
gourde, 448–9
gourdin, 448
Granada, 480, 482
Great Khans, 486
Grenada, 452
Guadalajara, 430
Guadeloupe, 452
Guanajunto, 430
Guatemala, 432–3
Guiana, British, 446–7
Dutch, 447
French, 447
guinea, Saudi Arabia, 495
guilder, 446–7, 451–2, 522, 556–7
Gujarat, 518
Gupta kingdom, 503–5
Gurkha conquest of Nepal, 529
Gurmukhi script, 529
Guyana, 446
Gwalior, 527–8

H

Hafsid dynasty, 418
Haidar Ali, sultan of Mysore, 526
Haile Selassie, emperor of Abys-
sinia, 464
Haiti, 448–9
halala, 496
Hamdanid dynasty, 483
Han dynasty, 540

Hanover, counter, 568–9
hao, 554
Hard Times token, 566
Harihara, king of Vijayanagar,
510
Harun-al-Rashid, Abassid caliph,
476, 479
hat money, 552
Hawaii, 459
Hejaz, 496
Hephthalites, 505–6
Heraclius, Byzantine emperor,
477, 485
Herzl, Theodore, portrait of, 494
Hidalgo, portrait of, 432
Hirohito, emperor of Japan, 548
Hog money, 420, 452
Honduras, 433
Hong Kong, 557–8
hop tokens, 566
Hormuzd II, Sassanian king, 474
Hoshang, sultan of Malwa, 517
Hoysalas, 509
Hsiao Tsung, emperor of China,
541
hu, 542
Hudson's Bay Company, 416
Hulagu, Mongol chief, 486
Humayun, Mogul emperor, 514–
15, 518–19
Hungary, Mongols in, 485
Turks in, 487
Husen, sultan of Jaunpur, 516
Huvishka, Kushan king, 502–3
hwan, 549
Hyderabad, 528

I

Ibrahim, sultan of Delhi, 514, 518
Ibrahim, sultan of Jaunpur, 516
Ichibu gin, 547
Idrisid kingdom, 480
Ifrikiya, 478
Ikkeri, rajahs of, 510
Il Khans, 486
Ilahi era, 519
Imadi, 496
India, 499–530
Indian States, independent, 526–9
Indo-China, 553–4
Indo-Parthian coinage, 502
Indo-Sassanian coinage, 506
Indo-Scythian coinage, 501
Indonesia, 557
Indore, 528
Inonu, Ismet, portrait of, 492
Iran, 495; see also Persia
Iraq, 494
Isabel II, queen of Spain, Philip-
pine coins of, 558
Isfahan, 484, 490

Islam Shah, sultan of Delhi, 515
Israel, 493–4
Iturbide, Augustin, emperor of
Mexico, 430

J

Jaffna, 532–3
Jagatai Mongols, 487
Jahangir, Mogul emperor, 520–1
Jaitil, 514
Jalalu-d-din Muhammad, sultan of
Bengal, 516
Jalayrs in Persia, 487, 489
Jamaica, 453
Japan, 545–8
Jaunpur, 516
Jayakesin, Kadamba chief of Goa,
509
jetons, 567
Jewish Revolts, 567
John III, king of Portugal, coins of
Goa of, 521
Johore, 552
Jordan, 494
Juliana, queen of the Netherlands,
451
Justin II, Byzantine emperor,
476–7

K

Kabul, Hindu kings of, 506
Kadamba chiefs, 509
kahavanu, 531
Ka'him coinage, 551
kaiki shoho, 546
Kairawan, 478
Kajar shahs, 489, 495
Kalachuri dynasty, 507
Kalakauai, king of Hawaii, 459
Kalinga, 509
Kamehamema III, king of Hawaii,
459
Kanauj, 507, 512
kanei tsuho, 547
Kangra, maharajahs of, 507
Kanishka, Kushan king, 502–3
Kao Tsu, emperor of China, 540,
544
kapang, 552, 557
karan, 489, 495
Kararani dynasty in Bengal, 516
Kart Mongols, 487
Kashmir, 507, 518
kasu, 510
Kausambi, 500
Kay Khusru II, Seljuk sultan, 484
kazbegi, 489
Kazvin, 490
Kedah, 551–2

Keicho era, 546
kengen daiho, 546
Kennedy, John, president, portrait of, 427
Kenya, 470
Kerim Khan, shah of Persia, 489
Kharoshthi script, 501—2
Khingila, 507
Khorasan, 483–5, 487
Khusru Malik, sultan of Ghazni, 511
Kipchak Mongols, 486
knife money, 538, 540
koban, 547
Korea, 548–9
   Mongols in, 485
   North, 549
   South, 549
Krauwinckel, Hans, 567
Krim Tatars, 487
Kruger, Paul, 467
Kuang Hsu, emperor of China, 542
Kublai Khan, 485, 541
Kujula Kadphises, 502
Kumaragupta, Gupta king, 504
Kumara-pala-deva, Tomara king of Delhi, 507
Kung, 542
Kurdistan, 487
kuru, 492
Kushan kings, 502–3
Kutbu-d-din, sultan of Delhi, 512
Kutbu-d-din Mubarak, sultan of Delhi, 513
Kuwait, 496
Kwantung, 542
kyat, 550
kyoho oban, 546

L

Labuan, 557
Lahore, 483, 511, 519, 528
Lakshmi, 503–5, 507, 512, 531
Lakśmana, 510
Läos, 554
La Paz, 441
larin, 532
lat, 551
Layang, 541
lead, 501
Lebanon, 493
lempira, 434
Leon, 432, 434
leone, 470
li, 542
Liberia, 466
libra, 441
Libya, 465
Lima, 440
Lincoln, Abraham, portrait of, 426–7

lira, 491–3
Lodi dynasty, 514
Louis XIV, king of France, 416
Louis XV, king of France, 416
Louis I, king of Spain, New World coins of, 429

M

Macassar, 555
mace, 542
macuta, 469
Madras, 523–5
Madura, 509–10, 517
Mahakasola kings, 507
Mahdia, 480, 482
Mahendra Vira Vikrama, king of Nepal, 529
Maheswar, 528
Mahmud, sultan of Ghazni, 511
Mahmud, sultan of Jaunpur, 516
Mahmud Shah, sultan of Deccan, 517
mahmudi, 489
Mahmudpore, 483
Makuta, 470
Malabar, 509
Malacca, 552
Malagasy Republic, 470
Malawi, 470
Malaya, 551–3
Malaya-varma, Rajah of Narwar, 507
Malharnagar, 528
Malwa, 500, 510
mameita gin, 547
mamelukes, 482–3, 485
Manchu script, 542–3
Manco Capac, Great Inca, 441
manghir, 488
Mangit dynasty, 487
mannen oban, 547
mannen tsuho, 546
maravedi, 428–9
Marco Polo, 541
Marinid dynasty, 481
mark, 458
Marrakesh, 480
Marti, president of Cuba, 450
Maryland, 421
Massachusetts, 421
Masulipatam, 522–3
Mathura, 500
matona, 464
Maues, Indo-Scythian king, 501
Maximilian Emmanuel, duke of Bavaria, 431
mazuna, 465–6, 481
Medinet-es-Salam, 483–4
Medinet-ed-Zahra, 479
meia, 521

Meiji era, 547
Menelik II, emperor of Abyssinia, 464
Mesopotamia, 483–5, 487
Mexico, 428–32
   empire of, 430–1
Mihiragula, Hephthalite king 505–6
mil, 493
mille, 470
millième, 464–5
milreis, 444–6
Minas Geraes, 445
Mindon Ming, king of Burma, 550
Ming dynasty, 541
Ming knife money, 538, 540
Mir Usman Ali Khan, nizam of Hyderabad, 528
Misr (Egypt), 482
Mogul Empire, 518–21
mohur, Indian, 519–21, 524–9
   Persian, 489
Mongkut, king of Siam, 551
Mongols, 485–7, 541
Montreal, Bank of, tokens, 417
Montserrat, 452
Morabites, see Almoravides
Morazan, president of Salvador, 434
Morelos, insurgent leader in Mexico, 430–2
Morocco, 456–6
Mozambique, 469
Muhammad I, sultan of Malwa, 517
Muhammad II, sultan of Turkey, 487–8
Muhammad III, sultan of Turkey, 488
Muhammad, sultan of Jaunpur, 516
Muhammad, shah of Persia, 490
Muhammad Adil, sultan of Delhi, 515
Muhammad-ibn-Sam, sultan of Delhi, 511–12
Muhammad Zahir, king of Afghanistan, 529
Muhammad-ibn-Tughlaq, sultan of Delhi, 513–14
Muhammadan coinage, 475–90
Muhammadan invasion of India, 511
Muhammadan states of India, 515–18
Mulai Hassan II, king of Morocco, 466
Mumbai (Bombay), 524
mun, 549
Murad I, sultan of Turkey, 488

Murad II, sultan of Turkey, 487–8
Murcia, 480
Murshidabad, 524–5
Muscat and Oman, 496
Mutsuhito, emperor of Japan, 547
Muwahids, see Almohades
Muzaffarid dynasty, 487
Mysore, 508–9, 526

N

Nadir, shah of Persia, 489, 491
Naga dynasty, 507
Nagari script, 501, 506–7, 510, 522, 527–9, 549–50
Napki Malik, Indo-Sassania king, 506
Narwar, 507
Nasiru-d-din, sultan of Delhi, 512
Nasr-ed-din, shah of Persia, 489–90, 494–5
Nayaka princes, 510
Negapatam, 522
Nepal, 507, 529
Nevis, island of, 452
New Brunswick, tokens of, 417–18
New England, 420
New Granada, republic of, 438–9
vice-royalty of, 432–3, 440
New Guinea, 458
New Hampshire, copper cents of, 422
New Jersey, token coins of, 421
copper cents of, 422
New Orleans, 424
New Spain, vice-royalty of, 428
New World, 415–53
New York, copper cents of, 422
New Zealand, 459
Newfoundland, 416, 419
Nicaragua, 434
nickel, 425–6
nien hao, 541
Nigeria, 468
Nisabur, 484
Nkrumah, Kwame, president of Ghana, 467
Norodom I, king of Cambodia, 553
Nova Scotia, 416–17
Nueva Guatemala, 432
Nueva Vicaya, 430

O

oak-tree coinage, 421
Oaxaca, 430
oban, 546
Ogotai, Mongol chief, 486
Ohind, Hindu kings of, 506
Oman, 483

Ontario, tokens of, 417
Orissa, 509
Orthagnes, Indo-Parthian king, 502
Othman, Turkish sultan, 487
Ottoman Empire, 487–92
Ottoman Turks, 406–7, 481, 483
Oudh, 526–7

P

padma-tankas, 508
pagoda, 509–11, 523–6, 555
pahang, tin hat-money, 552
pahlavi, 495
Pahlavi shahs, 489, 495
Pahlevi script, 506
paisa, 529–30
Pakistan, 530
Pakores, Indo-Parthian king, 502
pala, 531
Palembang, 555
Palestine, modern coins of, 493; see also Israel
Pali script, 530
Pallavas, 509
Panama, 435–6
Pandyan kings in south India, 509
in Ceylon, 531
Pan Liang coinage, 540
Panipat, battle of, 518, 524
Papek, Sassanian king, 473
Papineau, 417
para, 488, 491–2, 495
Paraguay, 444
Parakrama Bahu VI, king of Ceylon, 531
Parvati, 510
pataca, 444
Patani, 552
peacock rupee, 550
Pegu, 550
Pehlvi script, 474
Peking, 541
Persia, 483–5, 487, 489–90; see also Iran
Peru, 437–40
peso, gold,
Argentina, 443
Costa Rica, 435
Dominican Republic, 450
Honduras, 433
Mexico, 431–2
Philippines, 558
peso, silver,
Argentina, 443
Costa Rica, 435
Dominican Republic, 450
Guatemala, 432
Honduras, 433
Mexico, 431–2
Philippines, 558

Salvador, 434
Peter I, emperor of Brasil, 444–5
Pétion, Alexandre, president of Haiti, 448–9
pfennig, 457
Philadelphia, United States, 423–4, 447
Philip II, king of Spain, New World coins of, 429
Philip V, king of Spain, New World coins of, 429, 432
Philippines, 558–9
Phumiphol, king of Siam, 551
piastre, 464–5, 470, 488, 491–5, 553
pice, 523–4, 527, 528, 529–30, 552
piece of eight (reales), 420, 422, 446, 457, 532
Colombia, 437
Guatemala, 432
Honduras, 433
Mexico, 428–31
Peru, 440
pieces of eight, cut, 452, 457
Pillars of Hercules, 428–9
pine-tree coinage, 421
piti, 555
Pondicherry, 522
Popayan, 437–8
Porto Novo pagodas, 522
Portuguese coinage in Angola, 469
in Brasil, 444–5
in Ceylon, 532
in India, 521–2
in Mozambique, 469
potin, 474, 501
Potosi, 440–2
pound, gold, 465, 467, 493
Prajadhipok, king of Siam, 551
Prithvaraji, Indian prince, 511
prutah, 493–4
pu money, 528, 540
pul, 529
puli, 491
Pulicat, 522
Pulu Penang, 552
punch-marked coins, 499–500, 508, 530
purana, 500, 530
Pushkalavati, 501
pya, 550

Q

quarto, 558
Quebec, 416–17
quetzal, 433

R

Rajaraja, Chalukya king, 509
Rajput dynasties, 506–7
Ranjit Singh, Sikh chieftain, 528

Rama VI, king of Siam, 551
Rama Raja, king of Vijayanagar, 510
Ramatanka, 569
rand, 468
Rashtrakutas, 508
Rathor dynasty, 507
Raziya, sultan of Delhi, 512
real, Chile, 442
   Colombia, 437
   Costa Rica, 435
   Ecuador, 439
   Honduras, 433
   Mexico, 428–30
   Nicaragua, 434
   Peru, 440
   Salvador, 434
   Venezuela, 439
reis, Brasil, 444–5
   Mozambique, 469
Reza Shah, shah of Persia, 495
Rhodes, Cecil, 468
Rhodesia, Southern, 468
rial, 465, 495–6
Riebeeck, Jan van, 467–8
rijksdaalder, 533
rin, 548
Rio de Janeiro, 445
Rio de la Plata, Provincias del, 442
Rioja, 443
rix-dollar, 532
Roman coins in Ceylon, 531
   in India, 508
Roosevelt, Franklin, 427
Rosa americana, 421
round money, Chinese, 539
royalin, 522
ruba, 482
rupee, Burma, 550
   India, 515, 519–32
   Java, 556
rupia, 522
rupiah, 557
ryo, 546–7

S

Sadasiva Nayaka, Raja of Ikkeri, 510
Safavid dynasty, 489, 491
Saffarid dynasty, 483
St. Lucia, 452
St. Patrick, 421
St. Sebastian, 522
St. Thomas, 521
St. Vincent, island of, 452
Sakas, 501
Saktivarman, Chalukya king, 509
Saladin, Ayyubid ruler, 482
sales tax tokens, 566
Salvador, 434

Samanid dynasty, 483
Samanta-deva, 506
Samarkand, 473
Samudragupta, Gupta king, 503–4
San Francisco, 424
San Martin, South American Liberator, 443
San José, 432, 435
Sanskrit script, 483, 503
Santiago de Chile, 441–2
sapeque, 554
Sapor I, Sassanian king, 474
Sarawak, 557
Śaśanka, king of Gauda, 505
Sassanian coinage, 473–5
satang, 551
satu, 552
Saudi Arabia, 495
schilling, 450
Sebastian, king of Portugal, Indian coins of, 521
Seljuk Turks, 484–5
sen, 533, 545–8, 557
sene, 460
seniti, 460
senti, 470
sequin, 488
Seringapatam, 526
Seven Years' War, 416
Seville, 480
Shah Alam, Mogul emperor, 521
   EIC rupees of, 524–5
shahi, 489, 495
Shams Shah, king of Kashmir, 518
Shamsu-d-din Iliyas, sultan of Bengal, 516
Sharif dynasty, 481
Shejer-ed-durr, 482
Sher Shah, sultan of Delhi, 515, 518
Sheybanid dynasty, 487
Shih Huang Ti, emperor of China, 540
Shiraz, 483, 490
sho, 545
shu, 540
Siam, 550–1
siege pieces, 565
Sierra Leone, 466, 470
Sikander, sultan of Bengal, 515–16
Sikh League, 528–9
Singapore, 559
Sitten, 519
Śivaji Rao, of Indore, 528
Siyak, 555
Skandagupta, Gupta king, 504
skar, 545
skilling, 450–1
sol, 416, 440–1, 448, 452
Sombrerete, 430
Sommer Island, 420, 452
Soter Megas, Kushan king, 502
sou, 447

South Africa, 467–8
sovereign, 418, 457–8
spade money, 538
Spain, Muhammadan coins of, 479
srang, 545
star pagoda, 523
stiver, 447
Straits Settlements, 552–3
stuiver, 447, 451, 522, 532–3, 555–6
Sucre, General, south American liberator, 439, 441
sucre, 439–40
Sudan, 470
sueldo, 441
Suleyman I, sultan of Turkey, 488
Suleyman II, sultan of Turkey, 488
Suliman II, Seljuk sultan, 484
Sumatra, 557
Sun Yat Sen, president of China, 543–4
Sung dynasty, 541
Suri sultans of Delhi, 515
Surinam, 447
Syria, modern coins of, 492–3
   Muhammadan coins of, 482–3

T

Tabaristan, 476, 479
Tabriz, 490
tael, 540
Tai, emperor of Korea, 549
Tai Ping rebels, 542
taihei genpo, 546
talari, 464
Talugi script, 525
Tamerlane, see Timur
Tamil script, 522–3, 525
Tanesar, battle of, 511
Tang dynasty, 540, 544
tanga, 532
Tankah, gold, 512–13, 517
   silver, 512–14
Tanzania, 470
Tatar Chin dynasty, 541
Tatar Khans, 486
Taxila, 500
Tegucigalpa, 432–3
Teheran, 490
Teluga inscription, 508–9
Tempo era, 546–7
Temujin, Mongol chief, 485
Tenasserim, 530
tesserae, lead, 563–4
Thebaw, king of Burma, 550
three-halfpence, 533
three-swami pagoda 510, 522–3
tiao (ten strings of cash), 540
Tibet, 544–5

Tical, 551
Tiflis, 488, 490–1
Timur, Mongol chief, 487, 518
tin, 552, 555
Tipu Sultan, 526
Tirumala Raja, king of Vijay-anagar, 510
titsz (string of cash), 540
Tlemcen, 481
To, mythical Burmese animal, 550
Token coinage
  Australia, 457,
  Canada, 417–18
  New Zealand, 459
  United States, 421
Tokugawa Shogunate, 546
toman, 489, 495
Tomara dynasty, 507
Tonga, 460
Toramana, Hephthalite chief, 505–7
Tordesillas, treaty of, 415, 444
Tortola, 452
trade dollar, United States, 426
tradesmen's tokens, 565
Tranquebar, 522
Transoxiana, 483–4, 487
Transvaal, 467
tremisses, Merovingian, 477
Trincomalee, 532
Trinidad, 452
Tripoli, North Africa, 488
Trivhuvana Vira Vikrama, king of Nepal, 529
tughra, 488, 491, 516
Tughril Beg, Seljuk sultan, 484
Tukoji Rao II, maharajah of Indore, 528
Tulunid dynasty, 482
tung pao, 541–2, 545, 548–9
Tunis, 481, 488
Tunisia, 465
Turakina, Mongol chieftainess, 486
Turcomans, 489
Turkestan, 485
Turkey, 491–2; see also Ottoman Empire

U

Uganda, 470
Umaiyad Caliphate, 477–9
Union of South Africa, 467–8
United Arab Republic, 465
United States of America, 419–27
  coinage in Philippines, 558–9
Urkhan, sultan of Turkey, 488
Urtukids, 484
Uruguay, 443–4

V

Vasu-deva, Kushan king, 502
VEIC, 556
venezolana, 439
Venezuela, 439
Venkatesvara, Hindu deity, 510
Vermont, copper cents of, 422
Victoria, queen of Great Britain,
  Canadian coins of, 417–19
  Indian coins of, 525
  Singhalese coins of, 533
Vietnam, 554
Vijaya Bahu I, king of Ceylon, 531
Vijayanagar, 510–11
Villa Rica, 445
Vima Kadphises, Kushan king, 502
vintem, 444
Vishnu, 510, 513
Vishnu Chitta-deva, Kadamba chief, 509
Vishnu-Vardana, Chalukya king, 508
VOC, 522, 532, 555–6

W

wado kaiko, 545
Wajid Ali, nawab of Oudh, 527
WangMang, Chinese usurper, 540
wardrobe counters, 567
wark, 464
Wasit, 478
Wattasid dynasty, 481
weight money, 538

West Indies, British, 452–3
West Indies Danish, 450–1
West Indies, Dutch, 451–2
West Indies, French, 452
Western Samoa, 460
Western satraps, 501, 504
White Huns, see Hephthalites
Wilhelmina, queen of the Netherlands, 451
William IV, king of Great Britain,
  Indian coins of, 525
  Singhalese coins of, 533
willow-tree coinage, 421
Windward Islands, 452
won, 459
Wood, William, tokens of, 421
wu shu (5 shu), 540
Wu Ti, emperor of China, 540

X

xu, 554

Y

yang, 549
Yemen, 496
yen, 547–8
Yezdigird III, Sassanian king, 475–6
Yoshihito, emperor of Japan, 584
yuan, 543
Yuan dynasty, 541
Yuan Shi Kai, president of China, 543–4
Yueh-chi, 500–2
yuzlik, 488

Z

Zacatecas, 430
Zaire, 470
Zambia, 470
Zand shahs, 489
Zengid dynasty, 485
zer mabub, 489
Zodiac coins of Jahangir, 520–1
zolota, 488

PLATE 48

772

773

775

774

776

777

778

779

780

781

783

782

784

NEW WORLD COINS: NORTH AMERICA

PLATE 49

785

786

787

788

789

790

791

792

793

794

795

796

797

798

799

800

NEW WORLD COINS : NORTH AND CENTRAL AMERICA

PLATE 50

NEW WORLD COINS: CENTRAL AND SOUTH AMERICA

PLATE 51

816

817

818

819

820

821

822

823

824

825

826

827

828

829

830

831

NEW WORLD COINS: SOUTH AMERICA, CARIBBEAN

PLATE 52

AUSTRALASIAN COINS; AFRICAN COINS

PLATE 53

850

851

852

853

854

855

856

857

858

859

860

861

862

863

864

865

AFRICAN COINS

PLATE 54

866

867

868

869

870

871

872

873

874

875

876

877

878

879

880

NEAR EASTERN COINS

PLATE 55

PLATE 56

NEAR EASTERN COINS

PLATE 57

917

918

919

920

921

922

923

924

925

926

927

928

929

930

931

932

933

934

935

936

INDIAN COINS

PLATE 58

INDIAN COINS

PLATE 59

957

958

959

960

961

962

963

964

965

966

967

968

969

970

971

972

973

974

INDIAN COINS

PLATE 60

975 976

977 978

979 980

981 982 983

985 986

984 987

989 990 991

988 992 993 994

INDIAN AND SINGHALESE COINS

PLATE 61

995

996

997

998

999

1000

1001

1002

1003

1004

1005

1006

1007

FAR EASTERN COINS

PLATE 62

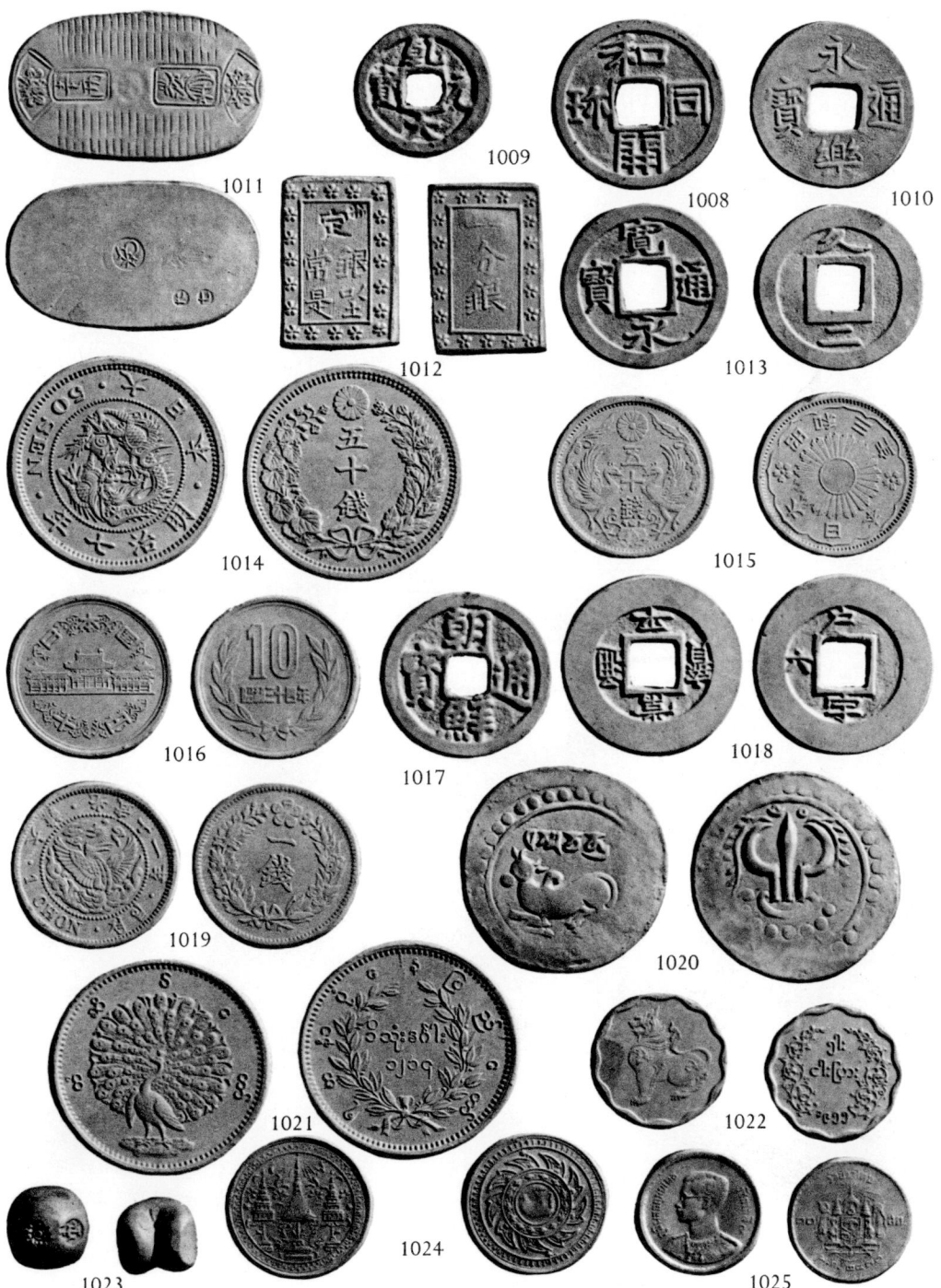

FAR EASTERN COINS

PLATE 63

1026

1027

1028

1029

1030

1031

1036

1032

1033

1034

1035

1037

1038

1039

1040

1041

1042

1043

1044

1045

FAR EASTERN COINS

H · J · £2-50
471